THE END IS ALWAYS NEAR

THE END IS ALWAYS NEAR

Apocalyptic Moments from the Bronze Age Collapse

to Nuclear Near Misses

DAN CARLIN

WILLIAM
COLLINS

William Collins
An imprint of HarperCollins*Publishers*
1 London Bridge Street
London SE1 9GF

WilliamCollinsBooks.com

First published in Great Britain in 2019 by William Collins
First published in the United States by Harper in 2019

1

A catalogue record for this book is
available from the British Library

ISBN 978-0-00-834092-6 (hardback)
ISBN 978-0-00-834093-3 (trade paperback)

Set in Bulmer MT Pro
Printed and bound in Great Britain by
CPI Group (UK) Ltd, Croydon

MIX
Paper from
responsible sources
FSC™ C007454

This book is produced from independently certified FSC™ paper
to ensure responsible forest management.

For more information visit: www.harpercollins.co.uk/green

To Brittany, Liv, and Avery

CONTENTS

PREFACE

DO YOU THINK that modern civilization will ever fall and our cities will ever lie in ruins?

It sounds like an overused science fiction theme, with the archaeologists of the future carefully poking around the rusting skeletons of New York, London, or Tokyo's skyscrapers, subways, or sewers; removing our dead from their graves and studying them like we do ancient Egyptian mummies; trying to decipher our language, unlock the code that is our writing, and figure out who we were. To imagine our tombs, buildings, and human remains being treated the way we today treat ancient archaeological finds might seem unimaginable, but there's a pretty good chance that's what the mummy being excavated thought about his time and place, too.

There's no right answer to a question like that, of course. Many of the questions raised in this book fall into that same unanswerable class. Maybe that's part of what makes them intriguing.

Just noting past evidence and extrapolating it out to future events can get weird quickly. To imagine things that have happened many times in history repeating in the modern era is to dabble in science fiction. It is a very thin membrane that separates factual history from unprovable and speculative fantasy. The instant in which we all live is the point at which those two things—the hard chronology of recorded names and dates and the what-ifs and alternate realities of possible futures—intersect. To imagine the twenty-first-century world being hit with a great plague like the great disease pandemics of the past is *fantasy*, yet it's also extremely possible and has happened many times before. What's the connection between the factual past and the speculative future?

I am told that any conventional book should answer questions or should at least provide an argument. If that's true, this will not be a conventional book. It's more of a collection of loosely connected vignettes. I have no argument, which is consistent with the approach we take in the podcast as well. My approach is that of a nonexpert, for that is what I am. Historians, political scientists, geographers, physicists, sociologists, philosophers, authors, and intellectuals in general have all weighed in over the eras on all the sorts of issues we ponder in this book, each doing so using their own methods and viewing them through their own eras, specialties, and cultural lenses.

While a modern geographer might cite global historical analogies to make an argument about a civilization "falling," or a physicist provide the math to determine the likely probability of a dark age–creating asteroid striking Earth, the approach of a storyteller or journalist is to look at the human angle.* What sort of human stories are going on as a civilization collapses? A bombing raid destroys a person's city, or a pandemic begins to unravel the bonds holding a society together? Seeing things through that lens engages different parts of the brain, including

---

*This is also the job of the historian. Often journalism and history have a somewhat interconnected/symbiotic relationship as journalists write of current events and then historians mine their work later as primary sources. Often journalists then use the work of historians to tell stories of the past that the historians unearthed, as we are doing here.

emotions, and can often have an impact that the data, graphs, and research studies don't. Think of it as another tile in a vast mosaic as many disciplines try to restore an image of the past.

Do tough times make tougher people? Does how we raise our children have an impact on society at large? Can we handle the power of our weapons without destroying ourselves? Can human capabilities, knowledge, and technology regress? There's a very Twilight Zone sort of element to such ideas, with subtle (and sometimes not so subtle) overtones that seem to speak to our present times. They are ideas that cross the boundaries of modern academic disciplines and tread into territory usually occupied by drama, literature, and the arts.

But even without agreed-upon answers, such questions are both fascinating and potentially valuable. Many of them are the types of proverbial "deep questions" that have always been at the heart of philosophical works. Simply thinking about them more often may have value. Others may offer some practical usefulness. Reminding us all, for example, of how many times similar occurrences have taken place in the past may help add a layer of believability to many future possible occurrences that seem more like far-fetched movie plots right now. A history professor once told me that there are two ways we learn: you can put your hand on the hot stove, or you can hear tales of people who already did that and how it turned out for them.

Hardcore History fans have long been asking about a book. I had so much existent material, research, and ideas in the archives that it just seemed natural to use them as the nucleus for such a work. Going back and sorting through it became something of a personal Rorschach test. When one considers all the reading and research that goes into these shows, it's imperative that the subject be of great interest to me.

If a person's bookshelf is a window into their interests,

apparently mine lean toward the apocalyptic—although it was a bit surprising just how often the shows eventually factored down to a related version of the same idea: the End of Civilization in one form or another and not just how we humans might react or respond to that based on past experience, but what kind of people these experiences might make us.

Can you blame me? The rise and falls of empires, the wars, the catastrophes, the high-stakes situations—the "Big Stories"—are intense and dramatic by their very nature.* The combination of material that is entertaining as well as (potentially) philosophical, educational, and practical is an age-old winning formula. Historians and storytellers from Homer and Herodotus to Edward Gibbon and Will Durant recognized that long before Ajax and Achilles were spearing their way dramatically and bloodily through *The Iliad* while making "History." There's a reason a guy like Shakespeare mined the past so often for his material.

But it isn't just about diversion or amusement. One is often moved to a form of historical empathy and personal reflection. These events happen to real flesh-and-blood human beings who were often relentlessly trapped in the gears of history. It's hard not to wonder how we would cope if we found ourselves in similar situations.

One of the things that I kept noticing when burrowing into the archives was a recurring, unanswerable either/or historical question. Will things keep happening as they always have, or

---

*My background is in journalism, and while a true professional should be able to get just as excited covering a dog show as a war, neither I nor most of my colleagues could do this. Judging from the ratings bumps that occur in news with huge events, it seems many people outside of journalism feel the same way about the "Big Stories." History, like news, has its big stories and sometimes "if it bleeds it leads" is a phrase that applies to both.

won't they? It is an unbelievably intense and scary question in some circumstances. Some of those types of case studies, if you will, are discussed in this book.

Will we ever again have the type of pandemics that rapidly kill large percentages of the population? This was a feature of normal human existence until relatively recently, but seems almost like science fiction to imagine today.

There have always been large wars between the great powers. Any next such war would involve nuclear-armed states. World War III sounds like a bad movie concept, but is it any more unlikely than eternal peace between the great states?

Finally, as we asked earlier, can you imagine the city you currently live in as a desolate ruin? Will it one day be like most cities that have ever existed, or not? Either outcome seems fascinating.

While much of what follows is rather dark, looking at history has a way of putting our circumstances in better perspective. Hearing about what, for example, people dealt with as their cities were carpet-bombed or while enduring monstrous medieval plagues has a way of making your problems seem small. Premodern dentistry alone is enough to convince me things are pretty good now, no matter what.

And yet, despite all the differences between people over the ages, some events and eras seem, as Barbara Tuchman wrote, like looking into a distant mirror. It's hard not to wonder how we would cope in similar circumstances. My grandfather loved the phrase "There, but for the grace of God, go I." Thanks to a bit of cosmic luck, we were born at the time we were, and in the place we were. It could've easily been any other time and some other place. I find that recalling that makes having historical empathy somewhat easier.

However, despite the seeming stability of our time, there's

also no guarantee that our current situation won't change drastically. The examples in this book dramatize some times in which this happened. At the risk of sounding like a low-rent Nostradamus wearing a sandwich board sign reading "The End Is Near," a modern version of the Bronze Age collapse *could* happen to us. Or the global superpower could implode unexpectedly, as ancient Assyria did, creating a huge geopolitical vacuum. Our version of Rome could fragment as the Roman Empire did. A pandemic could easily arise and if bad enough could remind us what life was like for human beings before modern medicine. A nuclear war could occur, or environmental disaster could await us. We may yet find ourselves in a reality that future ages read about in books on examples of extreme human experiences or warnings about things to avoid doing.

Hubris is, after all, a pretty classic human trait. As my dad used to say, "Don't get cocky."

THE END IS ALWAYS NEAR

Chapter 1

DO TOUGH TIMES MAKE
FOR TOUGHER PEOPLE?

FOR AS LONG as humans have been writing history, some historians have suggested that hard times somehow create better, tougher people, that overcoming obstacles—through war or privation or some other hardship—creates stronger, more resilient, perhaps even more virtuous, human beings.

"History is filled with the sound of silken slippers going downstairs and wooden shoes coming up," Voltaire reportedly said. The observation refers to the argument that fortunes of nations or civilizations or societies rise and fall based on the character of their people, and this character is heavily influenced by the material and moral condition of their society. The idea was a staple of history writing from ancient Greece until it began to decline in popularity after the middle of the twentieth century.*

Nowadays, the wooden shoes–silk slippers concept has been

---

*In many earlier eras of history writing, a large part of the historian's or author's goal was to impart or teach some sort of moral lesson, usually by historical example.

largely dismissed by modern historians. There are all sorts of very good reasons for this, starting with the lack of data. It is hard to prove or quantify an amorphous human quality such as toughness or resilience[*] and then justify its inclusion in a fact-driven, and peer-reviewed, academic history book. But that doesn't mean it has no impact at all.

Let's try a little mental exercise: Imagine that two boxers step into the ring together. They are the same height, weight, and skill level. They have had the same conditioning; they even shared a trainer. All possible variables have been eliminated. What is most likely to be the deciding factor in determining which boxer wins? Is it this hard-to-quantify concept we call "toughness"? It's difficult to say one boxer won because he was "tougher." For a start, why do we tend to assume that tougher is better? Toughness is this vague concept that we all believe exists, and we all use "tough" as an adjective, but it is a relative term, and one person's or culture's idea of what's tough may be different from another's.[†]

Now instead of individual boxers lining up against each other, imagine the contest on a larger scale, with entire societies facing off. For example, how about if the United States of America of today went to war against another country just like it—the same geographic size, the same population size, the same economic output, the same military capability, the same weapons

---

[*] Especially when you broaden it out to focus not just on individuals, but on whole societies.

[†] In fact, there are multiple words used instead of "tough" that in some contexts may mean the same thing. "Warlike" is a common example. Yet this defines toughness in purely military/violence terms. There are other potential aspects to this idea, such as emotional resiliency and the ability to withstand privation, which might constitute, in some combination, "toughness."

and equipment and technology. And this war is going to be brutal, fought to an unconditional surrender, with cities left in ruins on both sides. The only difference between the two countries is that the people we are fighting against, in that mythical mirror country, are our grandparents.

Most of the people born between 1900 and 1930 are gone now, but they were part of an age-group popularly dubbed "the Greatest Generation"*—but there have been so many tough eras and generations in history that singling out "the greatest" of anything seems a bit silly. Nonetheless, by our standards the members of the Greatest Generation seem very rough and tough indeed. And there's a reason for that. Even before they fought the Second World War, these men and women had lived through more than a decade of extreme economic hardship— the worst in modern world history.

Andrew Mellon, the secretary of the treasury under President Herbert Hoover when the 1929 stock market crashed, which initiated more than a decade of economic collapse, thought the coming hardship would be a good thing. "It will purge the rottenness out of the system," Mellon said, as reported in Hoover's memoirs. "High costs of living will come down. People will work harder, live a more moral life. Values will be adjusted, and enterprising people will pick up the wrecks from less competent people."

From Mellon's point of view, maybe he got his wish. The Depression put an end to the Roaring Twenties, a time remembered for high living, speakeasies, jazz, flappers, the Charleston, and the advent of motion pictures. What Mellon might have thought wasteful frivolity was simply fun to others. Things got a lot less fun when money became more scarce.

---

*This label was invented by the journalist Tom Brokaw for his 1998 book of the same name.

When the collapse came, it didn't ruin everyone, but about half the population found itself suddenly below the poverty line. It was a decade of hard times. And the accounts from that era are heartbreaking, so much so that it's hard to imagine any good coming from it. Certainly, few in our modern world would choose to experience an economic disaster like the Great Depression for the potential positive side effects.

By the time the Second World War arrived, an entire generation had been through deprivations. And then they got the worst war in human history right on top of it. The war itself was very bad, entirely different from twenty-first-century conflicts. Today, a first-class power might suffer casualties from a single incident that number in the dozens—perhaps from the mechanical failure of a helicopter, or maybe a blast from an improvised explosive device (IED). Compare this with the hundreds of thousands of casualties the United States experienced in the Second World War—at Iwo Jima, for example, the thirty-six-day conflict left nearly seven thousand Americans dead, of at least twenty-six thousand total casualties. And that's just American numbers; imagine the millions of casualties suffered by the Germans, or the tens of millions suffered by the Chinese and Soviets. It's interesting to speculate how we today would react to such mortality.

And it's not just about weathering the damage; it's also about inflicting it. Maybe we could take it, but as US general George Patton pointed out, that isn't how you defeat your adversary.* Think about the kind of bombing runs the American military had to make—a thousand planes loaded with tons of bombs

---

* "No dumb bastard ever won a war by going out and dying for his country. He won it by making some other dumb bastard die for his country." According to Lieutenant General James M. Gavin, Patton said this to officers in a wartime speech.

heading toward cities where ten or fifteen thousand people might be killed in a single night. Or imagine living through the Blitz in London, when German bombers unleashed their pay-loads on the city nearly every night for more than eight months. The Greatest Generation knew there was a solid wall of planes above them, and they also ordered the bomb bay doors to be opened.

And then there was the ultimate weapon, nuclear bombs. History shows that our grandparents certainly could, and did, use them.* Is there currently a scenario in which the citizens of our societies (as opposed to their governments) would find that an acceptable course of action?

We seem almost too civilized now to do something that seems so barbaric. But then, we haven't lived through what the World War II generation did. Assuming that one could measure a generation's relative toughness on a scale of one to ten, perhaps the Greatest Generation gets a seven; if we were to imagine ten of these people born between 1900 and 1930 together in a room, maybe seven of them meet our qualifications for "tough." Generation X has tough people, too—some became Navy Seals, a few have crossed Antarctica on foot—but maybe only two out of every ten members of that generation could be said to be tough enough to do such things. So rather than each individual being tougher, perhaps there is simply a higher percentage of tough people in what is considered a resilient generation. That is one way to try to conceptualize how toughness might apply to societies, and yet at the same time it helps highlight how strange it would be to try to quantify such a thing.

*For more on what it takes to drop a bomb or have one dropped on you, see chapters 7 and 8.

In the moralistic histories of the ancients, the "tough times make tougher people" formula worked both ways. Soft times made softer people. To Plutarch and Livy, for example, sloth, cowardice, and lack of virtue were the fruit of too much ease and luxury and money. And a lot of softer people in a society meant a softer overall society. In times and places where the citizenry might have to don armor and use a sword to defend their state in hand-to-hand combat, this could potentially be a national security concern. Perhaps we're living in a time when toughness in the old sense doesn't matter as much as it used to. If that is the case, then what advantages might a "softer" society have over a tougher one?

The great twentieth-century historian Will Durant wrote about the Medes, an ancient people who lived in what is now Iran. At the time Durant wrote,* the Medes were thought to have been a relatively poor, pastoral people who had banded together to help throw off the domination of the Assyrian Empire and who had then become a major power in their own right.† But soon after, wrote Durant, "the nation forgot its stern morals and stoic ways. Wealth came too suddenly to be used wisely. The upper classes became slaves to fashion and luxury, the men sporting embroidered trousers and the women cosmetics and jewelry."

The pants and earrings were not themselves the cause of the Medes' fall from power, but to Durant and many of his contemporary historians, they were outward signs of how this society had changed and become corrupted, along the way losing the

---

* In the 1930s.

† Since Durant's day, the view of the Medes has changed significantly. They are now thought to have been richer, more powerful, more organized, and more sophisticated than earlier historians gave them credit for.

qualities born of harder times that had made them tough enough to win the empire in the first place.*

The mid-twentieth-century historian Chester G. Starr wrote about Sparta, an entire society geared toward creating some of the finest fighting men in the ancient world. The soldiers of Sparta propelled this agrarian Peloponnesian Greek city-state to heights it had no right to expect given the size of its population and its relatively modest economic output. But the entire society and culture in Sparta supported and reinforced the army and soldiery. Every male citizen was trained for war and was liable for service until age sixty.

The trained citizen militia approach was common to many societies, especially in ancient Greece, but Sparta took it to extremes. There, it was nothing less than a human molding process that started at the very beginning of life: newborns were deemed the raw material of the military, and a Spartan baby was subjected to judgment by a council of Spartan elders who would decide whether the baby was fit enough to live. "Any child that appeared defective was thrown from a cliff of Mt. Taygetus, to die on the jagged rocks below," wrote Starr.[†]

The infants who were deemed worthy of living were subjected to "the Spartan habit of inuring their infants to discomfort and exposure." At seven years old, children were taken from their families and sent to a camp to train. As young adults, Spartans ate in communal military mess halls with their brethren, never

---

*Such comments may tell us more about the views of the mid-twentieth century than about the ancient Medes. Is it significant that Durant wrote this in the middle of the Great Depression?

[†] Starr wrote this more than fifty years ago. Many modern histories argue that Spartan children were left to die by exposure, and if they didn't, it proved they were tough enough to live. For more on views on children across societies and centuries, see chapter 2.

knowing the comforts of home. They were deliberately under-fed to encourage them to steal food and be resourceful, but then they were harshly punished if caught. These Spartan children grew up to be the best fighting men in Greece precisely because their whole culture worked to create them that way. Suppos-edly, the Spartans even eschewed money during their heyday,* because they thought it corrupted their upstanding morals and martial values.†

Then over time, according to the traditional narrative, the Spartans became "luxury-loving and corruptible," as Starr wrote, and this eroded their toughness and military superior-ity, eventually leading to their downfall on the battlefield. The Spartans of 380 BCE might not have beaten their very formi-dable grandfathers of 480 BCE, but the Spartans of 280 BCE would *definitely* not have beaten *their* grandfathers.‡ The hated Persians are sometimes credited with deliberately contributing to this. The "Great Kings" of Persia, who could not defeat the Spartans on the battlefield, found that gold was a more effec-tive way to neutralize them. Over time, the premodern sources portray Spartans, especially some Spartan kings, as a good deal more materialistic and money loving than the more "spartan" Spartans of old. It's as if these "soft" Persians, as the ancient

---

*Dating this would be subjective, but 550–400 BCE isn't a bad range to consider as the Spartan "heyday."

†This existed elsewhere, too. High-class people in Republican Rome thought commerce and money were beneath them. Money was what mer-chants and dirty people did. The Japanese samurai were that way as well; merchants were the lowest class in their society. Peasants were above merchants—at least they farmed the food you needed.

‡If we ignore the toughness aspect or "moral decline" idea completely, one might easily say that the ever-decreasing numbers of people in the Spartiate class (the group that composed the classic Spartan elite heavy infantry spear-men) was a bigger factor.

Greeks often portrayed them, spreading their softness like a virus, equalized the toughness between the two sides.*

There are other ways to explain Sparta's rise and fall than "toughness"—better training and conditioning, for example— but it seems strange to assign no value to it at all.

WAR AND POVERTY are not constants. They may create a heightened resilience on the part of the humans affected by them, but not all people are. Some people get lucky and avoid combat and economic privation. But everyone gets sick.

It may seem strange to suggest that high levels of illness might make human beings tougher, but the effect on a society of relatively regular and lethal epidemics and the mortality they cause certainly might have created a level of resilience that most of us today probably don't possess. A husband and wife who have lost several of their young children to disease and have stoically pushed forward with their lives would probably seem tough and resilient to us. People around the world still do this, and we consider it one of the great tragedies of life to lose even a single offspring. But it has been only relatively recently in human history that this experience has become less than commonplace. Before the modern era, the number of people who lost multiple children to illness was astonishing. One wonders what effects this might have had on individuals and their society as a whole. The historian Edward Gibbon, who wrote *The History of the Decline and Fall of the Roman Empire*, was one of seven children. All six of his siblings died in infancy. That was a pretty high rate even in the early eighteenth century, but the

---

* One member of the Greatest Generation offered this solution for bringing down the Soviet Union: "We should have been dropping *Playboy* magazines, blue jeans, and Elvis Presley records on them, and they'll do it themselves."

terrible regularity of losing children before they reached adult-hood was common. However, focusing on what disease might do to children is to ignore the wider effects that high levels of illness can have on a society. A really bad epidemic might kill everyone.

When it comes to disease, the world is a vastly different place in the modern era than it was at any previous time in history.* Yes, there are parts of the developing world that have been virtually unchanged since the Middle Ages and are still disease ridden, but by and large the technologically advanced societies of the modern world have scant concept of the way human existence was affected by disease from the beginning of humankind until just a generation ago. It's startling to think of the many pandemics that have erased large percentages of the global population over the ages. Reading the contemporary accounts is like reading very dark science fiction. If we lost a quarter of the human population to a modern plague, it would seem obscene to suggest there was the positive side effect of making us more resilient.

In some ways, illness makes us tougher, because immunities often develop in those who have been sick. That's hard science. But do people who suffer the regular loss of loved ones to disease become tougher or more resilient individuals? Do societies with large numbers of such people living in them become tougher societies? These questions fall into that gray area of things that we intrinsically feel *might* be important, but that can't really be measured or proved. Clearly, there were times in our history when only the strong survived, so a person had better be tough. But a case might be made that toughness isn't as important a qualification for survival as it used to be.

*For more on the effects of disease on societies, see chapter 6.

Connecting this to the wooden shoes–silk slippers ladder, one might suggest that timing is important. If tough times call for tough people, what if the times are less tough? In addition, the silk slippers stage can come with some potentially offsetting benefits.

The early-twentieth-century German military historian Hans Delbrück* had a theory that everything that characterizes the modern military—the organization, tactics, drill, logistics, and leadership—is designed to help offset the natural advantage of the toughness that people at a lower level of civilization possess. "Compared to civilized people," he wrote about the ancient Germans who kept getting beaten by the more refined Romans, "barbarians had the advantage of having at their disposal the warlike power of the unbridled animal instincts, of basic toughness. Civilization refines the human being, makes him more sensitive, and in doing so, it decreases his military worth, not only his bodily strength, but also his physical courage. These natural shortcomings must be offset in some artificial way. . . . The main service of the standing army consists of making civilized people through discipline capable of holding their own against the less civilized."†

By Delbrück's way of thinking, the whole reason that city-states first started organizing their farmers—who generally tended to be more peaceable than the barbarians right outside their borders—was to create a superior military, which requires training and discipline, so that they could hold their own against people whose harsher environment made them

---

*In the movie *Young Frankenstein*, when Dr. Frankenstein sends Igor to fetch a brain for his creation, it is Delbrück's that he wants. Then Igor drops it on the floor and grabs another brain labeled "Abnormal."

†For more on the ancient Germans, see chapter 5.

fiercer or more warlike.* "If a given group of Romans normally living as citizens or peasants had been put up against a group of barbarians of the same number," Delbrück wrote, "the former would undoubtedly have been defeated; in fact, they would probably have taken flight without fighting. It was only the formation of the close-knit tactical body of the cohorts that equalized the situation."

The seemingly softer society's use of technology, superior organizational capabilities, and money against a potentially tougher and hardier society is a dynamic that's visible in many historical eras. The modern Afghans may be one of the toughest people on the planet right now, but their individual and societal resilience is offset by Western military forces that might as well be playing the part of the Romans in this story. However, if the Western militaries were forced to fight using the same weapons as the Afghans—AK-47s, rocket-propelled grenades, and IEDs— and they, in turn, used our drones, fighter planes, and cruise missiles, then the question of our toughness versus theirs might be crucial. Remember, the Afghans have been a people at war for forty years, against a multitude of opponents. In some ways, they might be more like our grandparents when it comes to toughness than we are.

The weapons and technology are so advanced now that we can have a modern warrior engaging his foe in Afghanistan from an air-conditioned room in Kansas—a virtual pilot whose skills were likely honed growing up on video games the same way that a Japanese youth two centuries ago practiced for a future of sword fighting in kendo class. Instead of combat weapons drill, today's trained killers, many of whom may never see a dead

---

*Again, two words sometimes used that in some cases represent the same thing as toughness (as we, and apparently Delbrück, are defining it).

enemy up close, fly drones that shoot tough-as-nails tribal soldiers in the harsh, mountainous terrain.* Modern militaries have, like Delbrück's Romans, found ways to work around the toughness deficit.† Yet toughness may still make a difference in who wins or loses the war. It may be the key factor that decides who has the willingness to continue the ongoing body count and financial costs indefinitely.‡ But if it were, how could a historian prove it conclusively in a peer-reviewed paper?

---

*It gives a whole new meaning to the phrase "revenge of the nerds," as the designers of much of this super-technical gear used by drone pilots probably weren't playing quarterback in high school.

†The tip-of-the-spear Western troops today that are in combat operations on the ground are just as tough as their adversaries, just as Roman elite units were in the days of the legions. The support elements and civilian populations at home might be another matter, however.

‡This is a similar dynamic to that of the latter stages of US involvement in Vietnam.

Chapter 2

SUFFER THE CHILDREN

HISTORY IS AKIN to traveling to a distant planet, but one inhabited by human beings. Biologically the same, but culturally alien—and a major reason is that they were raised differently.

The importance of parents and parenting is almost universally accepted. Like toughness, it is an aspect of humanity that we almost intrinsically understand to be extremely influential in how a person turns out as an adult, but it's challenging to assess its impact on individuals in the past or on human history as a whole. Yet it would seem strange to suggest that the way parents reared children was of no great historical import at all. What if they reared everyone wrong?

"Wrong" is a culturally determined concept, of course. Every age and culture has its own ideas on the best way to raise progeny. But while parents in any place or time usually try to do what's best for their offspring, in the past much of the information they had was fallacious. Out of ignorance they may have harmed children while doing things they believed would be beneficial. Today the modern understanding of health and science, and the widespread dissemination of parenting information, has probably created the most knowledgeable generation of parents ever. Of particular emphasis is early childhood development. The effects of poor childhood nutrition, prenatal damage from alcohol and drugs, bad hygiene, child abuse, and just awful parenting during a child's formative years are well known. Parents deemed unfit or abusive or who can't meet minimum societal standards often lose custody of their children. In very bad cases, they can go to prison.

There's no doubt that these measures have, over time, tremendously improved the child-raising climate in our modern societies. The benefit to individual kids is incalculable. But trying to determine how this adds up at the societal level is extremely difficult. It's obvious that it has to make a large difference, and yet it's almost impossible to say exactly how or to what degree it actually has. Do huge cultural improvements in child rearing create a better society? Conversely, how much did poor childhood environments affect the societies of the past?

Some of the theories on the subject can seem far-fetched, but they definitely prompt us to think about things that might have slipped below the radar scanning for the traditional names, dates, and events we usually seek out when we're trying to understand history. Could you, for example, suggest that child-rearing practices can affect a nation's foreign policy? If it seems unlikely, imagine a world where half the adults are child abuse victims, and then consider the many strange and unforeseen consequences that might manifest. It's a fascinating question.

One of the earlier voices exploring the potential historical importance of child-rearing practices was Lloyd deMause.* DeMause specializes in psychohistory, a controversial discipline

---

*DeMause thinks child-rearing practices may indeed be capable of affecting a nation's foreign policy.

that focuses on, among other things, child-rearing practices and the effect they might have on the way history unfolds. He takes a rather dim view of parents in the past, writing in *The Emotional Life of Nations*, "Parents until relatively recently have been so frightened and have so hated their newborn infants that they have killed them by the billions, routinely sent them out to extremely neglectful wet nurses, tied them up tightly in swaddling bandages lest they be overpowered by them, starved, mutilated, raped, neglected, and beat them so badly that prior to modern times, I have not been able to find evidence of a single parent who would not today be put in jail for child abuse."

DeMause and the psychohistorians look at societies of the past in the same way psychologists and psychiatrists look at individuals today, trying to figure out if the early development of and influences on children affected the societies they created later.* DeMause believes that most children up until recent times would likely have met modern criteria as child abuse victims, which he and others like him believe may help explain why, for example, eras like the Middle Ages were so barbarous.†

But human cultures are so varied that such blanket statements seem too sweeping. While such theories might appear applicable to some complex urban societies, many premodern

---

*To date, the discipline of psychohistory seems to have garnered scant interest from higher academic institutions, with its critics going so far as to call it a pseudoscience.

†Critics of deMause say that rather than writing about standard child-rearing practices he has instead written a history of child abuse. Many of the terrible things he cites were done by parents of earlier eras often out of ignorance rather than malice. Much of his academic criticism focuses on the wide-ranging effects on history that he attributes to the way people were being treated while growing up. DeMause's critics rightly point out that his conclusions are often based more on speculation than data. But, in his defense, how could one collect and interpret data about a subject like this?

and tribal societies had age-old patterns of human upbringing that involved plenty of parental and extended family love and nurturing. Yet members of such societies too often involved children in practices and activities that we today would assume would cause lasting damage. But some of these things were merely aspects of living life in another era. The violence, for example, that a child growing up several thousand years ago may have seen on a regular basis may have had little or no negative effect on her compared with its effect on a modern child. It just might have been part of life in her world.

One of the important variables in this discussion concerns whether culture can be said to have shielded the children of past eras to any degree from the effects of what we today would call abuse, neglect, or emotional and psychological trauma. If a behavior that we moderns consider horribly deviant were viewed in a more positive and culturally reinforced way in the past, some argue that the effects would have been less damaging. It feels a bit like grading child abuse or bad parenting on a historical curve, but if something is more socially accepted and lacks the stigma it would have today, does that lessen its damage? Some would argue that the damage is a constant regardless of the society or era, others that it is culturally influenced. Either these people of the past were basically normal and well-adjusted adults despite their childhood experiences and the differences in parenting, or they were, as deMause argues, almost universally what we would today classify as abused children living in a society created by, operated by, and led by abused children.

The easiest way to imagine how bad things might have been for children growing up in past societies is to simply imagine what our own would look like if we removed today's prohibitions, investigations, and enforcement concerning such things as child abuse and neglect. Even with our modern attention and efforts, children are abused, mistreated, and neglected in every society on earth. Without those rules and enforcement, such mistreatment would almost certainly be much worse. Imagine how bad it might get if a society actually *encouraged* such behavior.*

BEATING CHILDREN WAS a common form of discipline from the earliest days of human history to relatively recent times. Many in the Greatest Generation, for example, grew up in a culture that did not think the general practice unusual whatsoever.† In fact, beating was considered by many to be the preferred and proper way to raise good, well-adjusted adults. It was routinely done to students in schools. And while a parent today who regularly struck his child with a belt twenty or thirty times would be considered abusive by the vast majority of people, he would have been considered positively lenient by the standards of past eras, when a belt might seem a poor substitute for something designed specifically for the task of beating kids.

DeMause's *The History of Childhood* describes various implements of corporal punishment, including

- whips of all kinds,
- cat-o'-nine-tails,
- shovels,
- canes,
- iron and wooden rods,

*Imagine popular culture offerings—movies, music, television—showing child abuse and sex with children in positive and provocative lights, some ancient society's cultural value system combined with today's modern media and marketing power.

† Attitudes on beating children, as opposed to giving them a quick swat or light spank on the rear, started to change in the 1960s, and changed quickly.

- bundles of sticks,
- "disciplines" (whips made of small chains), and
- "flappers" (school instruments with a pear-shaped end and a round hole, used to raise blisters).

Today there is almost no chance we would countenance the use of a discipline tool specifically designed to raise blisters on a seven- or eight-year-old child. Yet the oft-cited line "spare the rod and spoil the child" asserts that a parent who is too lenient with physical punishment on children is doing them harm. People took this admonition seriously for a long time.*

It's hard to blame parents for not seeing the potential damage they were doing to their children, because, after all, this is how they themselves had been raised. If we are imagining what a society of abused children might be like to live in, consider for a moment how they might raise their own offspring. The historian M. J. Tucker in an essay in *The History of Childhood* gives an account of the harsh treatment Lady Jane Grey† endured at the hands of her parents and then writes that "Jane's parents were typical. . . . Common usage decreed that parents who love their children will beat them." He says that this is how the children often saw it as well: "Little girls, like Lady Jane Grey, never doubted that her beatings issued from parental concern and blessed herself that her parents took their responsibility so seriously." Lady Jane Grey would be executed as a teenager after being caught up in a royal succession crisis. Had she lived, though, and wished to have been a good mother by the standards of the time,

---

*There are still the occasional voices suggesting that society would benefit from a return to the old corporal punishment approaches.

† British noblewoman and "Nine Day Queen" who lived in the mid-1500s.

how would this beaten child have been likely to behave toward her own kids?

While child beating has gone out of fashion, corporal punishment is still practiced in some public school systems in the United States, and there are still people who defend its use as valuable (albeit not to the degree of severity we just talked about). The same cannot be said for some of the other kinds of abuse that many children of past ages were subjected to. For instance, some societies and cultures of the past held wildly differing ideas of what should and shouldn't be okay sexually between adults and children.* It not only makes it difficult for us today to relate to those cultures and peoples but it's hard to imagine that such cultural perspectives didn't have a large effect on their reality. It wasn't particularly uncommon in many cultures in past eras for children to be viewed as sexual objects and sometimes to be used as such. There are four-hundred-year-old accounts of sailors who encountered overtly sexual women on Pacific Islands, but some of these "women" were as young as ten. To us, such sexual relations may seem bizarre or even obscene, but what if the society these sailors existed in didn't think so?

In other ages, antiquity for example, the mores were often very different from our own when it came to sex and children.† In the ancient Mediterranean, both heterosexual and homosexual sex between adults and children was in many places an accepted part of the culture. Would the children in those

---

*This is complicated by the fact that many societies over time have allowed or encouraged girls to marry at puberty.

†Antiquity is generally thought of as the period of human history before the fall of Rome in the fifth century CE.

ancient cultures experience the same long-term adverse effects we would expect to see in children who had sex with adults today? If they did, one wonders how this might have affected how those societies developed. If they didn't, that's also interesting—one would have to wonder why.

Even parents who wanted to do the best for their children and were perhaps less inclined to outright beat them could do great damage to them by simply following the prevailing wisdom at the time—inadvertent child abuse, if you will.

One common practice throughout much of human history was to give children liquor or opium to relieve teething pain or to help them sleep. As recently as the 1960s, it wasn't unusual for a doctor to prescribe sleeping medication for children, or for parents to rub whiskey on a teething infant's gums. We know now these substances are harmful, but there were some people who recognized the problem even hundreds of years ago. *The History of Childhood* quotes a British doctor named Hume, who complained in 1799 of thousands of child deaths caused by nurses "forever pouring Godfrey's cordial down little throats, which is quite a strong opiate, and in the end as fatal as arsenic."

Once upon a time, it was considered good parenting to teach your children a moral lesson in right and wrong by taking them to witness public executions. To make the lesson really stick, parents sometimes beat their children as they watched, forever linking the spectacle with physical pain. And the practice of beating a child so he or she wouldn't forget was done for other reasons, too. Anglo-Saxons sometimes beat kids so that they would recall a given day for legal reasons, such as presenting evidence at trial—physical violence as a kind of notary public service, or long-term reminder note.

In modern times, we worry about our kids' exposure to simulated violence on television or in video games and whether it desensitizes them to real-life atrocities. But in many past eras it may have been actual violence, not the made-for-TV variety, that desensitized children to more of the same. Think of the children who grew up in cultures where they would have seen real-life killings and torture up close by the time they were five, six, or seven years old. In some cases, they might have even participated in it.*

If we heard of a modern child with such a bloody or violent upbringing, we would assume he or she would be a very damaged person in need of counseling and help. It's hard to determine, though, if all children in all times and all cultures would be affected the same way by such experiences. It's possible that people in earlier eras who grew up seeing animals butchered and people killed as a matter of course weren't affected the way a person with modern sensibilities would be. Today we might assume certain things would hurt any human being at any time, but this may not be true. Actions don't have to cause obvious harm to create a significantly different version of a human being. A child (either today or in the past) who has witnessed several very violent live public executions is going to be different from the other children in our society. Any modern child with the same life experiences would probably be prescribed some sort of therapy and perhaps medications for a long time.

After considering such heavy-duty abuse, you might think something like physical or emotional child abandonment would sound like a lightweight issue—but modern experts who deal with children have no doubt about the lasting negative impact that a lack of sustained contact between parents and children can have. The psychohistorians assert that such situations may

---

*Some Native American tribes, for example, considered it culturally appropriate for women and children to participate in the torture of war captives.

have damaged a lot of children in the past. This seems like a no-brainer on the surface, but trying to determine how this might have affected the past on a macro scale is seemingly impossible.

In many past societies, parents and children had less contact than we are accustomed to today.* Even the bonding experience of a mother feeding her infant was something often farmed out. For thousands of years, in many societies and cultures, the human institution of the wet nurse was very popular. There are stories of wet nurses—women who breastfeed other women's babies—in the Bible and going back to ancient Babylon. Roman wet nurses gathered at a place called the Columna Lactaria (the "milk column") to sell their services. For mothers who couldn't produce milk or had died in childbirth, the wet nurse filled a real need, especially when many such societies didn't believe in giving infants animal milk.

Yet the practice often still meant sending children away from their homes to live with a wet nurse, sometimes for years. The casual giving away of children in past eras can astound; in various writings from the eighteenth and nineteenth centuries, children sometimes sound like litters of puppies rather than human beings. The mother-in-law of one nineteenth-century gentleman wrote about a baby that had been promised to another family: "Yes, certainly the baby shall be sent as soon as it is weaned," she wrote, "and if anyone else would like one, would you kindly recollect that we have others."

The trauma didn't end with the sending away. After the child spent years bonding with the wet nurse, they were eventually returned to their biological parents, essentially ripping him or

---

*This varies widely, and many traditional societies fall on the opposite side of the spectrum, with mother and child almost literally joined at the hip, as they spend so much time in close proximity to each other.

her away from the only parent he or she had known.* Sometimes the wet nurses were unkind to their charges, making returning home a blessing, but either way, the child was now faced with complete strangers. Lloyd deMause quotes a piece written by the chief of police in Paris in 1780 estimating that of the, on average, 21,000 children born in that city every year, only 700 were nursed by their biological mothers. (Marie Antoinette, writing in a letter to her mother, noted after her daughter recognized her as her mother in a room full of people, "I believe I like her much better since that time"—which suggests she hadn't liked her all that much before.)

Children could also be seen much more like a commodity than a family member. Selling children was a profitable business (and there are parts of the world where it still occurs). Children were also farmed out for labor. The Middle Ages institution of the apprenticeship took kids as young as five or six to a neighboring castle or community to begin their working life. This wasn't seen by parents as a form of punishment or abuse, but more like an internship in which the child would learn valuable foundational skills necessary for later adult success. And farm families since agriculture began have used every strong hand available to work the land and keep food on the table.† But seeing children as nothing more than easily exploitable low-wage labor was all too common. It wasn't until the late 1930s in the United

---

*Winston Churchill, a boy in the late nineteenth century, was raised this way. He had a wet nurse whom he called Womb, and she was the person he got all his motherly love from.

†Most people today would think kids growing up on a family farm working to help their parents was not only okay but taught the value of hard work. So where does such labor cross the line into something twenty-first-century people would call abusive? We don't want ten-year-olds working the register at McDonald's, but we celebrate their picking beans for Mom and Dad.

States that child labor in such dangerous industries as mining and manufacturing was outlawed. There was much more opposition to the reform attempts at the time than might be thought. But today the idea of sending a thirteen-year-old into a mine or a twelve-year-old onto an assembly line seems like one destined to stunt the child's development.

It makes one wonder why our ancestors—many of whom were perfectly smart people—didn't see how damaging these practices were. Yet perhaps our concept of what constitutes "damage" is different from theirs. They were raising kids to live in their world, a world alien to us. Besides, who knows what child-rearing experts of the future will think about our current practices? Maybe our best practices now will be deemed abusive or damaging to children by future standards. In our defense, we could probably say that we did the best we could knowing what we know now—but that's also probably what our ancestors would have said.

Chapter 3

THE END OF THE WORLD
AS THEY KNEW IT

THE IDEA OF "progress" is not without bias. Is transitioning from a hunter-gatherer society to one where humans live in cities an advance, or do we just think it is because that's where we mostly live now?* If a society that is literate is supplanted by one that is not, is that a backward step in the progress of civilization? If the economic vitality and wealth of a society is reduced to a level far below its highs, is that necessarily a "decline"?†

Since human civilization first arose, societies have "risen" and "fallen," "advanced" and "declined"—or so the histories written decades ago often said. More commonly now, historians refer to societies in "transition," rather than use terms that

---

*Many native peoples have expressed the opinion that they prefer their traditional way of existence to the one offered by the more "advanced" societies that have subjugated them. Could this be *their* bias at work?

†Some have suggested that, in order to create sustainable modern societies in the future, what we consider economic progress today might need to be reimagined. Could a "decline" in one aspect of a society's development be part of an advance in another?

denote forward or backward development. Continuity, too, is often emphasized, instead of the emphasis found in earlier historical accounts of hard breaks from a previous era.

So, did the Roman Empire "fall" to the "barbarians," or did it transition to an equal yet more decentralized era, one with a more Germanic flair?

In the period after the Roman Empire disappeared in the West (the time formerly called "the Dark Ages"), many of the capabilities of the people who lived in its wake deteriorated. Eventually, those who lived in what formerly were Roman lands couldn't repair or build anew the infrastructure that had previously existed. The aqueducts, monetary system, and trade routes were not what they had been. Literacy plummeted in most areas, and other groups and outlets began to perform some of the functions that formerly had been provided by an organized central authority.* What would we call it today if we could not emulate the technological, economic, or cultural achievements of our forebears?†

The 1968 film *Planet of the Apes* provides an instructive illustration of the inherent fallacy of the position that *our* version of humanity represents its final incarnation. In the movie, a bedraggled Charlton Heston (in a loincloth, no less) screams, "Take your stinking paws off me, you damn dirty ape!" In his character's mind, the apes are beneath him, but to the apes, *humans* are the inferior species.

At the very end, Charlton Heston escapes, and in the final

---

*Monasteries and other church entities are examples, as were more local authorities like cities and bishoprics. Local warlords or rulers also filled this role in some places.

† It's hard to even imagine something comparable. What if we lost the Internet, not just for a while, but forever? Or what if spaceflight became something humankind was no longer capable of?

moments of the film, you see him riding a horse down a beach with a preverbal (i.e., inferior) human girl he's rescued. When he rounds a bend, he's confronted with the Statue of Liberty, from the bust up to the crown, sticking out of the sand at an angle, and we realize that the movie is set on earth in a far-flung future.

"You maniacs! You blew it up!" Heston bellows, his fist pounding the sand.

We moderns almost unconsciously consider ourselves exempt from outcomes such as this, which is one of the reasons why that final scene in *Planet of the Apes* is so effective.* It is unimaginable to us that we could have descendants who might live in a world more primitive than our own. Likewise, it was just as impossible for Romans living in the era we now label "antiquity" to envision a future in which the place they knew as "the Eternal City" would ever be a ruin.

THE EARLIEST PIECE of storytelling in the Western canon appeared around the eighth century BCE. The *Iliad* was supposedly composed by the blind Greek poet Homer, though historians have long thought its text was actually distilled from an oral storytelling tradition that was far older.

The *Iliad* tapped into a potent mix of dramatic elements that humans have shown an enthusiasm for ever after. The epic poem features facets of superhero films mixed with the J. R. R. Tolkien–style mythical golden age of a far-flung past. It's the original and ultimate "sword and sandals" epic, an

---

*We have no problem imagining the plot as a science fiction or dystopian story. We can even contemplate the aftermath of nuclear war or climate disaster as an outcome we wish to avoid. But it's very difficult for most people to seriously think about such things as ever happening. We innately consider civilizational collapse an imaginary situation rather than something that has actually occurred to people living before us.

action-packed saga of gods, demigods, and swashbuckling heroes, where the "Greeks" leave their homeland to rescue the kidnapped oh-so-fair wife of a king and embark on a quest that leads them across the sea to fight a great war for a decade and eventually topple a powerful, glorious kingdom led by a rich and lofty monarch. The story has everything—magic and spearplay, dead characters that come back to life as ghosts, the gods fighting among themselves and taking sides with the mortals, sex and romance between star-crossed adversaries, bloody single combats, and heroic loss. It's even got a sequel, if you consider the *Odyssey* to be such. But whereas our modern fantastic tales and epics are intended—and are taken by the audience—as fantasy, the ancient Greeks, Macedonians, and Romans often considered their versions more like history.*

One of history's greatest military leaders, Alexander III of Macedon (known as "the Great"; 356–323 BCE), allegedly slept with a copy of Homer's *Iliad* under his pillow, and he may have considered himself inspired by, and a direct descendant of, the story's überhero, Achilles.† Before attacking the Persian Empire in 334 BCE, Alexander visited a site the locals said was the tomb of Achilles, and the classical writers say that he donned the "ancient" armor he found within.‡ To him, Troy was history from a long-gone great age, and he had the antique armor of a demigod to prove it.

---

* Some of the more skeptical Greeks would say that tales like the *Iliad* were true in the main, but exaggerated by storytellers.

† Achilles could easily be called an ancient Greek version of a superhero—he was the son of an immortal, after all!

‡ Let the record show that locals in many places throughout history have figured out the value of tourist attractions connected to local history. The Christian Byzantines would buy up "relics" the locals in the Holy Land "found" all the time, then bring them home, and venerate them.

Later scholarly opinion disagreed that the *Iliad* was history, however. Starting with increasingly skeptical and evidence-based academic approaches in the eighteenth century, historians trying to disentangle truth from fable considered the tale of the Trojan wars to be legendary. In the late nineteenth century, however, a German named Heinrich Schliemann, one of several people who believed in the existence of the ancient city and was actively looking for it, found the remains of one on a hill in modern-day Turkey. Over time it became clearer and clearer that the site Schliemann had found was indeed the location of the city at the center of the West's oldest written tale. Somehow, through hundreds of years of oral storytelling, the Greeks had kept alive a distant memory of an advanced and prosperous time that existed on the far side of an intervening dark age.[*]

This discovery of "Troy" by an amateur (as most archaeologists were in that era) searching for artifacts caused an international sensation and helped jump-start the modern era of archaeological discovery. Digs, excavations, and fieldwork all over the Mediterranean and the Near East began to unearth and illuminate a world that was already ancient when the Athens of Pericles (495–429 BCE) and the Sparta of Leonidas (540–480 BCE) were young. Troy was but a tiny fraction of it. A snapshot from about 1500 BCE would show a multipower geopolitical landscape encompassing the whole region: ancient Egypt at its pharaonic height in the New Kingdom; the powerful and important Hittite Empire, controlling a large chunk of modern-day Turkey and down into Syria; Assyria and Babylon, strong societies in what is now Iraq; the Elamite people, occupying

---

[*] The Greeks of the classical era sometimes called the age of the *Iliad* stories the "heroic age" or the "mythical age." It has echoes of J. R. R. Tolkien's "First Age of the Sun" in his realm of Middle-Earth.

southwestern Iran; Minoa, a great maritime trading state based in Crete; and the Mycenaeans, who occupied Greece.*

It was an era of great cities, many of them crowned with ornate palaces, and urban life was at its highest level of sophistication so far seen. It was a golden age of wealth, power, writing, trade, military sophistication, and long-distance communication. This era, which modern history calls the Bronze Age (approximately 3000 to 1200 BCE), represents a high-water mark in the region's development in many measurable areas. The last stage of the Bronze Age was the most golden of all.†

But the glory of the Bronze Age wouldn't last. By the time of the Iron Age, the classical Greeks of Athens and Sparta were beginning to rise to levels of wealth, trade, and literacy that were comparable to the lofty heights of the previous era (in

---

*The Mycenaeans are traditionally thought of as the Greeks of the Trojan War story.

†The time period categorizations of early history that we all know came about in the nineteenth century when historians labeled certain eras of the past in order to make it easier to study them. That's when people started using the terms "Stone Age," "Bronze Age," and "Iron Age." These eras got subdivided further from that point—the Stone Age, for instance, was broken down to the Paleolithic, Mesolithic, and Neolithic. The Bronze Age is divided into early, mid, and late periods. But it's not a neat rubric and doesn't denote an equal pace of change in every location. The late Bronze Age crosses over into the early Iron Age, and different societies were in different places in the arc of "progress." (Needless to say, the criteria is set by the designers, and this can influence how cultures and societies are rated and assessed. If you decide a society must have bronze to be advanced, does that mean no society without bronze is advanced?) When western Asia was in the early Iron Age, most if not all of Europe would still probably have better fit the criteria for the late Bronze Age. The further back in time you go, the more problematic dating specific periods becomes, and there is a lot of controversy about dates in the Bronze Age. But these specific eras are all human constructs; nobody alive in 1300 BCE knew he was living in the Bronze Age. It makes one wonder what label future historians might slap on our own age.

probably around 700 BCE-ish)—in fact, those earlier states and civilizations of the late Bronze Age could well have been represented to the Iron Age as *Planet of the Apes* represented ours. The remnants of their former greatness were nearly totally in ruins, and their history was relegated to myths and legend.

The "collapse of the Bronze Age" is a transformation on par with the fall of the Western Roman Empire, but what caused it has become one of the great mysteries of the past, a whodunnit that casts historians in the role of detectives trying to determine a cause of death for one of humankind's great time periods.

It apparently happened relatively quickly. That's why words like "collapse," "destruction," and "fall" are often used when talking about how this literal end of an era concluded. Unlike the Roman Empire, there would be no "decline and fall"—the Bronze Age would tumble from its highs like a stock market crash. An older person alive in the regions most affected during the steepest dive (from about 1200 to 1150 BCE) would likely have seen a very different world than the one she had been born into.

Histories written a century or even a half century ago have relatively definite conclusions about the fall of the Bronze Age (and a hundred other subjects). Times have changed. Modern standards and methods in many fields have subjected any and all theories to acid tests that historians of the past never dreamed of. From dating technology to DNA sampling to a thousand other tools, modern researchers have resources that can unlock—or debunk—information as never before.

It is in the nature of such scrutiny that existing theories get shot down more easily than new ones garner support. The historian John H. Arnold pointed out that history is an ongoing process—it never can, nor will, reach its final conclusion, and revisions will always be happening, as more facts and data become available and older theories are modified or disproved.

One by one, modern researchers are debunking (or at least casting reasonable doubt on) many of the theories about the end of the Bronze Age. But though today's experts have immeasurably more information about the time, they are less sure about what befell it than ever before.

A good detective might have two questions to set the parameters for any investigation:

1. What happened?
2. How (why) did it happen?

If question number one can't be answered, it becomes extremely difficult to answer question number two. And the truth is, experts still disagree about that first question.

Traditionally, the explanation behind "the fall of the Bronze Age" says that sometime between about 1250 and 1100 BCE, something horrifying happened to the areas in the ancient world that were anywhere close to the Mediterranean Sea. Some sort of phenomenon or event or series of events affected states and peoples from the central Mediterranean all the way east into modern-day Iraq. Hundreds of cities were destroyed or abandoned. Famine, war, disease, political upheaval, volcanoes, earthquakes, piracy, human migration, and climate changes such as drought are mentioned in the sources and found in the data. Somehow and at some point, the complex, interconnected system of trade and communication supporting the very centralized states in this era was disrupted. By about 1100 BCE, many of the formerly centralized societies had reverted (or fragmented into) more localized, smaller political entities, while wealth (such as evidenced by grave goods included in burials) declined in opulence.

Most of the states that did survive the era emerged looking

like bruised and battered boxers who'd survived a grueling bout—somewhat diminished, if not permanently reduced, in power and influence. Egypt would never be the same. Writing would almost die out in Greece. And the powerful Hittite Empire, a large and strategically placed kingdom for two and a half centuries, was somehow destroyed.* Several major states never made it out of the Bronze Age at all.

The historian Robert Drews has said that the end of the eastern Mediterranean Bronze Age was one of history's most frightful turning points and a calamity for those who experienced it. According to Drews, almost every significant city in the eastern Mediterranean was destroyed over a fifty-year period running from the end of the thirteenth to the beginning of the twelfth century BCE. He ran down the list of damages:

> In the Aegean, the palace-centered world that we call Mycenaean Greece disappeared: although some of its glories were remembered by the bards of the Dark Age, it was otherwise forgotten until archaeologists dug it up. The loss in Anatolia was even greater. The Hittite empire had given to the Anatolian plateau a measure of order and prosperity that it had never known before and would not see again for a thousand years. In the Levant recovery was much faster, and some important Bronze Age institutions survived with little change; but others did not, and everywhere urban life was drastically set back. In Egypt the Twentieth Dynasty marked the end of the New Kingdom and almost the end of pharaonic achievement. Throughout the eastern Mediterranean the twelfth century B.C.

*The Hittite Empire existed for about the amount of time the United States has been an independent nation.

ushered in a dark age, which in Greece and Anatolia was not to lift for more than four hundred years. Altogether the end of the Bronze Age was arguably the worst disaster in ancient history, even more calamitous than the collapse of the western Roman Empire.

So much for the "what happened" side of the investigation.

The second part of the investigation concerns how or why it happened.

Theories have never been in short supply:

1. The sea peoples (and related causes)
2. Famine/climate change/drought
3. Earthquakes/volcanoes/tsunamis
4. Plagues
5. Internecine warfare
6. Systems collapse
7. Any or all of the above in combination

There's more.* But the problem isn't one of finding evidence—there seems to be data available in one form or another to support cases for and against all of these suspects in some places and during some times—but rather, the damage that was done seems so extensive that it's hard to imagine any single cause capable of wreaking such widespread and long-lasting havoc.

In addition, the evidence is tricky.†

---

*Such as cultural collapse, revolutionary political upheaval, civil war, and others. Some of these can be classified as possible side effects of the other prime suspects listed.

†And inconsistent. For every researcher demonstrating widespread destruction of cities, there will be others who counter with the many urban

Take destroyed cities: Often when destroyed cities from thousands of years ago are found, visible signs of their end are present. Soot and ash layers from torched buildings are the most obvious evidence at most sites, but bodies lying where they fell, weapons such as arrowheads embedded in walls, and other forms of damage are also sometimes found. This certainly tells you that the city died a violent death, but it doesn't necessarily tell you who was responsible. One normally thinks of a force of alien outsiders, but the perpetrators could also have been the city's inhabitants fighting a civil war among themselves or going through a political upheaval.* It's hard to finger the culprit based solely on the archaeological evidence.

The written word might be used to cross-check the archaeological findings, but words come with their own problems. First, the Bronze Age was obviously a long time ago. The Hebrew Bible was still centuries in the future when the Bronze Age ended. Despite a surprising amount of written material (again, a sure sign of an advanced era), far less than enough is available to solve this riddle.

Yet there are inscriptions from this period that discuss subjects that might be germane to this mystery.

If, for example, you find destroyed cities in the archaeological record, and then get written accounts of invasions by marauders in that same area and around the same time, the evidence looks damning. In Egypt, there are official records

---

enclaves that survived and even prospered in this era. Cyprus, for example, may have thrived while other states around it suffered.

* In the Hittite capital of Hattusa, for example, the royal fortress and major public buildings were apparently destroyed, but private residences were left untouched. This seems more like the deliberate targeting of the symbols of state power than the wild ransacking of a foreign army. Could it indicate domestic political upheaval or revolution rather than war? The mystery deepens . . .

(with pictures!) carved into stone of violent encounters with the mysterious "peoples of the sea."* The Egyptians made it sound as though these sea peoples were raping and pillaging and burning cities throughout the entire eastern Mediterranean like a horde of Bronze Age Vikings. They were thought by historians decades ago to be a primary reason for the chaos at the end of the era.

But can the Egyptian records be taken at face value? Could they be misleading, or an outright lie? Historians are specifically trained in the fine art of disentangling and interpreting evidence with a skeptical eye, and they've found problems with the Egyptian account.

Multiple Egyptian rulers documented violent encounters with peoples whom they themselves connected to the sea or to islands. They would say of this or that tribe that they were "of the sea" or "of the countries of the sea," or mention them "in their isles." These sea peoples are made out to be different tribes or states of warlike and seaborne groups whose origin isn't clear.† Just as the crisis period of the late Bronze Age began, at least one pharaoh was using some of these tribes of "sea people" warriors as mercenary soldiers fighting for Egypt, so it's unlikely that they would have been totally alien or unknown. *We* may not know who they were, or from whence they came, but it's very possible the Egyptians might have.

Ramesses III (1217–1155 BCE) claimed to have defeated some groups of sea peoples in a battle that is often dated to right in the

---

*This is a modern term. These peoples, their origins, and often what became of them are mysterious to us today. The Egyptians labeled them individually by tribe.

†"Northerners from all lands," they are called in one account. From Egypt's vantage point, most peoples lived to their north.

middle of the crisis period (1180 BCE).* His surviving written accounts portray him as a sort of bulwark of civilization, fighting off a coalition of alien forces that he said had launched a conspiracy together and had been unstoppable. Ramesses tells that these peoples or tribes had already overthrown several other great states, raping and pillaging the coasts and seas like ancient Norsemen—until they ran into *him*: "The foreign countries conspired in their islands. All at once the lands were removed and scattered in the fray. No land could resist their arms, from Hatti, Kode, Carchemish, Arzawa, and Alashiya on being cut off at one time. A camp was set up in Amurru. They desolated its people and its land was like that which had never existed. They were coming forward toward Egypt, while the flame was prepared for them. Their confederation was the Peleset, Tjeker, Shekelesh, Denen, and Weshesh, lands united. They laid their hands upon the lands as far as the circuit of the earth, their hearts were confident and trusting as they said 'Our plans will succeed!'"†

The pharaoh said the plans of these many united foreign tribes failed, that the Egyptians crushed the invasion and the survivors fared badly: "As for those who reached my frontier, their seed is not, their heart and their soul are finished forever and ever. As for those who came forward together on the seas, the full flame was in front of them at the Nile mouths, while a stockade of lances surrounded them on the shore, prostrated on the beach, slain, and made into heaps from head to tail."

It's not unusual for people who aren't historians to assume

---

*Dates for Egyptian rulers can be difficult and have changed somewhat over the eras. In addition, some histories use reigns for dating while other date ranges use the ruler or historical figure's birth and death.

†This text is taken from the victory inscription of Egyptian pharaoh Ramesses III.

this is an accurate retelling of events, and indeed this could be extremely important information. But can we fully believe it?

Some historians point out that Ramesses III may have taken a small encounter and magnified it to enormous proportions to exalt his own greatness. Others suggest that he was simply retelling an event that had happened in the time of a previous Egyptian ruler (the pharaoh Merneptah, who reigned from 1213–1203 BCE and carved a victory report in the walls at the Temple of Karnak) and claiming the earlier pharoah's victory as his own. He was certainly fibbing to some degree, as historians and archaeologists have proved that some of the cities he says were destroyed were not. And it may have been that he was writing for a particular audience and had certain things he wanted them to know or believe. The question of motive and context are crucial when deciding how far to believe a contemporary account.

Finally, there's all the data that modern scientific methods and technology can add to the picture, the value of which is immeasurable. The list of specialties working on aspects of the Bronze Age mystery includes people who study climate, volcanoes, earthquakes, tsunamis, agricultural trends, underwater archaeology, the paleoenvironment, and a host of other fields. But extrapolating actual answers from such information to help clear up the mystery itself seems no easier to come by. At least not yet.

If we look again at our list of prime suspects and the cases for and against them, it becomes clear just how difficult solving a case as cold as this can be.

Suspect #1: The Sea Peoples (and Related Causes)

Part of what makes really ancient history so interesting is that there are lots of peoples who seem to just appear from nowhere in the historical records. It's like *Star Trek* without the space travel. One minute there aren't any people like the Arameans or Phrygians or Kassites, next minute they're seemingly everywhere you look.

History, especially the further back one travels, has a way of compressing the events of the past, so that trends that occurred over generations seem to us to happen almost in an instant. The "sudden appearance" of a new tribe or people into ancient history may have actually occurred over many lifetimes. What history has called "invasions" may sometimes have been more like migrations, and what history has termed "migrations" and portrayed as entire peoples simultaneously on the move may in many cases have been more like gradual long-term immigration.

It's possible that's how it was with the so-called sea peoples.

The sea peoples were public enemy number one in what might be termed the "invasion theory." In the mid-twentieth century, it was popular to portray the urban "civilized" world of the Bronze Age as an oasis of development ringed by a sea of antagonistic barbarism. There was an osmosis-like dynamic that kept attracting the hardscrabble tribal types on the outside to the rich (but perhaps soft) "civilized" peoples. That *human* sea was kept at bay only through great effort. At times, the barbarian tribes would break through and overwhelm a given city, region, or even state.

In this view, the crisis at the end of the Bronze Age was akin to a perfect storm that set in motion many of these outsider peoples, creating a "time of troubles" led by fierce tribal warriors who overwhelmed all but the strongest of political entities.

As the historian Chester G. Starr wrote in 1965:

The [Bronze Age] monarchs failed until too late to notice that new waves of invasion were mounting. From the desert Semitic tribes lapped against the strongpoints of the cities; from the north a terrific assault broke forth in the late thirteenth century. Ugarit was burned and destroyed forever, as were many other Syrian centers; the Hittite realm vanished from the map shortly after 1200, as did also the Mycenaean kingdoms in Greece. Egypt, attacked by land and sea under Ramesses III (1182–51), barely rode out the storm. So too Assyria survived, but lost any capabilities of expansion for the next few centuries.

Several other once popular hypotheses could also be wrapped into the invasion theory. For example, the idea that much of the calamity from this era can be attributed to the discovery and wide use (among some) of iron fits nicely into any idea that warfare was a prime component of the Bronze Age catastrophe. Many once thought that iron was the secret superweapon of the ancient world in this age, and that once some peoples acquired the ability and know-how to produce it, they gained a huge advantage militarily over their enemies. People who had this capability (such as the Hittites) were said to jealously guard the secret of its manufacture.

This idea is much less popular than it once was, but it has evolved somewhat and now forms a component in other theories relating to, for example, the collapse of regional trade. The exchange among developed states in copper and tin was a key pillar of the economy in the interconnected Mediterranean Bronze Age.* Few places had both those metals, so trade was vital and lucrative. Iron's main value had less to do with its hardness than

---

*Bronze is made from a mix of copper and tin. Archaeologists often find the metals stored on board trading ships in the exact ratio needed to make bronze.

with its abundance.* If it was cheaper to outfit soldiers with iron weapons than bronze ones, that certainly would have had military implications. If it severely damaged the economies of the major trading states, that would have had ripple effects as well.†

Then there are the last two elements at play here that may fall under the "sea peoples and friends" category—piracy and human migration. These also overlap with the next potential suspects on the list.

Let's start with piracy. Whether it's the Egyptians talking about "northerners in their isles," or written correspondence from the coasts of the Levant, there's a general feeling about the late stages of the Bronze Age (and what happened in the famed "Viking Age," from about 700 to 1100 CE) that periodic outbreaks of large-scale piracy were not an unusual historical occurrence. In addition to the raiding of coastal settlements and the burning of villages, towns, and even major cities, the taking of ships and cargoes at sea could wreak havoc on the all-important Mediterranean maritime trading network. A small amount of piracy in this region was no doubt normal,‡ but if conditions fostered an explosion in the number of seagoing

---

* "Iron" is a weird word here, since it basically transformed into some grade of steel as manufacturing became better over time. The image of armies with hard iron weapons shearing through the soft bronze arms of an opponent is definitely myth. Bronze weapons were still made and highly prized for a long time after this era. Iron, after all, rusts very easily, and polished bronze is ornamentally beautiful.

† Another theory put forward by the historian Robert Drews suggests that the sea peoples may have used new weapons and infantry tactics to overthrow the chariot-based military systems of the Bronze Age states.

‡ Piracy was never uncommon in the premodern Mediterranean. More than a thousand years after the Bronze Age ended, the Roman Julius Caesar would be captured by pirates and held for ransom. Almost *three thousand* years later, the US president Thomas Jefferson had to send naval forces to deal with the Mediterranean Barbary pirates!

bandits, it could be system threatening. The sea peoples were once blamed for the majority of pirate activity, but unearthed records have shown that in at least some cases the pirates may have been from the same city-state as their victims, a case perhaps of turning to piracy when economic conditions deteriorated.

But pirates are hit-and-run entities, and some of these humans may have wanted to move en masse to the more advanced or wealthy states permanently. The idea of a Bronze Age version of the Germanic *Völkerwanderung** (essentially, a migration), disrupting the equilibrium and setting in motion the collapse of the age, has been around for a long time. The Egyptian inscriptions depict families in wagons accompanying some of the "sea people" and Libyan tribes. The implication is that whole peoples were looking for new places to settle, and they were willing to conquer new lands with the sword if need be. The Egyptians were somewhat used to this, as they occupied a comparatively rich breadbasket in their region; Libyan peoples from the west, Nubian people from the south, and all manner of "Asiatics"† were often trying to gain entrance to raid or settle. It can be hard to draw a fine line between human migration and invasion in some of these cases.

The invasion theory assumes that this late Bronze Age outbreak of barbarian violence was a somewhat widespread phenomenon, perhaps one involving differing groups of peoples from the Balkans to the edge of China, and occurring at roughly close to the same time.

The theory is less popular today, if for no other reason than some of the invasions offered as evidence are now more doubted.

---

* See more on this in chapter 5.

† A sort of catchall term the Egyptians used for someone from the east and northeast of Egypt.

Did the "Dorians" invade and conquer Greece as part of this calamity? Eighty years ago, a majority of historians would have likely thought so and would have blamed those invasions for plunging Greece into a dark age. Today, fewer historians believe those "invasions" ever happened. If multiple invasions didn't happen—if, instead, warfare and raiding were more piecemeal and less widespread—it becomes tougher to blame them for bringing the entire system down. Some historians have even suggested they may be a historical myth.

While there are still big supporters of the idea that the peoples of the sea were of pivotal importance to the end of the Bronze Age, they are perhaps seen by most these days as more of an effect than a cause. The migrations, piracy, and even invasions may have been a response to something else . . .

Suspect #2: Famine/Climate Change/Drought

The Four Horsemen of the Apocalypse are commonly given the names Conquest (or Pestilence), War, Famine, and Death. In much of the modern world, the horsemen don't seem as scary as they used to. War and conquest are still around, of course, but no World War III (yet). We are no longer able to relate to what our forebears went through with disease (pestilence).* And mass, society-wide famine is almost unheard of in most of the world. It seems like much of the darkness that humankind lived with from time immemorial has been banished from our future.

But it's never wise to bet against any of the Four Horsemen long term. Their historical track record is horrifyingly good.

One of the things most of us take for granted is our access to food. There are malnourished and hungry *individuals* in

*For more on disease, see chapter 6.

every nation on earth, but times when food is scarce for whole societies is much, much rarer in most of the world than it's ever been. Mass food insecurity was more the norm than the exception up until very recently, though. It's only because of relatively recent changes that enough food can be produced to support our current population levels. Our modern delivery and logistics systems allow large amounts of food to be reliably shipped and to stock the shelves of even distant islands. When scenes of the ravages of modern famine appear on television charity ads, the reality displayed on camera is almost incomprehensible to most of us. But try feeding three hundred million people in the United States today with the farming technology of even two hundred years ago.

There *are* some incidents of mass fatality–level famine in modern advanced cities or states in the mid-twentieth century. The unusual sight of humans dying from starvation next to modern buildings and on modern streets clashes with the image in our minds of poor, war-torn, drought-stricken, underdeveloped societies on the edge of the globalized world. We are conditioned to think that way by recent history. It's hard to picture London or Tokyo or New York with mass deaths in the street from starvation.

But that's the human experience that we need to imagine when thinking about famine. The tales that modern observers and victims of famine tell are of societies that fall apart because there's no food. Imagine if the region where you live were cut off from food supplies today. As Garry J. Shaw suggests, it might explain why you get sea peoples, migrations, invasions, or insurrections.

When enough people are driven by desperation, not even the greatest state can stop them; symbols of wealth and prestige mean nothing if enough people reject their meaning. In such times, some will rise up, burn, and rebuild on the ashes. Others will leave. And so, in this time of instability, disease, violence, famine, and drought, the assorted 'Sea Peoples' took the second option: they travelled eastwards, bringing their families and possessions along with them, leaving their homeland behind. To support themselves or when attempting to settle, sometimes they turned to violence, probably supported by mercenaries, creating their legend.

There's good evidence for famine during the last few centuries of the Mediterranean Bronze Age in many places around the region. The Hittites, especially, seemed to be facing a dire food crisis over an extended period; a last desperate letter sent from the capital, before the destruction of the city, refers to starvation. In Egypt, cemetery finds show evidence that the population of this era often suffered malnourishment. And people from Libya seemed to always be threatened by hunger; they would raid or even migrate to Egypt periodically over many centuries for food.[*]

Lots of things can cause famine. Insects can eat or spoil food; rivers and water sources can dry up or change course, or complex irrigation systems can be destroyed; poor farming practices can deplete the soil. Usually, though, the weather itself is the greatest threat. Even in the modern age, the utter dependence of agriculture on the right range of favorable climatic conditions is humbling. No nation is immune. Arid weather in the American Midwest created the Dust Bowl of the 1930s, during the Great

---

[*]It is Egyptian records that allege this as a cause. Eventually, there would be Egyptian pharaohs of Libyan descent, after centuries of such migration and immigration had changed Egyptian society.

Depression, which in turn spawned a migration of people and sent forth ripples of historical change that are still felt today. Similar events must have happened innumerable times in humanity's past.

Weather-related explanations for the end of the Bronze Age are extrapopular right now given the general spotlight on climate change, but historians for many decades have theorized that drought was what really unleashed the Four Horsemen. A prolonged drought, leading to severe famine, could certainly have been the spark that set into motion chain reactions that in retrospect explain things like piracy, migrations, and perhaps internal unrest.

As the historian Malcolm H. Wiener writes: "Warfare and migrations may be both the result and the cause of food crisis, and particularly where the carrying capacity of the land is already stretched to the utmost. The effects may be cumulative, with food shortages leading to overuse and degradation of available land; to rebellions by troops, populace, or captives; and/or to the loss of legitimacy of rulers believed to have lost divine favor."

It's hard to know how much localized famine was normal and to be periodically expected, and how much a particularly bad situation represented an unusual larger threat. Studies have shown evidence of a prolonged drought roughly around the relevant time in some of these areas.*

A counterargument by some experts, however, is that droughts are not uncommon in this climatic zone, because much of the eastern Mediterranean is somewhat arid to begin with. Why, suddenly, did a particularly dry period bring down a chain of ancient societies in a region where droughts weren't so terribly rare? And

---

*But, as usual, these results have been questioned by experts who have different theories.

why, if drought explains why peoples began to relocate, did those people sometimes leave known dry areas and migrate to ones that have been shown to be even more arid?*

Famine prompts a similar question: If famine wasn't that rare, why did it topple the structure at the end of the Bronze Age rather than any of the other times it occurred? It certainly *may* have done so, but proving it is the task still facing historical investigators.

If something like drought or famine was the cause of the Bronze Age collapse, it didn't wreak its changes by starving everyone to death. Famine would have been more of a spark that set off side effects. Yet it's terribly difficult, especially thousands of years later, to tie the ripple effects back to whatever rocks were first thrown into the stream. How do you connect the dots, for example, between an attack by the sea peoples and evidence of a drought in their homeland? Having relatively accurate dates for when events occurred would be of great help solving such a puzzle. A drought, for example, a hundred years after the sea people invasions, couldn't possibly have been its cause, but if it happened ten years before the great attacks chronicled by the pharaohs, then it might indeed have spurred a subsequent migration. But how close can science get to actual specific years when something occurred more than three thousand years ago?

That leads to the next suspect:

Suspect #3: Earthquakes/Volcanoes/Tsunamis

First, let's step out of our timeline to the year 1815, when the Mount Tambora volcano erupted in what's now part of Indonesia.

---

*These are some of the findings that experts have made regarding people's migrations due to suspected drought or arid conditions.

It is the only eruption in the last thousand years that merits a 7 out of a maximum 8 rating on the Volcanic Explosivity Index (VEI).* It caused tsunamis and earthquakes, darkened the skies, and unleashed enough ash to cover a one-hundred-square-mile area to a depth of twelve feet. The effect on global climate was profound—1816 was known as "the year without summer." And, among other things, it was thought to have brought on famine.

There have only been a handful of volcanic eruptions to reach that high on the VEI since humans began keeping a written record of their history. One happened near the end of the Bronze Age, in the eastern Mediterranean, in an area that was right at the heart of the whole Mediterranean Bronze Age world.

Today, the location of the volcano is actually the Greek island of Santorini, but the ancient Greeks called the island Thera. Like Tambora, the Thera eruption was one of the most powerful volcanic events in human history; unlike Tambora, we have no surviving contemporary accounts of it. Scientists can find the evidence of its eruption all over the region, but they can't yet pinpoint the year it happened. If they could, it would become a specific marker that would help date other events.† Experts can get close to a date, within a century or so—usually between about 1630 and 1500 BCE—but while that's a tiny margin of error when compared with the intervening thousands of years, it's still enough to muddy this investigation. Since the fall of the Bronze Age is usually dated to around 1200 BCE or so, the later

---

*As with the Richter scale for earthquakes, each step up on the Volcanic Explosivity Index represents a huge increase in power.

†Some of the best potential data points for dating are astronomical events such as an eclipse. Since experts can often reverse-date these with precision, even far back into the past, any eclipse that can be synced up with contemporary records, accounts, or events can provide a hard, reliable data point to aid with dating other events.

the eruption is dated, the more likely it is to have had an effect on the catastrophe.*

Experts argue about most things connected to the Thera eruption. In addition to the dating, the amount of damage done to the surrounding areas is in question. If it somehow played a role in the downfall of that age, how did it do so? Tsunamis are one proposed vector of destruction. That one or multiple tsunamis were generated by the eruption seems universally accepted, but disagreements occur over their size and what sort of damage they would have caused. Most of the Thera volcano's tsunamis would have been created by the quick addition of massive amounts of material into the sea, which generates waves that can reach enormous heights (the same way that a glacier's calving produces large waves).† These waves, known as megatsunamis, are quite different from the more familiar seismic variety of tsunami. Whereas the seismic tsunamis are almost too small to be noticed while moving through the open sea, and they explode in height only when they approach land, megatsunamis start at maximum height upon generation and lose force and height as they move across miles of water. Seismic tsunamis are often preceded by a strange receding of the beach tide, only to have the water roar back later, but megatsunamis are more like rogue waves—they can come out of nowhere.

The reason waves matter is that one of the theories about how a volcano might be tied to the end of the Bronze Age argues that

---

*There were eruptions in other locations farther from the eastern Mediterranean (Iceland, for example) but perhaps closer in time to the catastrophe that have also been implicated as possible contributors to the end of the Bronze Age.

†Experts have found the huge amounts of expelled volcanic material underwater off the coast of Santorini.

the tsunamis may have decimated the coastal areas of nearby states. Ships in port would be damaged by a tsunami of any sort, but a megatsunami could also have wreaked havoc on ships in the open sea. A huge wall of water speeding across the ocean might sink anything in its path.*

The island of Crete, the heart and soul of the powerful maritime Minoan state, was close to Thera and is often thought to have been a likely victim of the volcano's explosion.† If the ships, facilities, and perhaps settlements and coastal population of Crete were badly damaged or destroyed by the sea, the resulting effect on the economy of the region *might* have been huge.

It's also been suggested that widespread damage on a large scale might have weakened the Minoans in a way that made them a tempting target for geopolitical predators in their region. Sometime between about 1450 and 1370 BCE, most of the great palaces from the heyday of the Minoans were destroyed, and eventually the area and culture was taken over by the Mycenaeans.‡ But if the Minoan state declined around 1400 BCE or so, that's still two or more centuries removed from the other parts of the collapse manifesting. It's possible that the volcano and the resulting tsunami might have been responsible for this, a chain reaction of events that destabilized what had been a stable system, but that would constitute a long lag time between cause and effect.

---

*Things like wave height, wave steepness, and the like come into play here. Some waves are more likely to be problematic for oceangoing vessels than others; near-breaking waves or waves with very steep faces, for example.

† And some have suggested that Bronze Age Crete was the model for Plato's legendary Atlantis.

‡ Who, if the whole Trojan War legend has any truth at all to it, are a key people who sacked Troy a few centuries after this period. The *Iliad*'s King Agamemnon was the king of Mycenae.

The other natural disaster that gets brought into the conversation about the end of the Bronze Age is earthquakes. There's overlap here, because the Thera eruption may have sparked or been preceded by earthquakes, and these might have contributed to the damage spawned by the volcano. And earthquakes are also one of the primary causes of tsunamis.

There's no doubt that earthquakes were a relatively regular ancient visitor to this very seismically active region. Damage from earthquakes in ancient times (sometimes including crushed bodies found where they fell) has been discovered in structures all over the eastern Mediterranean and western Asia. In fact, there seem to have been several big earthquakes dated to around the time of the Bronze Age's end, and lots of important cities in that area show earthquake damage. In the age before stabilized buildings and modern construction, and when open fires were common, the damage done by earthquakes may have been worse than what we'd find today. Certainly, the ability to deal with an earthquake's aftermath is better in modern times. An earthquake and a resulting tsunami that killed fifty thousand people today would be much easier for us to clean up and recover from than it would have been for a Bronze Age society.

Yet the evidence points often to rebuilding after the historical quakes, which shows that such events weren't totally fatal and that the affected society could continue. But it doesn't necessarily mean that population, prosperity, or geopolitical power and influence would return to predisaster levels.

A single phenomenon (such as earthquakes, droughts, volcanoes, or tsunamis) can explain why a particular city or area suffered damage, but it can't by itself explain why the entire Mediterranean and west Asian region was affected by something at the end of the Bronze Age. Just because there may have been a volcano on an Aegean island that erupted and caused tsunamis, why did Babylon and Assyria, located in landlocked modern-day Iraq, have problems?

Suspect #4: Plagues

Smallpox is one of the most infamous diseases in history. To give an idea of its virulence, it killed an estimated 300 to 500 million people in the twentieth century *alone*,[*] but the disease was eradicated from the planet in 1980[†]—meaning half a billion people were killed by smallpox in just eight decades. Those who didn't succumb to the illness were often left blind, and severely disfigured by scarring. Mercifully, we don't deal with smallpox anymore, but the illness goes back millennia. When the Egyptian mummy of Pharaoh Ramesses V (r. 1149–1145 BCE) was examined, the body revealed smallpox scarring. (He may have died from the disease.)[‡] Smallpox killed multiple reigning European monarchs and five Japanese emperors, and it was likely the cause of many early plagues of his-

---

[*] For comparison, the Second World War killed between 70 and 85 million people. This number includes deaths in the Second Sino-Japanese War that began several years before the 1939 German attack on Poland.

[†] "Eradicated" is a bit misleading. Smallpox exists in samples, and weaponized smallpox is a potential threat.

[‡] Dating is always suspect here, but assuming the standard dates used are close, this pharaoh would have been from a transitional era, perhaps born into what we today would call the late Bronze Age, dying sometime after its official end. Does the fact the pharaoh apparently had smallpox tie into the investigation here at all? Is this just smallpox taking its usual toll? Or could it be indicative of a larger outbreak? The Hittites thought they caught their plague from the Egyptians.

tory, such as the one in ancient Athens in 430 BCE.* Smallpox was also one of the main killers of the Aboriginal peoples of the Americas and Australia after first contact, the majority of whom may have died from the disease before the Europeans who first transmitted it across the oceanic disease barrier actually encountered them.†

Just as it is difficult for most of us today to imagine the food insecurity that was common in most human populations in most eras, it's difficult to conceptualize the range of illnesses and diseases against which earlier cultures had no defense. Pretty much nothing separates us more from human beings in earlier eras than how much less disease affects us. We are still victimized by illness and disease of all kinds, but unlike in the distant past, we now have so many more ways to fight back, and such a better understanding of the underlying reasons for maladies. Real plagues—a common experience in all of human history—are thankfully rare today. Some of our greatest modern fears over disease are simply that we might ever again have one plague as bad as any average plague in earlier eras.‡

Sources make it sound as though Hattusa (the Hittite capital) was dealing with both famine and plague in this general Bronze

---

*Sometimes the disease that caused an ancient plague can be known or identified from the documented symptoms, or from the testing of found remains, but often experts must guess at what disease was behind a given early historical outbreak.

†Once the disease had been spread directly to the tribes first contacted by Europeans, natives themselves spread the new contagion into the continental interior.

‡A terrible outbreak of Ebola is a perfect example. It's one of the greatest fears of communicable disease experts, yet even in their wildest nightmares such an event wouldn't do the sort of damage one of the great plagues of antiquity or the Middle Ages did, in which large percentages of a given population were wiped out.

Age era.* Two successive Hittite rulers succumbed to one plague in around the 1320s BCE. There are reports of plague in the Levant, Cyprus, and Egypt. Several regions in Greece saw depopulation during this era that might have been related to an outbreak of disease.

The Four Horsemen of the Apocalypse often ride together, though, and just as famine and pestilence are interconnected with each other, they are often also linked with war.

Suspect #5: Internecine Warfare

We've already discussed violence in different forms leading to the problems in the Bronze Age. From sea peoples to revolutionaries to the Trojan War, there was no shortage of bloody outbreaks as the era came to its close. How is one to make a distinction between the "normal" level of violence and something system threatening? Was there anything about the end of the Bronze Age in a military sense that was different or stood out? Yes, there was: Assyria.

Assyria would become the first of the great empires of the next era, the Iron Age.† It was in the later Bronze Age that this Semitic-speaking superpower-to-be began to alter the map of the Near East in ways that could easily upset the region's geopolitical equilibrium. The Assyrian state, located in modern northern Iraq, and centered on several already ancient cities,‡ had an extensive

---

*Famine and plague have a similar interconnected relationship to the one between drought and famine. Famine-weakened populations are more susceptible to disease, and epidemics can badly disrupt food production in agricultural societies, potentially causing famine.

†In this part of the world.

‡Incredibly ancient. At the tail end of the Bronze Age in 1200 BCE, several Assyrian cities were already well over a *thousand* years old.

history and had long been a part of regional power struggles. By about the 1390s BCE, Assyria was about to go on another multigenerational historical winning streak, and much of this would come at the expense of neighboring states in the region.

After falling under the domination of another powerful state in the region (Mittani) in about the 1450s BCE, the Assyrians wrested back their independence after a couple of generations, and then began to take their former overlords apart piece by piece. Leading an increasingly fearsome and effective fighting force, aggressive and energetic Assyrian kings like Ashur-uballit I, Tukulti-Ninurta I, and Tiglath-Pileser I expanded the boundaries of their kingdom and added to its resources.

Assyria's increasing might eventually began to alarm the other great powers. The Hittites, especially, were right in the crosshairs. The Hittite Empire's territory formed a key international crossroads in the Bronze Age, a potentially indispensable link in the structure of economic, diplomatic, and military interconnectivity that supported that version of an international system. If something damaged the Hittite state, many others in that system could have felt the effects.

Sometime around 1237 BCE, the Hittites were defeated by the Assyrians at the Battle of Nihriya. The resulting loss of territory meant ceding important resource outlets to the Assyrians.* There's a sort of death spiral that can be created in war when a state's treasury is drained by extended conflict, when manpower is decimated by battlefield defeats, and when possession of the resources that are indispensable for recovering from those losses is lost to the enemy. The year 1237 is right around the start of the

---

*For example, an important copper mining locality was taken from the Hittites by the Assyrians. That would be like conquering and taking over an oil-rich region today.

traditional era when the Bronze Age seemingly began to come under severe strain, so if we are trying to correlate dates with ripple effects, we can see that the extension of Assyrian power corresponds with some of the large geopolitical changes quite well.

War can be a net positive or negative to a combatant power.* War (and the resulting conquests) has often benefited the state doing the conquering. In this case, it might have benefited Assyria.

And while it goes without saying that wars are bad for those who lose them, in many circumstances, wars can be a negative for *all* involved. By the last year of the First World War, for example, all the nations that had begun the war four years before had been ground down by it. The economies that were paying for the costs of the conflict were in shambles. The damage the war caused to the global system meant that the conflict was harmful even to nations that were not a part of the fight.†

The subsequent negative effects of that early twentieth-century war involved many of the same factors we've targeted in our discussion of the end of the Bronze Age. By 1918, due to the conflict, Europe was experiencing famine and pestilence to go along with its war and death. The Four Horsemen of the Apocalypse were running rampant through some of the most advanced societies in the early twentieth century—an eventuality that was made possible only because the war opened the door to it. It's not hard to imagine, then, how a multigenerational and eventually losing struggle with another great power may have challenged the Hittite state.

---

*Obviously, this is why some are willing to risk it. If there were never any good outcomes for a victorious state, the whole war idea seems somewhat pointless, doesn't it?

†This does not include either the United States or imperial Japan, both of which came out of the First World War having arguably profited from their involvement in it.

Assyria's wars of expansion during this era were in the military history foreground and are hard to miss. But in the background were lots of conflicts that didn't involve the great powers fighting their peers at all (which doesn't mean they weren't potentially important, or possibly fatal, should a great power have been defeated). Lots of "barbarian" peoples and tribes, for example, nibbled at the fringes of the great states, always seemingly ready to exploit weakness or take advantage of opportunities. In the case of the Hittites, their local troublesome "barbarians" were people like the Phrygians and a lesser-known people known as the Kaska (or Gasga). The Kaska are portrayed by the Hittite sources as aggressive wild tribesmen who had sacked and burned the Hittite capital in the past. Some historians think that, as the Hittite state got weaker, its ability to resist these peoples declined. If major conflicts with other powerful states like Assyria weakened the Hittites, it may have made them less able to fend off their traditional "barbarian" neighbors. And, just to tie it all together, if those barbarian neighbors were starving due to a famine caused by arid conditions and poor harvests, does that explain why the Hittites might have had to fend them off in the first place?

If one credits the Assyrians with a large amount of responsibility for bringing down the state of Mittani,* and then possibly mortally wounding the Hittites, that would amount to a great deal of political and military change occurring around the

---

*The Hittites also fought with and benefited from the decline of the state of Mittani. At times, the Hittites and Assyrians were almost fighting proxy wars and cold wars with each other by using rival claimants to the throne of Mittani. But Mittani was a buffer state between the Hittites and Assyrians, and when it was gobbled up, the predators that devoured it were left sharing a border with each other.

thirteenth century BCE. And this might have been enough to spark a chain reaction that disrupted a whole system.

Suspects #6 and #7: Systems Collapse, Multiple Causes

We live in a world of complex systems—economic, cultural, social, administrative-bureaucratic. Many things must function together to make an interconnected system work, and a breakdown anywhere can mean a breakdown everywhere. For that reason, most systems have some flexibility and redundancy built into them to deal with stresses, breakdowns, and unforeseen circumstances—in short, they are made to be resilient. But when these backup systems become overwhelmed, the cascading nature of a problem can ripple throughout the entire system like an economic version of a communicable disease. So in a Bronze Age trading network that reached from Spain to Iran and from northern Italy to Nubia, a disruption of something like Mediterranean commerce could affect all those regions.

And while the loss of things like luxury products and the money generated from trading activity would have had an enormous effect, it's important to remember that food constituted one of the major categories of goods being shipped in the late Bronze Age. The Egyptians were sending food to multiple places (including the Hittite lands) via ship to alleviate starvation. If those ships were unable to reach their destinations, it wasn't a question of loss of income or a lowering of living standards, it was a potential famine.

When people don't have food, under certain circumstances all law and order and societal controls can break down. Plagues can cause the same problems if they're bad enough. Anarchy, revolution, and civil war can sometimes do to a society what outside invaders can't manage. All it can take is too little food or too much disease.

There are other scenarios that can lead to the same outcome. Mass migration in a short time (for example, the Libyan and sea peoples' "invasions" of Egypt) can disrupt norms and break down culture and amicable coexistence. Insufficient military defense can leave a population and its food supplies open to predation by other armed groups.

Some experts have suggested that the Bronze Age system was somewhat fragile or brittle. Undergirded by highly centralized, very bureaucratic states, with a small rich elite presiding over large numbers of peons,* such a system might have been vulnerable to all sorts of rebellion and social upheaval. Think of an ancient version of the French Revolution, for example. If such destabilization were sparked by a system's inability to deliver food to a starving population, what's ultimately to blame: The famine, or the brittle, inequitable social system? If the sea peoples' piracy helped destroy the maritime trading system, does the damage come from the piracy or the resulting collapse of the trading system? This is where the multiple-causes suspect begins to look like a good bet.

WHILE WE FEEL somewhat safer from those Bronze Age suspects than our ancestors did, we have managed to add new potential threats that previous eras never had to face: nuclear weapons, global environmental damage, potentially catastrophic scientific innovations, and more.† And the ongoing threat of certain

---

*Peons are how everyone but the palace elite is usually portrayed in this scenario.

†Something like a worst-case scenario with artificial intelligence or weapons technology, for example. Are we adding new horsemen to the Four Horsemen of the Apocalypse? Pestilence, War, Famine, Death, and Climate Change? Or Runaway Technology?

types of potentially dark age–inducing wild cards seems pretty consistent over the ages. Whether you live in an era when a scary-size asteroid hits the earth or a supervolcano explodes in Yosemite seems merely the luck of the celestial roulette wheel.

When the Soviet Union suffered a political system collapse[*] in the early 1990s, did some of the USSR's successor states have something we might consider a mini–dark age? That unsettled era saw an extended and difficult transition period. In newly created nation-states like Russia, birth rates and life expectancy dropped drastically. Alcoholism and suicide rates rose; the social safety net was shredded; the nation's military and infrastructure seemed to atrophy; its political system seemed unsteady, corrupt, and chaotic; and its national resources were seemingly up for grabs to the highest or most corrupt bidder. If the history of the post-USSR era were being written by historians a century ago, would they have called it "The Decline and Fall of the Soviet Union"? Would they have identified the period afterward as a "dark age"?

Perhaps how long any societal, economic, or civilizational downturn lasts is a key factor in whether or not we agree that something qualifies as a dark age. Both the Great Depression in the United States in the 1930s and the post-Soviet breakup of the 1990s lasted roughly a decade or so. That length hardly seems to meet the minimum standard for a dark age. However, had the direct fallout from either instead lasted a century or two, that might have been enough to turn a statistical civilizational blip into an extended negative trend.

One of the modern theories on societal collapse argues that because of the entire planet's connected nature in the twenty-first

---

[*]Which then cascaded into many other areas of the interconnected system that kept Soviet society running.

century, individual or localized "dark ages" of the sort that formerly occurred are nowadays absorbed by the rest of the global body and civilization as a whole.* Others have suggested that the depth and severity of any potential "dark age" are lessened due to modern interconnectivity. So you might have another Great Depression or the fall of a superpower, but you won't have a century of global decline and technological backsliding. It's sort of a global diversification of risk in our modern civilization, a redundancy that allows the system to survive local blackouts.

But perhaps our bias is showing. Maybe such changes are not decline or backsliding at all. It all might depend on the criteria we've decided to use. Depending on your point of view, things might not be considered better or worse . . . just *different*.

Earlier we brought up the idea of "progress" having an innate bias attached to it. If literacy declines in a later era because reading is less important, is this indicative of living in a "dark(er) age"? Or would it be more a case of people adjusting their skills based on their needs? And who gets to decide this—we moderns looking backward at the past, or the people actually living in the earlier era? Our ideas of what was good for the inhabitants of an earlier time might be different from their own.

This brings up the question of how much the people living in a dark age would even realize it. If you were born in Greece in 1000 BCE,† did you know (or care) that there was a greater age before yours? Take a kid born in the United States in 1929,

---

*For example, if the United States fragmented into many nation-states, it certainly might count as a "decline" in some ways by local standards, but global knowledge and capabilities and the like might be affected only marginally. When the Bronze Age ended, no other society in the world existed to pick up the pieces or keep the lights on.

†About 1177 BCE is sometimes considered the period the Bronze Age's civilizational stock market crashed.

at the beginning of the Great Depression. On his tenth birthday, the world was still mired in the effects of the crash. To that child, the privation and lowered sense of expectations felt normal; he had no experience or memory of anything else. His parents, however, likely felt that times had gotten tougher. While it sounds like a bad thing to be living in a society off its technological, cultural, or economic highs, it's very possible the happiness level of individual human beings adjusted and evened out comparatively quickly. It's hard to know what you're missing after it's been gone for a couple of lifetimes.

Maybe we are looking at this entirely wrong. If we lived in an era when our history books taught us that Ben Franklin's eighteenth-century Revolutionary War generation had landed a spacecraft on Mars and could completely cure cancer (which of course we can't do or haven't done yet), would we care? Of course we would want the things of the past that seemed like improvements, but would we want the rest of the package that came along with it? If, for example, a Native American from five centuries ago had a bad tooth, she might really want our modern dentistry to deal with it. But if in order to get the modern medicine she had to become modern in all the other aspects of her existence, she might not consider the deal worth it.

There are multiple ways that any account or story can be viewed, but it's helpful to be reminded from time to time. Certain narratives, such as "golden ages" and "rise and falls," are so ingrained in our thinking that it's easy to forget there might be other ways to see things. The anthropologist Joseph Tainter said that in some regions the Roman Empire taxed its citizens so highly, and provided so few services in return, that some of those people welcomed the "conquering barbarians" as liberators.

A similar theory exists about the Bronze Age: that perhaps the very bureaucratic and tax-heavy structure of the palace cultures of the Mediterranean states stopped working well for the majority of people, and one way or another they abandoned or stopped actively supporting it. In such a case, if things become too complicated to work well, or too centralized to be in touch with ground-level problems, is reverting to a greater level of simplicity and local control moving in a negative or a positive direction?*

As with so many things, it may depend on whom you ask. No doubt at least some of those living back then would think we were romanticizing how wonderful the "good old days" of their lives were. Indeed, the successors of Rome would spend hundreds of years trying to put it back together again (in some form or another), and a certain blind poet named Homer would make a living recalling tales of the good old heroic days of the Bronze Age centuries after it ended.

---

*This could be as simple as, "The empire far away is letting us starve while the local warlord is feeding us."

Chapter 4

JUDGMENT AT NINEVEH

TWENTY-ONE YEARS AFTER *Planet of the Apes* was released, at an excavation of the city of Mosul in northern Iraq, archaeologists from the University of California began slicing into what, to the naked, untrained eye, appeared to be a naturally occurring hill. But like so many other mounds in the area, it was actually a man-made stone-and-brick structure that the passing of thousands of years had worked to transform. Underneath twenty-five centuries' worth of dirt, evidence of disaster was revealed: a layer of destruction and burnt material just beneath the soil. Pieces of weapons were discovered, and a corridor of sorts emerged, with cut stonework and a pebbled floor.

Then the archaeologists found the dead.

There were at least twelve skeletons in the passage, multiple adults and children, and also a horse. The bodies appeared to lie where they had fallen. There was no indication of looting, which in any case would have been difficult, because at or near the time of these people's death, the corridor had collapsed and buried them. Investigators determined the roof had been burning when it fell, and some of the dead were scorched before they expired on that terrible day two and a half millennia ago.

Had the site been discovered closer to the time of the events, the findings would have been grisly in the extreme, but time has a way of sanitizing even a mass killing. There is no longer any flesh or blood or viscera, and the facial expressions have been erased by decay.

The Halzi Gate, as the site was later identified, was one of fifteen external openings in the walled defenses of perhaps the greatest urban center of the ancient world—Nineveh, the heart of the Assyrian Empire in northern Mesopotamia.

At its height, around 650 BCE, the city and its surrounding villages may have had as many as 150,000 inhabitants and covered an area of about two thousand acres, or just under three square miles. The city was a wonder of its age, huge and grand, the center of gravity of the Assyrian Empire's government and the primary residence of its ruler, a figure whose many self-proclaimed titles included "king of the universe." The defenses of this metropolis were mammoth, with walls sixty feet tall and fifty feet thick stretching more than three miles on each side, and deep ditches carved out below them. The Halzi Gate itself had a 220-foot-tall facade and was flanked by six towers.

Yet in the same way the ash-covered corpses from the Roman-era volcanic destruction of Pompeii are frozen in the moment of their death, the dead at the Halzi Gate are frozen in the instant of their final agony. The bodies show the unmistakable signs of mortal hand-to-hand combat, including defensive wounds and, in some cases, clear evidence that a final killing blow was administered. They died as their city was dying.

What had Assyria done to deserve such a fate?

In the scope of human history, there are two kinds of cultures that have had a large geopolitical impact on the historical stage. The first are the societies and cultures that can trace their lineage back to much earlier versions of themselves, like the Chinese and Egyptian civilizations. They've had their high points and low points, but they've always been a political force to reckon with through thousands of years of history, and they're still here. Perennial players.

The second are societies that seem to have had a glory-filled golden era, then fell into obscurity. Their historical moment in the sun, so to speak. The Mongol people are one example. Today, the Mongols are on the periphery of world events, a seemingly poor and out-of-the-way and behind-the-times culture, at least compared with what we call the "developed world." But the Mongol people at one time ruled most of the known world and did so for several hundred years. This may have seemed like a long stretch at the time, but it was a blink of an eye compared with the ancient Assyrians.

The great state of Babylonia, to the south of Assyria, was the empire's great adversary throughout their Bronze and Iron Age histories. Babylonia's capital city, Babylon, located some fifty-five miles south of modern Baghdad, was one of the greatest cities ever built. It was likely the first metropolis inhabited by more than two hundred thousand people, and at its height had maybe twice that many. Remarkably, in this era before modern sanitation and modern medicine and with so many people living in such close proximity, Babylon managed to stay largely plague-free. (Babylon would outlive its great Assyrian rival to the north and would eventually seem like an urban refuge from a previous age in the new world to come.)

Some two hundred years after Assyria's fall, a Greek general named Xenophon recorded an encounter with what was left of Assyria's grandeur when he saw cities—places that were larger and more formidable than anything he'd seen back in Greece—dissolved into ruins. Xenophon wrote the *Anabasis*—now considered a classic of Western literature—about his experience commanding Greek mercenaries in a Persian civil war. As

Xenophon and ten thousand Greeks fought a running battle trying to escape from their pursuers after fighting on the losing side
of that war, they stumbled upon enormous fortifications and cities decomposing in the sand in what's now northern Iraq—the
ruins of something greater than his own civilization had ever
produced. Almost 2,500 years ago Xenophon wrote, "The
Greeks marched on safely for the rest of the day and reached
the River Tigris. There was a large deserted city there called
Larissa, which in the old days used to be inhabited by the Medes. It had walls twenty-five feet broad and one hundred feet
high, with a perimeter of six miles. It was built of bricks made
of clay, with a stone base of twenty feet underneath."

Later, they came upon yet another city.

From here, a day's march of eighteen miles brought
them to a large undefended fortification near a city
called Mespila. . . . The base of the fortification was made
of polished stone, in which there were many shells. It was
fifty feet broad and fifty feet high. On top of it was built
a brick wall fifty feet in breadth and a hundred feet high.
The perimeter of the fortification was eighteen miles.

These cities were gargantuan by Greek standards, and Xenophon asked the locals about them; they said the structures had
been built by the Medes, because that's who'd preceded the Persian Empire they were then living under. But in fact these weren't
Median cities, they were Assyrian. The one "near a city called
Mespila" is thought to have been Nineveh—Xenophon was mar-
veling at its majestic remains two hundred years after its demise.

Xenophon was someone whom we today would think of as
inhabiting the old world. Ancient Greece is, after all, a very
early European civilization. But he was looking at something

that was already ancient in *his* day—the equivalent of a Statue of Liberty in the sand from a Near Eastern empire that had been the superpower of its age a mere two centuries previously, and one that now seemed so thoroughly erased that the locals didn't even know to whom it had belonged.*

Before its fall, the Mesopotamian culture that Assyria was a part of was akin to Civilization 1.0. Babylon and Assyria represented the apex of that civilization's version, with a growth in power, sophistication, and development that had begun in places like Ur, Akkad, and Sumeria. This basically unbroken civilizational tree lasted longer than any of the versions since. By way of comparison, if we were to date our modern civilization to the beginning of the Renaissance, we could count it as so far lasting around five or six hundred years. Assyria and its world was three to five times older than that, depending on how you date it, but their own records show an unbroken line of kings dating all the way back to the 2300s BCE,† and Nineveh, their greatest city, fell around 600 BCE. That's nearly two millennia that these people were a recognizable regional entity. The oldest work in European literature is often credited to Homer and dated between 800 and 1000 BCE—compare that with *The Epic of Gilgamesh*, from Mesopotamia, which was put into writing in about 2100 BCE and had been an oral story earlier than that. Civilization 1.0 had deep roots.

It's difficult to understand just how urban this culture was,

---

* It's very possible some of these people were themselves of Assyrian stock. It's also possible that the Assyrian remnant kept alive oral traditions of their great past even as the non-Assyrian locals forgot about it. Perhaps Xenophon was simply querying the wrong locals.

† This may not reflect historical reality, but it reflects what those people *thought* was reality. Such records go back to the mythical "great flood" period that made its way into the Hebrew Bible.

and how much in some ways it reminds us of our own modern society. If you were to look at a map of the Mediterranean and west Asia in the Bronze and Iron Ages, it would look a lot like a map of early twentieth-century, pre–First World War Europe. There were several powerful states intertwined with one another through diplomacy and alliances. When they went to war, they often went as coalitions, as the Triple Entente and the Central Powers did in the First World War, and the Allied and Axis powers did in the Second.

To continue the analogy, the Assyrians would be the Germans, because the Germans have always had a reputation for being militarily tough, not just in the twentieth century, but throughout history. An oft-cited rationale proposed for this is that the area of modern Germany is surrounded by other powerful peoples and doesn't have a lot of natural frontiers, making it difficult to defend. From a social Darwinian perspective, you might say the only people who could survive in an area like that would be those who were tough and warlike. The same is often said about the Assyrians, because ancient Assyria was also ringed by powerful states and suffered a lack of natural frontiers, so the Assyrians had to be very tough, very centralized, very efficient, and very good warriors to survive.

As with the citizens of most powerful states throughout the ages, though, it is highly unlikely that the citizens of ancient Nineveh ever thought their culture would be wiped off the map.

But the fall of Nineveh is probably one of the most significant geopolitical events in world history. It is certainly *the* geopolitical event of the Near East Iron Age. It's like the fall of Berlin in the Second World War in that it forever and decisively ended an empire, but the destruction of Nazi Germany toppled a twelve-year regime while Assyria's fall meant the end of an ancient power. And the Assyrians were often cast, especially by their neighbors, as the equivalent of the Nazis in the biblical era.* These were people who appeared to be proud of the terrible things they did. They created great carvings in stone of their armies at war and the punishments their kings meted out to those who had rebelled against them. In some cases, these reliefs are essentially advertisements publicizing what would amount in the modern day to crimes against humanity.

As if the grotesque illustrations weren't enough, the Assyrian kings provided cuneiform text narration of their atrocities, too. When one reads what they wrote about their feats, one feels as though the Assyrians didn't have just one bad Hitler-esque ruler, but rather that they were *all* like that. The artistic "court style" of Assyria's royal reliefs is genocidal.

Take, for example, Ashurnasirpal II (r. 883–859 BCE), one of the most brutal of the Assyrian kings. He had this to say about how he handled a rebellion: "I built a pillar over the city gate, and I flayed all the chiefs who had revolted, and I covered the pillar with their skin. Some of them I walled up in the pillar, some I impaled upon the pillar on stakes. Others I bound to stakes around the pillar. And I cut the limbs off the royal officers who had rebelled."

Ashurnasirpal II goes on to describe burning captives with fire; cutting off their noses, ears, and fingers; and putting out their eyes. The tens of thousands of warriors who weren't burned or walled up or beheaded or mutilated were driven into the scorching desert like cattle and left to die of thirst.

Lest Ashurnasirpal II be seen as an aberration, hundreds of years later, another Assyrian king, Ashurbanipal (r. 669–627 BCE), not content with defeating the Elamites in battle,

---

*In fact the Hebrew Bible can sometimes make them sound like evil personified.

described what he did to their long-dead ancestors, so that they would have no peace in the afterlife: "The tombs of their earlier and later kings, who did not fear Ashur and Ishtar, my lords, and who had plagued my fathers, I destroyed, I devastated, I exposed to the sun. Their bones, I carried off to Assyria. I laid restlessness upon their shades. I deprived them of food-offerings and of water."*

Many historians will point out that this Assyrian behavior was pretty standard for the era, and that there was a practical purpose to all this boasting of brutality. The Assyrians are considered by many to have built the first major empire in human history, and every empire that has followed has adopted many, if not all, of the strategies and techniques the Assyrians used to govern and administrate theirs. And one of their preferred techniques to keep their subject peoples in line was a form of state terrorism. The formula is well understood today, as it's been used many times in history. Cities, regions, and peoples that rebel will be utterly destroyed, and the retribution will be devastating. The goal is to keep the conquered in line, but as so often happens, the repression breeds dissatisfaction, and the Assyrians were forever putting down, and then harshly punishing, revolts. The Assyrians made sure that those who might consider revolting understood the stakes involved. Some of the grisly scenes found during archaeological excavations had been intended to intimidate the very people who might be seeing them while waiting to meet with the king. Imagine being the gov-

---

*"Shades" is a reference to spirits or ghosts. The Assyrians were punishing the ancestors of their current enemies, and through them making the retribution that much worse. In a move common in the ancient world, the Assyrians would also snatch the statues that represented the deities of these societies and cart them off into captivity, too. That brings a whole new meaning to the term "Total War."

ernor of any such troublesome city, and you're summoned to see
the ruler. Arriving, you might come upon a scene carved in stone
(and perhaps painted in color) showing what happened to a city
and its prominent citizens that had thumbed its nose at Assyria.
One such scene found in the ruins of an Assyrian palace shows
a rebellious governor named Dananu before his horrible torture
and execution—as Dananu walks to his own death, the relief
shows him pictured with the severed head of one of his cocon-
spirators hanging around his neck as he is being abused, spat on,
and beaten by Assyrians passing by.* Simply having a severed human head draped around one's neck seems macabre enough, but
to have known the dead person makes it particularly horrific and
psychologically torturous. The ancient era, as the biblical Old
Testament attests, excelled at such exquisite bloody symbolism.

While many historians say such acts were not deliberate cru-
elty so much as a way of controlling an empire, one does wonder
if the Assyrians took pleasure in them. When Ashurbanipal was
done laying waste to the Elamites, his army brought back the
Elamite king's severed head, which Ashurbanipal hung from
one of the trees in his garden so he could look at it while he
feasted with his wives. This macabre scene itself was carved in
stone, too, and it can still be seen on a relief in the British
Museum today. What was the king trying to say? Was it plea-
surable to see one's enemies' dead faces while one ate and drank
in luxury? Or is this symbolic, and the king didn't really eat
with a dead human head watching over his plate? Either way,
he wanted everyone to think that's what he did. When Ashurnasirpal II had his captives' skin pulled off their bodies while
they were still alive, apparently he made sure his throne was set

---

*Eventually, Dananu's head was put on a pole outside the gates of Nineveh
to serve as a warning.

up where he could watch. Was this part of his royal responsibility, or was it just too enjoyable to miss? Again, many historians will say that's how the Assyrian imperialists maintained unity and thereby created conditions that moved civilization forward. The trade routes, the stability, the protection from outside barbarian attacks—all are traditionally cited positives in the classic trade-offs-of-empire argument.* The Assyrians were not the first or the last state that maintained itself through frightfully putting down its opposition.

While there were advantages to this violent, perhaps evil, way of running their empire, the backlash it created put new meaning to the phrase "as ye reap so shall ye sow." When Assyria's neighbors finally got their chance, they destroyed the Mesopotamian juggernaut so completely and so quickly that, as we have seen, subsequent societies—ones that followed only a couple of generations later—seemed ignorant of its former greatness.

So what happened?

The decline of Assyria was not a long, slow one, as it would be in the case of imperial Rome. The last great Assyrian king, the aforementioned Ashurbanipal, inherited the empire at the height of its territorial expansion and ruled for more than forty years.† But his last statements are tales of woe and bad tidings. The empire did not long survive his death. One factor in the decline of the Assyrian Empire can be traced, paradoxically, to its conquest of surrounding populations. For centuries, the armies

---

*The trade-offs of empire involve the military conquests, deaths, and repressions versus the stability, organization, and consolidating advantages the imperial state brings through conquests and incorporation. The idea that this moves "progress" forward may of course be culturally biased.

†At the time of Ashurbanipal's reign, Assyria had recently added Egypt to its empire, which was a monumental conquest.

of the early Assyrian Empire were made up of the stout and comparatively loyal native Assyrians from the heartland of the territory. By the end of the empire, its armies comprised fewer and fewer Assyrians and more and more mercenaries and subject peoples who had been conscripted from places the Assyrians had conquered. The army was still an organizational and institutional marvel, but its manpower and loyalty were much more brittle and less dependable than they had been.

In addition, the Assyrians, like all the peoples of ancient Mesopotamia, had a problem with succession. When a ruler died, there was often a major struggle over which son would ascend the throne in his place—and that's when there wasn't a coup. Civil wars happened a lot throughout Assyria's history, and a significant number of its kings were killed by their own children. Dynastic struggles probably did more damage to the Assyrian state than any of its enemies, and they opened the door to what happened at Nineveh.[*]

But similar events in Assyria's past hadn't always had negative repercussions. The kickoff to arguably the most glorious period in Assyria's history[†] began with a particularly bad coup that could perhaps be compared with the Bolshevik takeover in Russia in 1917. In 745 BCE, the entire Assyrian royal family was apparently wiped out, and a general who afterward adopted the name Tiglath-Pileser III took the reins. It was Tiglath-Pileser III who reorganized the army into the most sophisticated fighting force the ancient world had ever seen. Assyria was the first of the major settled societies to employ cavalry in the modern,

---

[*] It's been said that the most dangerous armies the Roman Empire ever faced were its own during the civil wars. The same might be said for Assyria.

[†] The era is called the Neo-Assyrian Empire and is traditionally dated from about 911 to 609 BCE.

drilled sense, probably the first to have a real modern-style general staff,* the first to put large numbers of troops in the field routinely—as many as fifty thousand men, and up to three hundred thousand men across the empire. Just consider the logistics of putting that many people on the battlefield—feeding and watering and supplying and maintaining that many people through marches across hundreds of miles, through all sorts of terrain and conditions, in the era of the biblical Old Testament.†

The Assyrians were better trained and drilled than any army up until the time of Alexander the Great, and maybe even more than some of Alexander's troops. Looking back at all the great armies in the history of the Middle East, we can see that the one thing they usually lacked was good, disciplined close-order infantry, men whose job it was to stand shoulder to shoulder and engage in hand-to-hand melee with the shock troops of the enemy. Think Roman legionary, or Greek hoplite. Western Asia has always been home to some of the best cavalry in the world, but its infantry historically was often much less formidable than, say, Europe's. The Assyrians bucked this trend. They fielded drilled infantry formations as the main core of their armies. Their units often combined archers and spearmen, which provided great tactical flexibility.‡

As befits an empire that came of age in what used to be called

---

* Depends on how one classifies this. Other armies had councils of war, and the pharaohs of Egypt also had what might have amounted to general staffs of military advisers in an even earlier period.

† This isn't easy for modern states to do *today*. In fact, how many nation-states can field fifty thousand soldiers and supply them while they're fighting in distant lands?

‡ The mixed units would have allowed the archers to weaken advancing foes before the Assyrian spearmen engaged. They also would have been invaluable against foes who skirmished and fought in a hit-and-run style that could often frustrate and wear down heavy shock troops.

"the biblical era," the Assyrians fielded wonderful chariotry. Before the appearance of true cavalry,[*] armies took advantage of the mobility of horses by hooking them up to carts and chariots. The Assyrians, like most other powers, employed light chariots that were fast and usually contained archers. After about 900 BCE, as true horsemen began to take the place of charioteers in mobility-related tasks like scouting and pursuing beaten foes, chariots began to get bigger and heavier and their role evolved. The chariots of Ashurbanipal's era (686–628 BCE)[†] were huge vehicles drawn by four horses with three or four fighting men in each one. They were like biblical-era tanks or armored personnel carriers. Being on the opposing side of the battlefield must have been awe inspiring and terrifying. Hundreds of these machines lined up wheel to wheel—taking off across a plain at ten or fifteen miles per hour, the men inside them shooting arrows at their targets as the distance closed, then crashing into the closely packed mass of humanity facing them—must have been psychologically hard to bear. So much of war is about nerve and morale and avoiding panic,[‡] and it's interesting to speculate how many of the units in front of such an oncoming assault stood their ground to await the collision.[§] By this era, the chariots'

---

[*] Human beings riding on the backs of horses.

[†] These are commonly given as birth and death dates for Ashurbanipal.

[‡] The Greek god of panic, Phobos, was believed to run rampant on human battlefields.

[§] There are a lot of long-running questions over how the actual physics of ancient battle worked. One would expect these things to be known, but they aren't. Did troops or closely packed bodies of men actually crash into each other? The horses, too? Or did they instinctively halt at the last minute? Were opposing forces intermixed after charging? Or did both sides have an intervening "no-man's-land" where troops threw things at each other and occasionally came to blows? The ancient sources that might help resolve this often are silent on many crucial details. They usually assumed wheels were themselves six feet high and covered in metal studs, which were necessary (as one Assyrian account makes clear) because otherwise the chariots would slip and slide amid all the blood and gore.

The Assyrian horseman—perhaps the first true cavalry in history that was drilled and organized by modern standards[*]— was the most fearsome thing in their army. Multiple references in the old Hebrew Bible describe it as a "thunderbolt" and a "whirlwind." It was likely developed to deal with the barbarian Cimmerian and Scythian horse archers that swept out of what is now southern Russia after 1000 BCE (in what was probably the worst military threat to the civilized world of that time and place, and perhaps also the inspiration for the Gog and Magog of the Bible). Many historians say the Assyrians deserve credit for saving the civilizations of the Fertile Crescent from these tribal onslaughts because they were the only military power with the strength, flexibility, and manpower to blunt these invasions. If they hadn't done so, human history might have been vastly different. The Assyrians were certainly brutal, but their efforts may have saved the Iron Age civilization of west Asia from the rape, pillage, and brutality of the ancient world's version of the Mongol or Hunnic hordes.[†]

Alas, the Assyrians' enemies who were being slaughtered at

---

contemporary audiences would understand the universal basics and often commented only on the unusual things.

[*] Cavalry appeared among the nomadic horsemen of the Eurasian steppe before the settled societies adopted it. First came chariots, then men on horseback followed later. The Assyrians began using men on horseback somewhere between 1000 and 900 BCE; the Chinese wouldn't start using them in war until between 400 and 300 BCE.

[†] The Cimmerians and Scythians were some of the first peoples of the no- madic steppe culture of horse peoples who were themselves the cultural ancestors of the Mongols, Turks, and Huns.

the time weren't so grateful as later historians sometimes would be. It's easy to attribute altruistic or heroic motives to a "preserver of civilization," but in truth the Assyrians may simply have been trying to preserve their conquests and booty from being purloined by another. The magnificent army that the Assyrians created wasn't just a tool for the protection of their state but also for the furthering of their interests. Such interests included mass-scale piracy. Annual razzias and large raids were more common than not. Such forays were vital for keeping the Assyrian economy thriving.

A catalog of what one raid netted against an insignificant opponent gives a good idea of what constituted movable wealth and assets in that place and time:

40 chariots with men and horses
460 horses broken to the yoke
120 pounds of silver
120 pounds of gold
6,000 pounds of lead
6,000 pounds of copper
18,000 pounds of iron
1,000 vessels of copper
2,000 pans of copper
Assorted bowls and cauldrons of copper
1,000 brightly colored garments of wool
Assorted wooden tablets
Couches made of ivory and overlaid with gold from the
    ruler's palace
2,000 head of cattle
5,000 sheep
15,000 slaves
Assorted daughters of noblemen with dowries

The ruler's sister
An annual tribute of 1,000 sheep, 2,000 bushels of grain,
   2 pounds of gold, and 26 pounds of silver

While minor foes might be regularly sheared like sheep for profit, the other major Near Eastern states faced much more permanent levels of destruction. Elam, located in modern-day Iran, was a long-term implacable foe that Assyria "permanently crushed" several times over the eras. Obviously these conquests were less permanent than the boasting Assyrian rulers thought. Babylon, much closer to home, was a different sort of problem, one that they never managed to completely solve. The Assyrians had always treated Babylon better than they'd treated most of their other adversaries because the city was the cultural center of the very, very old world—the Paris of its day. Many historians have compared the relationship of Babylon and Assyria to the one between Greece and Rome. The Romans were militarily superior, but they had a real admiration for Greek culture, and they adopted aspects of their statue making, philosophy, literature, and architecture. The Assyrians were similar in their estimation of Babylon's ancient—and for that time and place, very advanced—culture. This regard and admiration had saved Babylon from the fate so many other cities and states had suffered at the hand of the Assyrians.

But every empire has its limits, and after yet another rebellion by the famously hard-to-pacify Babylonians (after the Assyrians had tried the "soft" approach with them), the Assyrian king Sennacherib got fed up and initiated what we might call the "final solution" to the Babylonian problem in 689 BCE. Stone reliefs narrate what happened next in the voice of the Assyrian ruler: "As a hurricane precedes, I attacked it, and like a storm, I overthrew it. Its inhabitants young and old I did not spare, and with their corpses, I filled the streets of the city. The town itself and its houses, from their foundations to their roofs, I devastated, I destroyed. By fire, I overthrew in order that in future, even the soil of its temples would be forgotten."

The historian Gwynne Dyer has said that Sennacherib destroyed Babylon as thoroughly as a nuclear bomb would have. In fact, the only difference between the ancient world and the modern is that it took a lot more human muscle power to accomplish the same thing. The Assyrian soldiers pulled the walls down and burned the city. (Imagine what would be involved trying to create a Hiroshima or Nagasaki if human hands had to do the work.)

In addition to killing the citizens of Babylon, the angry "king of the world" diverted a river over the city, and then had salt and thorny plants sowed into the soil to create an environmental wasteland.

The end for the Assyrian Empire may have come in part because of its success. In waging all these wars, the Assyrians ended up beating down some of the most ferocious and powerful tribes in the Middle East. Some historians have suggested that many of the peoples battered into submission remained pacified even after the Assyrians had left the scene. By the time the Persian Empire that succeeded the Assyrians stepped in, it's possible that the Persians may not have had to have been as brutal, because Assyria had already cowed many of the tribes, peoples, and states who otherwise would have posed a threat.[*] It's even been suggested that the reason Alexander the Great's invasion of Persia three centuries later seemed easier than per-

---

[*]That Achaemenid Persian Empire was, in fact, known for its relative tolerance and leniency. Was this a lesson learned from the Assyrians? Or had the Assyrians, by "breaking the Near East to the yoke of empire," made it less necessary?

haps anyone thought it would be was because the region had already been broken to the yoke of empire after centuries of wars with Assyria.

Tracing the reason great states decline or fall is always difficult. In Assyria's case, civil war and military overextension are popular culprits. Of the last of several great kings, Sennacherib, the destroyer of Babylon, was assassinated by his sons. Tradition says his brains were bashed out from behind while he was praying and that the murder weapon was a religious icon representing Babylonian deities. The Babylonians considered this payback for what Sennacherib had done to Babylon. His successor, Esarhaddon, might have thought so, too, and he went to work rebuilding the great city. (Nobody wants a god mad at him.)

Esarhaddon, a son of Sennacherib, brushed off internal rebellions and did what his forebears had only thought to do: attack Egypt. It's this attack on such a large, powerful, and faraway land that some historians cite as the Assyrian "bridge too far." Defeating the field forces of the Egyptians proved to be relatively easy for the still formidable Assyrian armies, but holding the region proved to be a nightmarish and expensive endeavor. The main Assyrian army was tied down for a long time in the Egyptian quagmire while things festered back at the heart of the homeland. It was a classic trap of empire: military overextension.

Meanwhile, in the vacuum created by Assyria's regular smashing of the formerly powerful Elamites, a once insignificant and little-known tribe was rising to power in what's now western Iran. A people known to history as the Medes began to coalesce into a more organized state, all under a king named Cyaxares, whose father had reportedly been killed by the Assyrians. Cyaxares is credited with reorganizing the Median army into a formidable force.* While the bulk of Esarhaddon's forces were tied down in Egypt, Media started giving Assyria trouble in a way it hadn't been given in a very long time.

In 615 BCE, Cyaxares attacked Assyria. He was initially thwarted, but the following year he came back and managed to destroy the ancient religious center of the empire, the old capital at Ashur. This was a shock. The Babylonians—always looking for a way to break free of Assyrian domination and smelling blood in the water—then allied themselves with the Median army in a ceremony under the ruined walls of Ashur. A powerful anti-Assyrian alliance was coalescing.† Cyaxares gave his daughter to the Babylonian king as a traditional cementing of the alliance. The tipping-point moment, if such things can be assessed so long after the fact, came when the barbarian Scythian mounted archers joined forces with the Medes and the Babylonians, and together all three powers moved on Nineveh in 612 BCE.

After several battles and a three-month siege, the great ancient metropolis fell. The Medes treated Nineveh just as the Assyrians would have treated a Median city. Legend has it that the last Assyrian king gathered all his precious goods and artifacts around him and set them on fire with him in the middle, burning to death as the allied armies were breaking down the walls of Nineveh.

Modern archaeologists have found ruins of the pottery and glazed bricks and other debris thrown into the city's moat to facilitate attacking the walls. They've also found the breaches made in those walls. Among the layers of burned ashes and soot, researchers have also discovered evidence of a fire so hot

---

* Or so the ancient sources say.

† Yet the Assyrians had smashed such multipower coalitions facing them in the past.

that glass might have melted, as well as human remains showing clear evidence of fatal violence from all over the site.

The biblical prophets, who allegedly predicted Assyria's downfall, wrote its epitaph:

'Behold, I am against you,' says the Lord of hosts . . .

It shall come to pass that all who look upon you
Will flee from you, and say,
"Nineveh is laid waste!
Who will bemoan her?"
Where shall I seek comforters for you?' . . .

Your injury has no healing,
Your wound is severe.
All who hear news of you
Will clap their hands over you,
For upon whom has not your wickedness passed continually?

And two hundred years later, when Xenophon stumbled upon the ruins, no one could even tell him they were Assyrian. The ghost city, however, remained in mute testament to the greatness and majesty of its builders, whomever they might have been.

We assume such a fate won't be ours. But once upon a time, so did they.

Chapter 5

THE BARBARIAN LIFE CYCLE

IT'S EASY TO take for granted all the things that keep the lights on in our society—the complex, interconnected system that provides things like power, food, and military or police protection. The financial system seems to run on autopilot. The same is true of the electrical grid; most of us hardly notice it until a storm knocks it out and we light some candles and wait for the power company to fix it. But what if the electricity were *never* fully restored? How would a people as reliant as we are on modernity deal with a forced, permanent reduction in it?

No generation of humans has ever had the capabilities ours has, or has relied on them to the degree ours does. And our minds are hardwired to think in terms of continuous improvement and modernization, an unspoken assumption that capabilities will always be advancing and the pace at which technological discoveries and innovations occur will only speed up.

It may be one-directional thinking, but it broadly reflects how things have been for many centuries. It's understandable that over time we would forget that things could ever move in the opposite direction. After all, when was the last time anything went the other way?

The fall of the Roman Empire is perhaps the most classic example. The experience of the Romanized areas of the British Isles is perhaps the starkest specific case. It was Julius Caesar who in 55 BCE famously made the first foray by a Mediterranean power over the English Channel to explore the misty, little-known (at least by non-natives) land on the far side. He fought with the local inhabitants, who he said* seemed culturally similar to the Celtic tribes he'd encountered in Gaul;† they rode and fought from chariots and many warriors dyed their skin blue to make them more frightening in battle. He portrayed the natives as a people primitive by Roman cultural and technological standards. After defeating them in several battles, Caesar crossed back over the channel with his troops and proceeded on toward his destiny in Italy. The tribes in Britain had almost a century of respite before the Romans returned. In 43 CE a Roman army of conquest crossed the channel and defeated and pacified the locals. They did this the usual way, and it involved large amounts of killing and repressing. Roman nastiness in what we might today call counterinsurgency warfare was often taken for granted and its immediate downsides to the local inhabitants were terrible. But the long-term gains for the descendants of the conquered inhabitants were immense. The Romans brought the proverbial "blessings of civilization" to much of the world.‡

---

*In a weird way here, Caesar is part conqueror and part Age of Discovery or Star Trek galactic explorer. His written account of these events, read all over the Mediterranean world, is the first confirmed eyewitness report the Mediterranean world gets of this ancient equivalent of an alien planet. Caesar is introducing a new civilization to his readers. Think of how fascinated we would be today by anything comparable.

†Essentially modern-day France.

‡That's one way to view it. "The Romans create a desolation and call it peace" was another way "Roman civilization" was viewed by those who had it forcibly inflicted on them. The Europeans also brought "the bless-

But when they eventually left and returned to where they came from, they often took those blessings back with them. And it's at that point that the local version of the Statue of Liberty begins the long process of melting into the sand.

Britain, under Roman rule, had been part of one of the great cutting-edge empires in world history, and then it rather rapidly lost that status. It's hard for us living today to relate to that. Several centuries of living as Romans had changed the formerly "barbarian" tribesmen into "Romano-Britons," a people who enjoyed their hot public baths, wonderful public buildings, fantastic roads, powerful walls, and any manner of forts and defenses—all manned by Roman soldiers from all over the empire. The Britons had been connected to the great Mediterranean and Near Eastern civilizational version of a power grid (the roots of which stretched all the way back to ancient Mesopotamia)—and then in the early 400s CE that direct connection was disrupted. The troops and money that supported the system in Britain were badly needed back in a threatened Italy. After several centuries of Roman governance and administration, the emperor essentially told the inhabitants of Britain that they would have to look after themselves.

The result was that a hundred years after Rome's power receded, the inhabitants of Britain were living in a less cutting-edge age than the one inhabited by their ancestors. What would be the result if that happened today—if a central government ceded all power over a given area? Some problems, such as food and fuel shortages, would appear almost instantaneously, while others would develop over a longer period, as systems and structures deteriorated and degraded.

---

ings of civilization" to Aboriginal people on multiple non-European continents throughout history. It certainly is a mixed blessing.

Metaphorically speaking, how long did the lights stay on in the Roman Empire after its disintegration? How long did the public baths last in the outlying former provinces before they broke down and there was no one left who remembered how or had the materials on hand to fix them? What about the aqueducts that supplied the water? Who manned the walls and fortifications that kept out enemies and invaders? How did anyone pay for anything if taxes weren't being collected or allocated? Who stepped in and took over the basic roles that government usually assumed?

HUNDREDS OF POTENTIAL scenarios have been proposed for the "fall of the Roman Empire."* Just as with other "falls," some experts believe that, instead of a dramatic "fall," there was a transition—a change in management, if you will—that may have better met the needs of people on the ground than the Roman administration did. But regardless of the truth, it's hard to ignore the fact that the new managers of many of these formerly Roman provinces in the West, even though they usually tried to preserve Roman practices, were Germanic tribes.

To look at a map of the formerly Roman world circa 600 CE is to see what an empire looks like when it's fragmented. That's basically what occurred. The Roman lands in North Africa had been occupied by a Germanic tribe called the Vandals. Spain and parts of what's now southwestern France were under the control of the Visigoths, while the Burgundian tribe dominated and administered southeastern France. What is today northern France was ruled by a "barbarian" Frankish king, and the heart

---

*This phrase refers to the Western Roman Empire. The eastern chunk of the old Roman Empire (centered in modern-day Turkey) lasted a thousand more years after the western half of the empire fragmented.

of the old Roman Empire, Italy, was Ostrogothic. Many other formerly imperial territories were controlled by even smaller ruling entities. It had all been Roman in 400 CE. In many places the "barbarian" warlords were still trying to keep it that way as much as possible. The historian Chris Wickham writes, "The larger western polities were all ruled in a Roman tradition, but they were more militarized. Their fiscal structures were weaker. They had fewer economic interrelationships, and their internal economies were often simpler." He adds, "Over and over again, 'barbarian' armies occupied Roman provinces, which they ran in Roman ways; so nothing changed; but everything changed."

How had it ever come to this? At its height (around 100 CE), the Roman Empire was probably the greatest state the world had yet seen. Only contemporary Han dynasty China could be considered to have been on par with Rome. The empire was incredibly sophisticated, controlled an enormous landmass, governed something like seventy million[*] citizens, and kept the "barbarians" at bay. The fact that Rome was also one of the most warlike states in human history is not a coincidence. None of this empire building would have been possible if Rome hadn't possessed one of the finest armies in world history.[†]

The Roman army still fascinates modern military historians. As with other armies from the ancient world, the actual physics of how it functioned in combat on the battlefield isn't entirely understood. At the empire's height, the army was a multinational force of long-serving professionals composed of men recruited from all over the empire, bound by an institutional tradition

---

[*] This number is unknown and argued about.

[†] This doesn't mean that Rome could beat any army it faced, however. In boxing, there's a phrase "styles make fights," meaning that some styles naturally beat other styles. The same applies to warfare. But the Romans were as dominant a military force in their day as anyone will find anywhere.

going back centuries. The troops were disciplined, drilled, equipped by the state, and highly motivated. Leadership at the unit level was provided by the famous centurions, and Roman armies did things on the battlefield most other armies couldn't.[*] It is a wonderful example in microcosm of just how sophisticated the ancient world really was. Simply feeding and supplying such a force on campaign requires logistics on a scale that we don't normally associate with long-ago societies. The entire Roman state was protected at any given time by between three hundred and five hundred thousand[†] men, guarding outposts from northern Britain to North Africa, and from Spain to Syria.

And in combat they dominated. As the historian Arther Ferrill writes: "Contrary to the usual rule of pre-modern military history, Romans inflicted heavy casualties even when they were defeated. Normally Romans did not run, which is when the heaviest casualties are taken. Against untrained troops, they simply could not be defeated, even when they were greatly out-numbered. Only when a Roman army was caught by surprise on unfavorable terrain did barbarians have a chance to win a tactical victory."

If one could transport the Roman army one thousand years into the future, it's hard to imagine them losing to any European army until the high Middle Ages.[‡] How far into the future

---

[*] Rotating spent troops with fresh troops in combat was a part of the Roman system that, if not unique, was rare due to its difficulty, if nothing else. The advantage of being able to do the sports equivalent of "substituting" with reserves would wear down even the best and most highly motivated of foes.

[†] Considering the numbers of enemies the Roman army faced, this is a re-markably small number of soldiers.

[‡] If for no other reason than the Romans would have had a far larger army than almost anyone in Europe. Charlemagne's Carolingian army is some-times estimated to have been very large, but other than that most post-Roman era European armies were tiny by comparison. The Normans

could the best military today be transported and still compete successfully?

If a neighboring state was at peace with the Romans, it was usually for one of three reasons:

1. They'd already been beaten. Many states at peace with Rome had been made client states or incorporated into Rome, with their population often becoming Roman citizens.
2. They hadn't yet been beaten. Sometimes Rome's own occasional weakness—like any long-lasting state, it experienced ebbs and flows of power—forced its diplomats, usually very aggressive, to make long-term, peaceful relationships with the neighbors. These relationships often ended when Rome's fortunes turned for the better.
3. They were unknown to Rome.

Number three reflects a facet of an earlier time in human history. Occasionally, we moderns will stumble upon a small, hitherto undiscovered community living in complete isolation in some very remote location. In ancient and medieval history, not knowing

---

invaded Saxon England with (maybe many) fewer than fifteen thousand men in 1066 CE. The Romans invaded Britain a thousand years before that with twenty thousand legionaries and about twenty thousand more auxiliary troops. How would William the Conqueror's eight to twelve thousand or so early medievals have done on a battlefield against a likely better supplied forty-thousand-man ancient Roman army? Also, William probably couldn't have raised or hired much more than this number, whereas the Roman invasion of Britain used but a percentage of the overall Roman army. On the grand strategy level it would have been a wipeout. The Roman Empire of seventy million or so people and immense money and resources steamrolls the Duke of Normandy's minor provincial territory. The Romans would have given any tribally organized pregunpowder army in history a very tough fight. They would have beaten most of them.

what the world looked like beyond a certain point on the map and bumping into a previously unknown state, culture, or people was not just possible, but, as empires expanded, inevitable.

We live in an age when all the world has been mapped and satellite imagery has turned the entire surface of the planet into a known commodity. No longer do our maps have sea monsters on them representing the vast edge-of-the-world territories that aren't charted or known. Modern defense strategists wouldn't know where to start if they had to account for, and plan for, areas of the globe that were as hidden from them as the dark side of the moon. What might be lurking in an undiscovered hemisphere? It could run the civilizational gamut from a terrestrial version of H. G. Wells's *The War of the Worlds*—in which a more technologically advanced, hitherto unknown society swoops into your hemisphere and suddenly starts shredding your backward armed forces—to the opposite, in which primitive barbarians not much different from hordes of Neanderthals come out of the dark unknown and smash against your empire's defenses.

This happened to military planners in the past repeatedly.*

And while we moderns wouldn't be particularly frightened of any newly found society if it were discovered to be far below our technological, economic, or complexity levels, some of the most frightening peoples in history were the ones who fit these criteria, the ones we've come to know as "barbarians."

The terms "Roman" and "barbarian" have become closely associated with each other, in large part because of the role the latter had in stripping the former of its western territories. But there were so-called barbarians long before there were Romans. The general public perception of a "barbarian"—a badass, bearded, horned-helmet-wearing, battle-ax-wielding warrior who prays to heroic

---

*Mongol invasions anyone? Huns?

gods, drinks a lot, and rides the line between sane and insane in battle—is more period and culture specific than the ancient Greek conception. It was they who invented the root of today's term, and by it they basically meant anyone who wasn't Greek.* That covered a lot of different types of people; most, in fact. The Romans used the word in a similar sense, often classifying even very refined peoples such as the Persians and Carthaginians as "barbarians." But the term has long been used by the settled agricultural states and societies as a denigrating label for tribal peoples and nomads. When we think of barbarians today, that's the stereotype we have: a fierce, uncivilized, illiterate, dangerous, and yet almost childlike destroyer of fine places and things.

It seems that any ancient city-state in its long-ago formative years had local barbarians, nomads, or tribes living nearby. Often these tribes made their homes or set up their tents or shelters in the rugged terrain avoided by the farmers and city dwellers—the hills or mountains, the desert, or the treeless steppe. There was trade, interaction, diplomacy, and, yes, friction between these two groups, and the city-states often subdued the local tribes or nomads—or vice versa.

Somewhere in the misty, semilegendary past of Italy in the eighth century BCE, this is how the city of Rome began. By the fourth and third centuries BCE it was a small city-state— fighting wars against its local neighbors who lived a mere day's walk away. Two centuries after that it had swelled into a vast empire operating on all three of the then-known continents.†

---

*It could even get more exclusive than that. Were Macedonians Greek? The Macedonians often liked to think so. The sniffy Athenians might disagree. It was they who labeled the king of Macedon, the father of Alexander the Great, "Philip the Barbarian."

†Europe, Africa, and Asia. The Americas, Antarctica, and Australia were obviously unknown to them.

The Roman writer Livy wrote that Rome conquered the world in self-defense, but this idea seems more than a little self-serving for a patriotic Roman writer to claim.[*] It rests on an assumption that conquest and the smashing of dangerous foes was often done to pacify the unstable frontier, but the frontier never seemed to stay pacified. There seemed always to be new enemies (usually ever tougher and fiercer) beyond the ones recently defeated. Caesar's conquest of Gaul, for example, stabilized the Gallic situation, but added a new Rhine River border to Rome's frontiers with new ferocious tribal neighbors that had previously been Gaul's problem. Now they were *his* problem, and Rome's ever after. From the perspective of the Romans, it must have seemed like every barbarian tribe had another even more barbaric tribe behind it forever stretching off to the ends of the earth. If you are seeking border security, where does it end?

Rome's most dangerous "barbarian" foes would originate from locations that, unlike relatively nearby Gaul, were beyond Rome's reach—places that appeared to belch forth fierce new tribes and peoples the way volcanoes do new islands. It's a fascinating historical human geographical phenomenon. The most famous of these regions sometimes referred to as "wombs of nations" or "factories of tribes" was in the general area of the Altay Mountains in Mongolia.[†] This very remote, oft-frozen, rugged steppe country may have been ground zero for a whole slew of central Asian nomadic horse tribes over the ages—the Scythians, Sarmatians, Huns, Avars, Turks, and Mongols all may have first appeared[‡] in this region. If this is true, it's quite

---

[*] That rationale can be debated, but conquer they did.

[†] Also often called/spelled Altai Mountains.

[‡] Whatever "appeared" means. Aliens weren't dropping them off from mother ships, so this is a bit of a historical trick the lack of sources plays on

a "barbarian" pedigree. It's also an enormous distance from Rome. The Romans would have had to conquer to the borders of modern-day China to shut down this wellspring of barbarism at the source the way they did in Gaul.

Scandinavia was another region that seemed to be a sort of womb of nations. It was also another place that would have been difficult for Rome to permanently subdue and colonize: comparatively remote, with a low carrying capacity in terms of food to support growing populations, and a harsh environment. It certainly didn't look like a rich and enticing place to invade. In fact, the inhabitants themselves periodically left in search of better things. Large, enthusiastic blond, blue-eyed warriors had for centuries been both a willing and unwilling export from the far north. The Vikings were one of the last of the great eruptions of these traders, seafarers, colonizers, pirates, and warriors from Scandinavia, but that region is popularly credited with producing many more offspring over recorded history. This is where Germanic tribes like the Goths, Lombards, Vandals, and many others were supposed to have originated before at some point moving southward.* Those specific tribes, however, all arrived (or coalesced) in central Europe centuries after the Romans first encountered peoples there that they classified broadly as "Germans."†

---

us. Hopefully, technology will solve the question of where all these wonderfully interesting people came from and to what other peoples in history they might be related.

*Many of these tribes had oral histories that told of a Scandinavian origin; work on DNA evidence is ongoing.

†In Latin, *Germani*. Trying to nail down what's really going on here ethnicitywise is impossible. DNA tests may someday sort this all out, but for a thousand reasons, trying to figure out what's a "German" versus what, for example, is a "Celt" or the supposedly mixed "Belgae" is impossible. The Roman writers were somewhat lazy ethnographers to begin with,

"Germany" is a modern creation. Territories that include peoples or cultures often identified as "Germanic" encompass a much larger area than that occupied by the modern nation-state we know as Germany. Stretching roughly west to east between the Rhine and Vistula Rivers, and from the North Sea and the Baltic south to the Danube and even the Black Sea, an ever-changing number of several dozen tribes and tribal confederations the Romans would (usually) classify as Germanic made their home.*

For much of ancient history, most of this area was off the known map, the terrestrial equivalent of the dragons and sea monsters that inhabited the oceanic edge of the world or the unknown interiors of "darkest Africa" on early charts and globes. Certainly, traders and friendly barbarian tribes would have provided some secondhand information about what the people were like in the interior across the Rhine, but it's doubtful that what they'd heard prepared the Romans for the *furor teutonicus* when they finally got to experience it firsthand.

The "first contact" moment—when German tribes en masse ran into the world of the Mediterranean (where the cultures were literate and could record information like this)—occurred when the supposedly enormous Cimbri and Teuton[†] tribes started to migrate south as part of what's known as "the Cimbric War."[‡] In 113 BCE, these tribes moved into the territory of a Celtic

---

and writers had their own reasons for describing these people as they did. Sometimes it may have been just to create a better story.

* Often the lines would blur at the borders where different peoples and cultures met, creating a sort of cultural estuary. So there could be a Germanic-Celtic tribe or a Thracian-German blend, etc.

† Of course, connected to the modern term "Teutonic."

‡ The point of origin of these "Germanic" tribes is debated, but near the coasts of the North or Baltic Sea is a popular theory.

people allied with Rome. According to (basically hostile) writers in the ancient world, both the Cimbri and the Teutons were huge tribes of particularly intractable "barbarians" in search of new homes; they had brought their families, possessions, and wagons with them.* Those authors claimed that these tribes were joined by other tribes and individuals as they moved along, swelling their numbers even more.†

By this time, Rome had been squaring off with so-called barbarians for centuries. But this new group was portrayed as extreme even by the standards of the uncivilized: they scared *other* barbarians. The ancient writers depicted them as physically enormous human beings with white hair and gray eyes. They were dressed primitively in the skins of animals, were inhumanly strong, and nearly crazed with bloodlust. They destroyed Roman army after Roman army seemingly with ease as they moved toward Italy, threatening the Eternal City itself. The battlefield casualties among the Roman legionaries were horrendous, and desperation gripped the Roman state.

And then, as the ancient writers describe it, the barbarian tribes, like a bunch of distractible children, saw the equivalent of something shiny over in the regions of modern Spain and France, and took a detour in that direction, giving the Romans

---

*It might be helpful to imagine the "barbarian" tribes the way the Romans and Chinese often saw them, on a sliding scale of how uncivilized they were seen. "Cooked" or "uncooked" was the Chinese way of describing the difference between tribes that had had the rough edges smoothed by contact with settled societies versus the totally wild ones that hadn't. In the Roman version, the Cimbri and Teutons weren't just uncooked, they were raw and still twitching.

†Including Celtic peoples. In fact, there's been debate over how much these northerners were Germanic (the dominant opinion) and how much might have been Celtic. Some theories suggest some sort of amalgamation of the two peoples.

time to come up with an emergency backup plan, which, as the Romans often did, was to find a transcendent leader and vest him with command.

By the time the Cimbri and Teutons (and friends) resumed their march on Rome in 104 BCE, the Romans had put the army general and multiple-time consul Gaius Marius in charge. This man—who would actually play an important role in the Roman Republic's downward spiral—arguably saved it from one of the worst threats it ever faced when he first smashed the Teutons and their allies at the Battle of Aquae Sextiae in 102 BCE (and supposedly left 90,000 dead Germans on the field). Gaius Marius then did the same to the Cimbri at the Battle of Vercellae the following year (killing a further 65,000 to 160,000 tribesmen).[*] So ended the first terrible German menace in Rome's history.

A generation later (55 BCE-ish), one of the greatest figures in Rome's history, Julius Caesar (a nephew of Gaius Marius), was dealing with his own scary German problem. According to Caesar's own account, the Celtic tribes in what's now western Europe (mostly in the Rhine River region) were being attacked by these ferocious people Caesar referred to as "Germans." Caesar portrayed them as just as scary and unstoppable as they were a generation earlier (that is, if they were related at all to the Cimbri and Teutons) and said the Celtic tribes begged him to help them fend off this attack or invasion from over the Rhine.

When the Roman legions arrived in the area to help their Gallic/Celtic[†] allies, they began to hear accounts of the terrible, unfamiliar foe that they would be up against, and Caesar said

---

[*] Again, who knows on these figures. The ancient sources are so unreliable, and even the very best experts disagree. This is a pretty standard range usually given.

[†] "Celtic" identity is as argued about as "Germanic" identity. For our purposes, the terms "Gaul" and "Celt" might be considered interchangeable.

they became intimidated. "Our men started asking questions," Caesar wrote, "and the Gauls and traders replied by describing how tall and strong the Germans were, how unbelievably brave and skillful with weapons. Often, they claimed, when they had met the Germans in battle, they had been unable to stand even the way they looked, the sternness of their gaze."* According to Caesar's self-serving and biased (though seemingly firsthand) account, the terrifying descriptions of these "Germans" caused a panic among the Roman military tribunes and prefects.

> Some of them started offering various excuses for urgent departure and asked his permission to go. Others stayed behind out of shame, wanting to avoid the taint of cowardice. These men could not conceal their fearful expressions, nor, at times, could they restrain their tears. They hid themselves away in their tents and bemoaned their fate, or among their friends lamented the common danger. Throughout the camp, all the men were signing and sealing their wills.

It should be noted that by Caesar's time the Roman military had been conquering everybody and was seen as pretty unstoppable. The troops whom Caesar describes as intimidated by this unnerving foe were themselves an army of intimidators.

Later ancient writers such as Tacitus and Plutarch would say much the same thing Caesar had: This group of people who

---

*Julius Caesar's more than two-thousand-year-old account depicts what was essentially the earliest Franco-German conflict of the many over the centuries. He had all sorts of personal motivations for writing such a piece, and while it is considered a very important and valuable source, it needs to be treated with skepticism in many places. He may have created a wholly artificial distinction between peoples for his own purposes.

Caesar claimed belonged on the eastern side of the Rhine River were physically large and very warlike.* The women and children of the tribe are often said to have come to the battlefield in wagons, tending the wounded and screaming encouragement for their warriors from behind the fighting lines, putting themselves in harm's way so that if the men lost the battle, everybody died or was enslaved.

Tacitus wrote that the Germanic warriors hated peace, and if their own tribe wasn't at war, they might seek out one that was and join their cause: "Many noble youths, if the land of their birth is stagnating in a long period of peace and inactivity, deliberately seek out other tribes which have some war in hand. For the Germans have no taste for peace; renown is more easily won among perils, and a large body of retainers cannot be kept together except by means of violence and war." He then added: "A German is not so easily prevailed upon to plough the land and wait patiently for harvest as to challenge a foe and earn wounds for his reward. He thinks it tame and spiritless to accumulate slowly by the sweat of his brow what could be got quickly by the loss of a little blood."†

Finally, Caesar talked about how these great tribes created zones where they had forcibly depopulated the land around their home area to form a defensive perimeter. The greater the tribe, the wider the dead zone. "The highest praise among the

---

*By insisting in his account that such peoples be kept to the east of the Rhine, Caesar was laying out a conception of where the "Celtic" peoples belonged and where the "Germans" belonged. He may have been creating artificial boundaries for his own reasons, but it's interesting to note that in many ways those boundaries have remained roughly in place to this day.

†There are elements of what we would call today racism, ethnocentrism, and stereotypes involved here. There may be truth mixed in with the bigotry, but it's not always easy to tell where one ends and the other begins.

German states goes to those who ravage their borders and so maintain the widest unpopulated area around themselves." (Caesar claimed to have heard of one zone that was six hundred miles wide.)*

An interesting relationship developed between the Romans and the Germans over the next several centuries, which would take two divergent paths. The first, and most obvious, in the history books at least, was a relationship through war.

From the time of the great invasion/migration of the Cimbri and Teutons, to the very end of the Western Roman Empire, Germanic tribes and Roman armies would regularly square off. Despite the Germanic armies' celebrated physical attributes, fighting qualities, and the *furor teutonicus*, the Romans beat them much more often than they lost to them, and when they did suffer defeats there were usually extenuating circumstances.

A perfect example of that happened in 9 CE, in what to us now resembles a Roman version of Custer's Last Stand. But where US lieutenant colonel George Armstrong Custer lost fewer than three hundred men in his disastrous encounter with a larger force of Native Americans, his Roman equivalent lost something like twenty thousand of his soldiers to tribal warriors. The Roman general Publius Quinctilius Varus led an army of three legions, plus thousands of auxiliaries, deep into forbidding north-central Germany . . . and never came out. Varus was led into a trap by a Roman-trained German tribesman he thought was friendly but who was instead secretly working with

---

*The mileage may not be exact once you convert Roman distances to modern distances, but it was still a huge dead zone—nearly the distance from Inverness in the north of Scotland all the way to Bristol on the southern coast of England; or from Washington, DC, to Indianapolis.

several allied German tribes hostile to Rome.* Varus and his troops were ambushed in the dark forests and were virtually exterminated—the story was, to a civilized Roman's mind, a complete nightmare.

Several years later, a Roman force exacting revenge on the tribes would find the nightmarish aftermath of the battle, including the overrun Roman camp defenses, the locations of the last stands by the final resisters, and the places where the Roman captives were tortured to death.

The ancient writer Tacitus portrayed it in stark terms:

Varus' first camp with its wide circumference and the measurements of its central space clearly indicated the handiwork of three legions. Further on, the partially fallen rampart and the shallow fosse suggested the inference that it was a shattered remnant of the army which had there taken up a position. In the center of the field were the whitening bones of men, as they had fled, or stood their ground, strewn everywhere or piled in heaps. Near lay fragments of weapons and limbs of horses, and also human heads, prominently nailed to

---

*At some point while the legions were strung out for many miles on narrow muddy forest trails, the tribesmen sprang their ambush. The sources say that it was pouring rain, that the Roman shields and bows were waterlogged, and that the legionaries were surrounded in many places with missiles raining down on them. One gets a sense of panic and claustrophobia, as the Romans in any given position likely couldn't see much more than what was directly around them and were prevented from forming up and fighting in any sort of traditional battle formation. They were deep in hostile country and the Germanic tribes were intimidating and frightening, especially on their home turf. In a running affair that would last several days, the three Roman legions were destroyed. Varus and many of his officers killed themselves rather than fall into their enemy's hands.

trunks of trees. In the adjacent groves were the barbarous altars, on which they had immolated tribunes and
first-rank centurions.*

Emperor Augustus Caesar was supposed to have pounded
his head against a door from time to time while declaiming,
"Quinctilius Varus, give me back my legions!"†

The Battle of the Teutoburg Forest (*Teutoburger Wald*)
didn't end Roman involvement in the region, yet it was deemed
by many historians to have been a turning point of sorts, one
in which the Germans smashed any hope the Romans would
turn Germany into another imperial province as they had Gaul.
The region was too big and the terrain and climate too challenging. To "Romanize" it would have been difficult for Rome's
taxpayers and military at this stage of the empire, and, frankly,
it was not a rich enough area to warrant the effort that would
have been needed to subdue and hold it. The emperors Trajan
(r. 98–117 CE) and Marcus Aurelius (r. 161–180 CE) would both
fight terrible wars against the Germans, but ultimately it was
decided that the frontier of Rome would pretty much stop at the
Rhine, not far from the borders of modern Germany. Along the
Danube in the south, the Romans would build massive fortifications to guard the empire from Germanic incursions.

The martial aspect of the Romano-Germanic relationship at-
tracts more historical attention, but it may have been the peaceful
interaction between the two peoples that eventually changed the
actual balance of power. It's easy to see how sustained contact,

---

*The battle site itself may have been found in the twentieth century; so far,
archaeology seems to be confirming some of the general points of the written accounts.

† So says the ancient writer Suetonius.

even just a shared border, can change societies, as goods, money, ideas, and people move back and forth across it. This is especially true if there's a cultural or technological imbalance between the two sides. The native peoples of the Americas in the sixteenth century weren't the same five hundred years later, after sustained contact with the more centralized and technologically advanced Europeans. The Germanic tribal peoples in central Europe weren't the same after five centuries of contact with the Roman world, either. Germans who fought with Rome as allies, auxiliaries, or mercenaries were an obvious conduit for the transmission of Roman ideas and culture to the tribes. This was especially true for any of the tribes in the interior of Germanic territory who lacked direct physical contact with Roman lands. Even before the Roman Republic morphed into the empire, the value of using German warriors had been recognized. Often, these German fighters in the empire's service would get to travel to Rome and experience one of the greatest cities the world had ever seen, then go out to fight on the frontiers of the empire, rubbing elbows with other cosmopolitan peoples in far-flung places. They would then return to their tribes in Germany, bringing with them a massive transfer of experience gained by operating in an advanced society. Multiply that by hundreds of thousands of individual warriors over many lifetimes and it's not hard to see how transformative it would have been.

By the time the Roman Empire in the West was beginning to totter (say, the 400s CE), many of these Germanic "barbarian" tribes and their leaders looked quite a lot like Romans themselves. The historian Roger Collins writes, "It would be easy to imagine ['the barbarians'] as little more than savages—naked, hairy and doubtless garishly painted. In practice, however, by the fourth and fifth centuries, the various Germanic-speaking peoples were, in terms of material culture, little different from the Roman provincials." Although they often had blonder or redder hair and the ubiquitous ancient German mustache, Collins points out that the Germans were even wearing many of the same clothes as the Romans. In fact, both sides were wearing each other's clothing and shared adornment styles, too. German skintight pants and long hair became fashionable among the cool crowd in Rome—much to the distaste of the traditionalists in the Eternal City.

It's been long argued that what was going on in the Roman army was a type of fusion that might have been far from harmless, a kind of Germanization of the army. It started with the practice of employing Germanic troops—sometimes whole tribes—often fighting and equipped as tribal warriors.* The practice of creating allies (or *foederati*) out of tribes and peoples, and then using their soldiers in Rome's armies, went way back in Roman history. The Romans handled the Germans as they had so many others, creating client states on their Germanic tribal borders, ruled by tribal leaders who were beholden to Rome, and who then formed buffer states between Rome and the interior German tribes. These client states also often provided warriors en masse to fight when needed with the Romans. Some historians have even referred to these arrangements as essentially "contracts."†

There was never a problem having *some* Germans fighting in the Roman army, but the question of whether there was such a thing as too many Germans in a Roman army has been debated extensively. At what point did it become more German than Roman? Did this even matter anyway? For the Romans this may have been an existential question as much as a theoretical

---

*As opposed to being trained as Roman regular troops and incorporated into the standard drill and organization of the Roman army.

†"Treaties" is the more traditional term.

one, especially since this army would be called on to defend Rome in its darkest days against the armies that would eventually topple the western empire—armies often made up of, you guessed it, Germanic tribesmen.[*]

Over just a couple of centuries, the Roman armies became so Germanized that Germanic warriors began to rise into the ranks of the command structure. There were times in the Roman Empire when the major field army in the West and the major field army in the East were *both* commanded by generals of Germanic descent. And these Roman armies over time began to look and eventually to fight differently than Roman armies of earlier eras. Instead of being integrated into the legions and becoming virtually indistinguishable from other Roman troops (as had happened with the Gauls after they were tamed), more and more German troops were fighting with the Romans using their traditional "barbaric" weapons, armor, group leaders, and fighting style.

It's hard to quantify how much this contributed to what would eventually happen to Rome.[†] Archaeology has recently shed light on previously unknown developments occurring "behind the barbarian iron curtain." It seems that much was changing in the dark interior of central and northern Europe, from increasing wealth and economic activity, to evolving political systems, to new agricultural techniques, all of which con-

[*] And while this sounds very dangerous, it's worth pointing out that the vast majority of the time the Germanic troops did this loyally and well. But it also meant the Germanic enemies were not "outgunned" as they were in earlier eras, either. If you were a Roman commander, would you rather have a whole bunch of first-century legionaries fighting a barbarian force, or would you rather be commanding one fifth-century barbarian force against another?

[†] And, as usual, there are differing opinions on the importance of this by the experts.

tributed to huge population increases. How much was due to contact with people like the Romans and how much of it was internally germinated isn't clear,* but this change was part of the reason the Germanic tribes of the very late imperial era were more dangerous than those of previous centuries.

As the historian Peter Heather has written: "The massive population increase, economic development and political re-structuring of the first three centuries AD could not fail to make fourth-century Germania much more of a potential threat to Roman strategic dominance in Europe than its first-century counterpart." He also points out that this greater threat was less stable than it had been: "It is important to remember, too, that Germanic society had not yet found its equilibrium. The belt of Germanic client kingdoms extended only about a hundred kilometers beyond the Rhine and Danube frontier lines: this left a lot of Germania excluded from the regular campaigning that kept frontier regions reasonably in line. The balance of power on the frontier was, therefore, vulnerable to something much more dangerous than the periodic over-ambition of client kings. One powerful exogenous shock had been delivered by Sasanian Persia in the previous century—did the Germanic world beyond the belt of closely controlled client kingdoms pose a similar threat?"

Maybe.

The period often cited as the crisis era in both Romano-Germanic relations and the eventual dissolution of the Western Roman Empire is thought to have been sparked by the arrival of

---

*The Germanic tribes on the borders with Rome were getting much wealthier than interior tribes through commerce and interaction with the Roman state directly. This created imbalances and may have prompted the poorer tribes to raid the wealthier ones, contributing to the unsettled dynamic in the Germanic interior.

an outside people into the story in 376 CE—the year the ferocious and still somewhat mysterious Huns broke like a storm on Europe.

It's hard to say what really happened in the dark depths of the "barbarian" interior, where great wars might have been fought between tribes and tribal confederacies, but no one knows of them because they were never recorded. The traditional story— which originated with ancient sources and was taken as gospel by most until recently—was that the Huns, a fierce tribe of nomadic steppe horse peoples, had broken into the European side of Eurasia and were driving all before them. Whole tribes were supposedly fleeing from them in utter desperation and smashing into one another in a chain reaction.

The Ostrogoths, we are told, fled from the Huns in panic toward the west, where they then collided with the Visigoths. Together, these Germanic tribes were driven against Rome's Danubian frontier, where they begged to be allowed in, creating a vast humanitarian crisis.

Some more modern theories, however, suggest that the Huns may not have been involved in a vast military offensive at all, but that lots of small-scale raids and attacks had made the home areas of the Gothic peoples unsafe and insecure.

Regardless of the reasons, the Roman emperor in the East was confronted with a difficult situation.* A crisis can also be an opportunity, however, and the emperor Valens (r. 364–378 CE), who may not have had a lot of great options in this situation, at least saw a potential upside in possibly adding a bunch of tough Visigothic soldiers into his armies. He agreed to allow the tribes to cross the Danube River frontier and settle within the presumed safety of the boundaries of the empire if they gave up

---

*Rome sometimes had two emperors during this period, one in the West in Rome (or another Western capital), the other in the East in Constantinople.

their arms. It wasn't an unreasonable request—having more than a hundred thousand armed Germanic tribespeople inside your borders is not without its potential dangers.[*]

The refugees expected salvation; instead, as the historian Arther Ferrill writes, "late in 376"—in the dead of winter—"the river crossing began. The Visigoths, perhaps 200,000 strong, were starving, and insensitive grasping Roman officials exploited them unmercifully. To avoid starvation, the Visigoths traded their children into Roman slavery for dog's meat at the rate of one child per dog."

Perhaps not all Romans treated the newcomers so viciously, but, as Ferrill notes, "the crossing of the Danube was badly mishandled." That's one way to describe the functional equivalent of pouring gasoline onto a situation that the panic and desperation caused by the Hunnic attacks had already made potentially explosive.

Beaten down, hungry, freezing, and disorganized though they were, the Visigoths were still a formidable and strong people. Eventually, the combustible situation ignited, and the warriors went on a rampage, taking what they needed from the region for the next eighteen months in what became known as the Gothic War (376–382 CE).[†]

By the time the Romans and Goths met in a real full-scale field battle, it was 378 CE, and the Eastern Roman emperor was at the head of a Roman army in modern-day European Turkey. He had to broker peace with his bitter foes the Sasanian Persians to make the army available, but Gothic depredations had the

---

[*]The numbers here are totally unknown, and speculation abounds. "More than a hundred thousand" for two large Gothic groups of entire families seems safe. But one can find both higher and lower estimates.

[†]One of several "Gothic wars."

public up in arms; in this era when emperors could come and go rapidly, the truth was that an emperor who allowed the Gothic problem to continue for too long might end up fighting his own rebellious people instead of the barbarians.

Even though it's natural to think of these "Goths"* as "Germans," it's hard to know what they really were by this time. These tribes had been absorbing other tribes and groups and individuals for so long since they'd left their Scandinavian homeland,† and were now residing in so many areas populated by non-Germanic types, that these "Goths" must have been a mix of ethnicities by this time. They probably retained core elements that bound them together, such as a Germanic tongue and shared origin myths, and they certainly had many people who fit the traditional Germanic physical stereotypes, but, like other Germanic tribes who moved into non-Germanic regions, they picked up adventurers, freed slaves, Huns, Slavs, Alan warriors, and even disaffected Roman citizens along their route. That's the sort of heterogeneous "Gothic" force that lined up against the Romans at the Battle of Adrianople in 378 CE.‡

Adrianople (also called Hadrianopolis) has always been considered one of history's pivotal battles. *If* this is true, it's only because of the outcome. Had the Romans prevailed, it would likely be chalked up as just another Roman triumph over the barbarians. But the Romans didn't triumph, Adrianople was a disaster (for them), and this made the battle extremely important.

---

*Again, the Romans often used specific tribal names for each of these peoples rather than the generic term "Goth."

†If that's even true.

‡Founded by the emperor Hadrian, Adrianople is located in the modern city of Edirne in northwest Turkey near the border with Greece.

The Roman army of this era may have been a shadow of its former self,* but it was still effective, especially against tribal peoples. But multiple errors in command, intelligence, and diplomacy put the troops in a bad situation and ensured that there would be fewer of them at the battle than could have been assembled if things had gone to plan. The Roman soldiers arrived at the battlefield tired after an estimated eight-mile march in rough terrain. It was very hot, and the Goths set fire to the surrounding grass to make things worse.

After their arrival, the Roman troops faced a massive circle of wagons perched on a hill, which the Goths had arranged as a defensive structure. Inside this makeshift battlefield fortification were the Gothic warriors and their families.

The battle seems to have started spontaneously when some Roman units began advancing to assault the wagon circle before so ordered. Initially, it looked like a typical Roman victory, with the tribesmen being pushed backward and the circle of wagons about to be stormed.

And then disaster struck.

Gothic[†] cavalry that had been away when the battle began returned to the Gothic camp as the fighting was raging, and charged into the already engaged Roman left flank "like a thunderbolt near the mountains."[‡] This Roman flank was rolled

---

*This is truer in quantity than quality. The troops were often still good, but the armies were generally getting much smaller and were harder to raise. The historian J. E. Lendon said that Roman armies of the fourth century were "small, expensive and fragile."

[†]Again, the Goths' numbers are said to have swelled, and some of the new friends the Goths traveled with were Huns and Alans, both powerful cavalry elements. The Alans were a mostly nomadic steppe tribe that seems to have acquired some Germanic characteristics over time.

[‡]Most of this information, along with this quoted line, comes from the Roman historian Ammianus Marcellinus.

up, the troops in the center crowded so closely together that they became encumbered by their shields, weapons, and fellow comrades, and after what seems to have been a rather spirited Roman resistance, the Gothic forces eventually prevailed. The ancient sources say that two-thirds of the Roman force died— probably between fifteen and twenty thousand[*] men in an era when raising an army of fifteen thousand was a major feat. The emperor Valens himself was killed somewhere on or around the battlefield. (His body was never found.)

Adrianople was not a large battle by the standards of Rome at its height, but at this point in its history, the losses were extremely hard to make up. Roman citizens in this era had long had professional troops to do their fighting for them and couldn't just be drafted out of the civilian ranks into the army and pitted against savage, experienced warriors. The money to hire professionals was in short supply, and when warriors were hired, they tended to be Germanic tribesmen.

Roger Collins says of the post-Adrianople era: "Between the years 395–476, Roman armies virtually disappear from the literary sources relating to both the eastern and western halves of the Empire." He points out that while there was still plenty of military activity going on it involved mercenary and barbarian allied troops, not Romans. After Adrianople, things got only worse for the empire. The Romans were plagued with a multitude of huge problems, chief of which may have been the power struggles among would-be emperors for control of the western empire. They also had social problems, tax base problems, military recruitment problems, and a host of other issues. All of this might have been survivable in less perilous times. But the arrival of the

---

[*] Peter Heather thinks the whole battle was smaller, and the Roman deaths more like ten thousand men.

Huns and the resulting agitation of many Germanic peoples seems to have had the same effect geopolitically as plunging a stick into a beehive. The number of tribes causing problems for the post-Adrianople Romans—the Vandals, the Alemanni, Burgundians, Lombards, Visigoths, Ostrogoths, Frisians, Saxons, Franks, to name a few—was huge. And their strength swelled with the addition of Roman slaves, "discontents and fortune-seekers." The Roman historian Ammianus Marcellinus wrote that the numbers were also increased by miners escaping the harsh conditions of the state's gold mines and by people oppressed by the burden of imperial taxation. So social discontent within the Roman Empire may have been merging with and found an outlet in barbarian activities.* Call it a perfect storm, or Murphy's law, or just the end of a centuries-long winning streak, but the problems facing fifth-century Rome in the West were monumental and came at a time when their armies were far weaker than in bygone days and their leadership of a much lower caliber.

One way to cut down on the sheer number of problems the Romans faced was to double-down on the practice of making contracts/treaties with tribes. This is what the Romans eventually did with the tribes they fought at Adrianople. More than in the past, though, the deals involved settling the tribal peoples on Roman land and allowing them to maintain a separate political identity while they defended the territory for Rome.

Some have described this as a sort of feudalistic relationship that would become a feature of the Middle Ages. In 418, for example, the emperor Honorius settled the Goths in Aquitaine, and in 435, the emperor Valentinian III gave Roman lands in

---

*One can't help but think of the slaves of the American South who often fled to native tribes like the Seminole and Cherokee to join them as tribal members.

North Africa to the Vandal tribe. The Visigoths were ensconced in Spain, and the Franks in much of modern-day France. Without realizing it, the Roman decision makers were parceling out the empire to the people who would eventually run these regions when the central authority fell apart—in effect creating their own successor states. As the historian Roger Collins writes: "What is genuinely striking . . . is the haphazard, almost accidental nature of the process. From 410 onwards, successive Western imperial regimes just gave way or lost practical authority over more and more of the territory of the former Empire. The Western Empire delegated itself out of existence."

Central authority in the West fell apart over the course of the fifth century. The Visigoths—whom Rome had allowed into the empire and who had beaten them at Adrianople—ended up sacking Rome itself in 410. This was the first sacking of the Eternal City by an alien power since another tribal people, most likely Celts, had done it eight hundred years earlier.

But unlike the Assyrian city of Nineveh, which was down for the count after being knocked out, Rome rose from the canvas for a few more rounds. It survived the sacking of 410 only to be sacked again in 455, this time, it is said, much more brutally by the Germanic Vandals. It was a German military leader of the Roman *foederati** who all but dismissed the last emperor of the Western Roman Empire in 476.

This is the point where the old histories would say the "Dark Ages" began in the areas where the Roman civilizational tide had receded. This was truer in some of those areas than others. Italy, for example, was less deeply affected and seems to have recovered more quickly than areas that were more on the Roman periphery. The areas to the north of Italy, though, which in-

*Odoacer.

cluded much of the old western empire, were on the equivalent of impulse power.* Elements of the Catholic Church (monasteries for example), local groups, and warlords or petty kings tried to manage a soft landing from modernity as best they could, but it wouldn't be long before some of the places that had once done their business in coinage—coinage that had a Roman emperor's image on it—reverted to a barter economy.

But was the decay and decline of infrastructure and the replacement of coinage by barter a sign of civilization moving backward? Or is that simply evidence of our modern bias?

The anthropologist Peter Wells writes of a "continuity of occupation" in several major cities that had been part of the Western Roman Empire even through to the Middle Ages. He says that several cities, which included Rome itself, seem not to have contracted in size or decreased in population "even though the traditions of Roman architecture and road building and maintenance of aqueducts and sewers effectively ceased with the end of the official Roman administration."

Wells cautions against the automatic assumption that Roman traditions were superior to local cultural traditions. He cites the example of the Roman city that is now London. At the end of the first century CE it was a "stunning center of the Roman Empire on its northern edge, with the monumental architecture, a thriving commercial center, and a military base characteristic of the greatest of Roman cities." When the Western Roman Empire fell apart, "much of the formerly urban area seems to have reverted to a non-urban character."

But to call these changes a decline, he says, is to adopt a conservative Roman attitude toward change. Wells writes, "As evidence accumulates in London, it is becoming clear that the

---

* For you Star Trek fans. "Backup" or "emergency power" for everyone else.

site was not abandoned, as earlier researchers had thought. Life went on in place. . . . It was just different."

For several centuries, Germanic tribal successor states would fight among themselves, as well as with and against the Eastern Roman Empire.* Over time, one of these Germanic successor states—that of the Franks—began to accumulate power and territory that set it apart from the others, and the Catholic Church,† in search of some military protection in a world with no Roman army in the West, began to form a mutually supporting relationship with this group of formerly fearsome tribal "barbarians." (The Germans still call the nation of France *Frankreich*—the empire of the Franks.)‡

The Franks had been one of many tribal groups to be given *foederati* status by the Romans; in turn, they simply became the political authority in their region when Rome fragmented in the West. There were in fact several branches of the Franks—centered in modern-day France and western Germany—but they were eventually brought under the rule of one king, Clovis I (c. 466–511 CE). Clovis seems to have been an even mix of Viking warlord, Mafia don, and outlaw motorcycle gang leader. The sources portray him as a guy who tells somebody to look for something on the ground and then splits the guy's head open with a battle-ax when he bends over to comply.§

---

*The Eastern Roman Empire, with its capital at Constantinople (which had formerly been called Byzantium), is often referred to by historians as the Byzantine Empire when discussing the period after the fall of the western empire. The inhabitants always referred to themselves as "Romans," though.

† Also sometimes called the Western Church or the Latin Church.

‡ And the French name for Germany is *Allemagne*, after the Alemanni tribe in this very story.

§ There are a lot of good Clovis stories in the history books. His historical press got better after his conversion, but it seems pretty clear Clovis was a badass.

In an enormously important political event, Clovis converted from paganism to Christianity in 496.* Now this rising European power of Franks was in many ways allied to the Western Church. As the traditional story goes, the church smoothed the rough edges off these Franks, helping them to transition in a few generations from violent barbarians to pious medieval Christians. But a case can also be made that the Franks added something to Western Christianity, too—more muscle power with a barbaric edge, perhaps.

Whatever the truth of it, both the Franks and the church thrived in the relationship, and Clovis—a man who is sometimes hailed as the first king of what eventually became France—marks the start of the Merovingian dynasty. This was followed by a later dynasty—the Carolingian—which, under some key rulers, and using extreme violence, managed to unite a very large chunk of territory, much of which formerly was the Roman West. The transformative figure among the Carolingians was Charles I (known as "the Great")—a.k.a. Charlemagne.† His rule as king of the Franks would last a monumental forty-six years—he isn't called "the Father of Europe" for nothing.

As a historical figure, Charlemagne seems a wonderful synthesis of the "Dark Age" Germanic barbarian stereotype and the pious Middle Ages Christian ruler stereotype. He was intelligent yet illiterate, but the sources say that he dearly wished to learn to read, and continually tried. He was physically imposing compared with his contemporaries, and had light hair and sported the classic Germanic mustache the Romans thought a

---

*Apparently in large part due to the influence of his wife Clotilde, who was sainted by the church for her actions.

†This is obviously the Gallic/French version of his name. In the German version, he's "Karl der Grosse." His native tongue was Old German. The question over which name should be used has prompted disagreement in the past, and some feel it has political overtones in Europe even today.

barbaric adornment.* In 768, Charlemagne was crowned king of the Franks and began a long career of adding territory to their already sizable realm. By 800, the Frankish kingdom controlled what is now modern-day France, Belgium, the Netherlands, Switzerland, Italy all the way south to Rome, most of Germany, and Austria. For the first time since the fall of Rome in the West three centuries previously, much of its former territory was united under one ruler.

On Christmas Day 800, something weird happened with Charlemagne and the pope in Rome in front of a lot of people. The event is traditionally one of history's "great" moments, but there's a great deal about this event that is unclear. It had a huge effect on subsequent history, though. Supposedly, Charlemagne went innocently to mass at Saint Peter's Basilica to pray, and while kneeling at the altar the pope suddenly slipped a crown on the great king's head and proclaimed him *Imperator Romanorum*.† Historians have debated ever since whether the claim that Charlemagne was unaware of the pope's intention to do this should be believed. But all of a sudden Europe

---

*He'd be somewhat taller than average today, but in the seventh century he towered over most of his subjects. His bones seem to show a man probably about six feet tall and weighing about 175 pounds. That height would be six inches taller than the average man of his day. A weight of 175 pounds seems thin, but Charlemagne died an old man for that era and may have been somewhat withered (sixty-five to seventy-two is the usual range given, but his exact age is disputed).

†"Emperor of the Romans." This act by Pope Leo III opened a Pandora's box of issues that would plague Europe for centuries. The primacy of church or state, for example. If the pope crowned the emperor, does that mean the pope made the emperor? Who is superior in this symbolism? Lots of people would die over questions like this. Charlemagne altered the title to read: "The Most Supreme Augustus, Crowned by God, the Great and Peace-Loving Ruler of the Roman Empire, as well as by the Grace of God the Franks and the Lombards."

had its first emperor since the Roman Empire in the West had fallen apart.*

There were a whole host of things going on with this move, a lot of it aimed at the Byzantines in the East (the part of the "Roman Empire" that had continued to exist . . . but whether it should be allowed to claim such a mantle was part of the issue). The branding and marketing questions connected with this new empire are fascinating.†

As the historian Alessandro Barbero writes, "On the whole, the symbolism of power adopted by the Carolingians after 800 always referred back to that of the empire of Rome. Charles had himself portrayed on coins with the laurel crown and purple cloak and his seal carried the wording that was to remain an extraordinarily effective political slogan for centuries: *renovatio Romani imperii*."‡ That is, "the renewal of the Roman Empire." If you were the people who still called themselves "the Roman Empire" off in Byzantium/Constantinople, this had to be galling.

But, in a way, this new empire *was* renewing some elements of what Rome had formerly been. This period, which is sometimes called the Carolingian Renaissance, offers perhaps an example of a more centralized government in the West, if not restoring the full civilizational, organizational, and bureaucratic power from

---

* In fact, if you take the Western Church's interpretation, the newly crowned Charles was the only "Roman emperor." At this time, an empress had taken power in Constantinople, and that to them was deemed illegitimate *femineum imperium* ("a woman's rule"). Hence the Western Church jumped at the chance to nominate not merely a new emperor for itself but *the* new emperor for all.

† Many historians think this "branding" was part of an effort to find a sort of ideological glue that could unite all the different peoples under the empire's dominion in a way similar to what Rome had been able to do.

‡ Translated usually as "renovation," "renewal," or "updating" of the Roman Empire.

Rome's heyday, at least ramping it up after the "Dark Age" lows. Levels of literacy* improved, architecture became more elaborate, wealth increased, and writing became more important again. There were concerted attempts to recover lost knowledge from antiquity and to recopy old written works to preserve the past.

Yet, there's some interesting historical irony—or perhaps karma—involved in this "renewed Roman Empire,"† run, as it was, by descendants of the Germanic tribesmen who helped end Roman rule in the West. These new emperors were plagued with one of the same problems the Western Roman emperors had faced when they last ruled from Italy: ferocious Germanic tribes. In fact, they could well have been the *same* tribes.

It's almost as though nothing had changed. In Roman Britain, for example, the Roman Empire had protected the island from the sea raiding of the Germanic Saxons. The legendary King Arthur supposedly fought these same Saxons after Rome left, and now three hundred years later Charlemagne was still fighting the pagan Saxons.‡ He was the one who finally beat them, but it was a brutal twenty-year conflict that seems eerily like the era when Varus and his legions were being snuffed out in the German forests.

Alessandro Barbero writes: "It was a ferocious war in a country with little or no civilization, with neither roads nor cities,

---

* Roger Collins says that Charlemagne was aiming for his educated "literate" class of people to possess the equivalent of about a Roman-era primary-level education. But he says that before we disparage that, we should consider "the base from which they started." This was more about educating people for positions in the clergy rather than educating laypeople.

† That will eventually morph into central Europe's "Holy Roman Empire," of which Voltaire famously quipped, "This body which was called and which still calls itself the Holy Roman Empire was in no way holy, nor Roman, nor an empire."

‡ Were these the same people? Good question.

and entirely covered with forests and marshland. The Saxons sacrificed prisoners of war to their gods, as Germans had always done before converting to Christianity, and the Franks did not hesitate to put to death anyone who refused to be baptized."

The effort was infused with religion. The pagan Saxons were known to kill those who tried to preach to them, yet the conversion of the Saxon tribes was part of the conditions of victory.* This is a perfect example of how different the optics are between "defending the church with the sword" and, as Roger Collins has phrased it, "armed evangelizing." Either way, it's difficult to keep the faith clean during such a brutal religious conflict.

Saint Lebuin—who it was said devoted his life to converting the pagan German tribes—is, according to Barbero, supposed to have given his famous ominous warning to the Saxons about Charlemagne: "If you will not accept belief in God, there is a king in the next country who will enter your land, conquer it, and lay it waste."

The Saxons apparently ignored the warning, continued to kill evangelizing clergy, and never ceased their usual small-scale raiding and banditry on the border. Charlemagne fought campaign after campaign against them, and eventually succeeded in cutting down the sacred tree they venerated as holding up the universe† and allegedly beheading 4,500 of them in a day at Verden in 782. And, like the Roman emperors who preceded him, Charlemagne found out that there always seemed to be more ferocious barbarians behind the ones he'd just subdued.

---

*Hard to define the line here between actual religious reasons for doing things and what might have been seen as a sort of power politics. If Christianized Saxons give the empire less trouble than the pagan variety, that might explain the "convert or die" aspect to the struggle.

†The World Tree, a.k.a. Irminsul, in the Teutoburg Forest, was the seat of worship.

In this case, behind (and to the north of) the Saxons were the Danes. And the era of the great Viking attacks that swarmed out of Denmark, Sweden, and Norway was just ramping up.

There's an apocryphal story about Charlemagne seeing Vikings near the end of his reign. They were not yet the large problem they would be a few decades hence, but the story is relayed as a sort of premonition. A monk named Notker, writing in about 887 (Charlemagne died in 814), claimed that the emperor was visiting what is now modern-day France near the coastline and saw a lone Viking ship. Affronted by its boldness, and with tears in his eyes, Charlemagne could supposedly see the future—that is, that it wouldn't be long before these Vikings would become a nightmarish headache.

While the story reeks of an after-the-fact prediction coming true, there's an aspect of it that seems to make some sense—if anyone should understand the potential danger posed by warlike "barbarians" from the frozen north, it would be a Roman emperor. This "Roman" emperor might have been expected to know this better than most; he was, after all, a tall, light-haired, mustachioed, blue-eyed German-speaking warrior king. And he was a man who had been fighting "pagan" German tribesmen long before he became the first Roman emperor to rule in the West in three hundred years.

Sometimes in history, what goes around, comes around. Charlemagne might have known that, too.

Chapter 6

A PANDEMIC PROLOGUE?

IT'S MUCH SAFER to be alive now than it used to be. Before the middle of the eighteenth century or so, the environment humans lived in was unfathomably lethal.* One of the things that makes our modern existence so different from that of almost all the human generations before us is that the threat of death, and especially untimely death, by disease is so much more remote. The fact that we live in an age when we don't expect a large percentage of our children to die in childhood makes us the historical anomaly. Does it make us different? How so? The everyday illness and epidemics that people in the past faced, and the pandemics they occasionally dealt with, are beyond the scope of our understanding. Imagine all the ripple effects if our modern world were hit with a pandemic that killed just 10 percent of the human population. That's not close to the worst sorts of numbers of some earlier plagues, but given how many people there are in the world today, that would mean seven hundred million deaths in a short span of time. One out of every ten people. About ten times the deaths of the Second World War. What's the aftermath of that like?

*This date applies only to the most medically advanced societies. In less advanced areas, medical progress came later.

Yet even a modern plague still wouldn't give us a good idea of what the experience of our ancestors was like, because we moderns understand the basic science of it all and they didn't. It's easy to minimize the effect of this, but throughout most of human history, no one really understood disease or germs, so sickness was attributed to all sorts of causes. Once again, it's easy to note that the damage done by disease over the ages, combined with the lack of understanding up until recently of what causes illness, must have affected people and societies deeply. It's terribly difficult, though, to say in what ways and to what degree this must have been so. It's possible, perhaps even likely, that people in eras when such death rates were common and expected were more emotionally insulated than we would be. But what this might mean falls into the same unquantifiable gray region that such things as toughness and the effects of child-rearing practices do.

Disease has always been a constant human companion; as soon as records began to be kept, accounts of epidemic and plague appear. It's often hard to determine from the ancient descriptions what the actual illnesses were, but some specific maladies have been identified. William Rosen, in his book *Justinian's Flea*, offers a sampling of the nightmarish plagues our forebears dealt with.* Ancient Greek physicians as early as the fifth century BCE diagnosed outbreaks of tetanus, mumps, and possibly malaria. All three of these diseases were much worse to contract back then than nowadays—many of today's common childhood maladies were fatal before the availability of modern vaccines and medicine.

---

*These are just the ones for which records are available. Most of these ancient events have no surviving accounts to document what occurred.

The ancient historian Thucydides was an eyewitness to the devastating Plague of Athens that began in 430 BCE during the Peloponnesian War when the city was under siege by Sparta. As many as a hundred thousand people perished over the ensuing three years—approximately a quarter of the population, according to Robert J. Littman. The deaths included the general and statesman Pericles, one of the greatest Athenians who ever lived.* There has been disagreement about the nature of this plague, but the discovery of a mass grave in 2006 revealed that the likely culprit was typhoid fever.

The Bible, Rosen notes, lists a catalog of diseases, including, of course, the plagues of blood and boils and locusts visited upon the pharaoh. The Book of Lamentations, describing the siege of Jerusalem by Nebuchadnezzar in the sixth century BCE, notes the "blackened skin"† that is characteristic of scurvy.‡ Some other highlights:

- In 396 BCE, the Carthaginian army was "stricken with a plague featuring dysentery, skin pustules, and other symptoms."
- During the first century CE, malaria and bubonic plague infected the citizens of Rome.
- 165 CE marked the beginning of the fifteen-year Antonine Plague brought to the Mediterranean from Mesopotamia by

---

* Pericles lost two sons to the same epidemic and is supposed to have been despondent about it. Who wouldn't be?

† Caused by hemorrhages under the skin that occur in the late stages of the disease.

‡ When they presumably had no access for months to fresh fruit or vegetables that are usually an easy source of vitamin C.

legionnaires of Marcus Aurelius. It is believed to have been smallpox.

- From 251 to 266 CE, the Plague of Cyprian reared its head; consensus says the disease in question was measles.[*]

Certainly these instances represent spikes in mortality, but people in the premodern world lived with what we would consider to be extreme levels of death by disease at all times. If we moderns lived for one year with the sort of death rates our pre-industrial age ancestors perpetually lived with, we'd be in societal shock. Their disease- and death-heavy environment perhaps gave them some increased level of emotional or cultural immunity to such things.[†] From time to time, though, the rogue waves of history were large enough to overwhelm even those with the sturdiest psychological constitutions. In 541 CE, what's been described as the world's first true pandemic arrived, and huge numbers of people died.

The Plague of Justinian, as historians have dubbed it, was once believed to have killed a hundred million people.[‡] That number is now thought to be far too high, but it gives a sense of what a large event this was. It was the precursor to the Black Death of the Middle Ages, and it was caused by the same thing—the plague bacillus *Yersinia pestis*, which was spread by fleas hosted by rats. It was a horrific way to die.

William Rosen describes its effects on Constantinople when the outbreak hit the city hard: "Every day, one, two, some-

---

[*] Note that modern childhood illnesses, William Rosen writes, have evolved from "far more dangerous versions" that killed "hundreds of thousands, possibly millions."

[†] This was one of the very valuable roles religion played for the people in these cultures.

[‡] In a world that obviously had a fraction of our current population.

times five thousand of the city's residents—one in one hundred of the preplague population—would become infected. A day's moderate fever would be followed by a week of delirium. Buboes would appear under the arms, in the groin, behind the ears, and grow to the size of melons. Edemas—of blood—infiltrated the nerve endings of the swollen lymphatic glands, causing massive pain. Sometimes the buboes would burst in a shower of the foul-smelling leukocytes called pus. Sometimes the plague would become what a modern epidemiologist would describe as 'septicemic'; those victims would die vomiting blood."

Rosen goes on to say that these were the lucky ones, because "at least they died fast."* In earlier eras or in other places, an epidemic this deadly would usually burn itself out because infected people die before they can travel far, slowing the spread of the disease. But the pandemic of 541 CE got onto ships departing from the large Egyptian port at Alexandria, and this allowed the plague to make it to new harbors before it could wipe out an entire crew; in cases where the crew died before arrival, the contagion continued via what had effectively become a ghost ship.

The disease spread far and wide, but details of the contagion are available only from a small percentage of the affected areas. Constantinople is one of them. According to Nick Bostrom and Milan Ćirković, the editors of *Global Catastrophic Risk*, 40 percent of that large urban center's citizenry was felled. And Rosen notes that more widely, over twenty-five million people—perhaps as much as half the population of the known world at the time—died in about one year. The plague would bedevil Europe for two centuries or more . . . and then, after about 750 CE, it seems almost to have gone away.

---

*According to Rosen, "bubonic plague kills 'only' four to seven out of ten victims, [whereas] septicemic plague is virtually 100% deadly."

The next time the plague came, in the 1340s, it had a new name: the Black Death. Eight hundred years after the Plague of Justinian burst on the scene, the terrible disease once again visited itself on the known Western world. It was thought to have possibly started a decade earlier in Asia—there are reports of Chinese cities almost being wiped out, perhaps a 90 percent mortality rate in some places.

Nothing like this plague had ever hit humankind before, dwarfing even the Plague of Justinian. One reason it produced such high casualties might have had to do with the fact that human population levels had reached a critical mass. More effective transportation, too, facilitated societies interacting in ways they never had before—and these factors didn't just affect the spread of the plague, they also affected its persistence. Persistence is a key factor in how deadly any pestilence will be, because if an illness burns out a village and kills everyone in it, the disease is usually eradicated along with its victims. But because the plague kept coming back, thanks to the numbers of people on the planet and how much they now traveled, the plague's effects only widened.

The first reports of the disease describe ships showing up at Western ports from the East with entire crews dead, or dying, of some unknown pestilence. Any possible survivors would then unload the ship's cargo, interacting with unsuspecting people on the dock and in the town—and very quickly, the pestilence spread.

Soon Europe was seeing death rates similar to those that had afflicted the Chinese. Whole towns simply disappeared from the map. Aerial photos today show the outlines of places where settlements existed before the Black Death. In the big cities, hundreds and hundreds of corpses were carted off every day, while the nobility and the rich fled to the countryside, hoping to escape what they didn't understand. One chronicler described the devastation:

> Great pits were dug and piled deep with the multitude of the dead. And they died by the hundreds, both day and night. And as soon as those ditches were filled, more were dug. And I, Agnolo di Tura, called the Fat, buried my five children with my own hands. And there were also those who were so sparsely covered with earth that the dogs dragged them forth and devoured many bodies throughout the city. There was no one who wept for any death, for all awaited death. And so many died that all believed it was the end of the world.

The victims of the plague didn't have the tools to understand that they were dealing with a biomedical contagion. In fact, from time immemorial people have thought plagues to be divine anger or justice; in the case of the Black Death, many people thought the pandemic was God's will or a manifestation of the devil on earth.

Barbara Tuchman's book *A Distant Mirror* chronicles how Europeans of the fourteenth century dealt with the rippling effects of the plague. She quotes one Brother John Clyn, of Kilkenny, Ireland, who wrote a message, in essence, to the future. Sensing "the whole world, as it were, placed within the grasp of the Evil One, I leave parchment to continue this work, if perchance any man survive and any of the race of Adam escape this pestilence and carry on the work which I have begun." The last sentence of his note was written in another hand and said that Brother John had died of the disease.

The human ripples of pain are still heartbreaking when made visible to us now.

Our friend Agnolo the Fat wrote: "Father abandoned child, wife husband, one brother another; for this illness seemed to strike through the breath and sight. And so they died. And none could be found to bury the dead for money or friendship. Members of a household brought their dead to a ditch as best they could, without priest, without divine offices."

The essence of that account is of an epidemic destroying the very bonds of human society. When was the last time the developed world experienced such a rapid descent into a microbial hell?

And if parents abandoning children wasn't destabilizing enough, other support elements in society were shattered by the justifiable fear of the pestilence. The natural human inclination to seek companionship and support from one's neighbors was short-circuited. No one wanted to catch whatever was killing everybody. In an era when people congregating together was so much more important than it is in our modern, so-called connected world, people kept their distance from one another, creating one of the silent tragedies of this plague: that they had to suffer virtually alone.

Religion, too—which in the Middle Ages in Europe formed the entire conception of how the universe was ordered—took a battering. Fear of joining the ever-growing piles of bodies stacked in graves like cordwood destroyed the Middle Ages version of a "social safety net," the element of the system designed to cope with tragedy, loss, and, literally, "acts of God": namely, the clergy. The church was one of the key support pillars of that society, and the clergy played very important roles, only some of which we would call religious; they were also medical practitioners, lawyers, and notary publics. They held management positions in society and formed an entire middle level of the medieval social strata. And of course, they were indispensable for religious functions like marriages and, notably during a plague, last rites.*

But the clergy were only human.† At one point during the raging epidemic, the pope was compelled to give mass absolutions and allow citizens to give the last rites to other citizens because there weren't enough priests willing to do the job and face a likely death sentence.

In the end, the clergy suffered fatalities at the same rate as the rest of the population, and their deaths led to unexpected consequences. For example, to replace losses in their ranks, the church lowered the ages at which people could attain positions of authority. This led often to very young, hardly prepared people in positions that had previously been held by much older, more august figures.

Before the epidemic, members of the clergy had devoted their whole lives to the church. The people who replaced them weren't necessarily as committed or as educated. Corruption began to creep in, especially as men attained elevated positions in the church due to money changing hands, not thanks to their lifelong commitment or qualifications. Over the course of around two centuries, the clergy's reputation diminished, tarnished by abuses and excess and a lack of high standards. This dissatisfaction led to the development of the many complaints that the German theologian Martin Luther is said to have nailed to the door of the church at Wittenberg Castle in

---

*In an age, let's remember, when the people were religious, and frankly, superstitious, to a degree that most people today, even very devout people, would consider fanatical.

†Not just that, but many of these people probably joined the clergy to get into a career. Many of these men were more scribes than preachers of the Gospel or leaders of a religious flock. It's probably not fair to hold them all up to a modern "priestly" standard.

1517, marking the onset of Protestantism and a break with the Catholic Church.*

In the wake of so much death, society was hammered down, and darkness filled people's thoughts. Having witnessed so many of their neighbors and loved ones die, survivors had no confidence that life was going to last very long. This attitude is reflected in the art of the period, which is a window into the psyche of these traumatized people. For a start, the physical manifestation of death, usually portrayed as a skeleton of sorts, begins to appear everywhere. When the great mortality began, people turned to holy relics and prayers, anything that they believed could help protect them—but when people saw their loved ones die anyway, it shook their confidence in their belief systems. A generation after the plague struck the West, a terrible pessimism permeated society. Having witnessed a scourge that had carted off perhaps seventy-five million people—up to half of the world's entire population at the time—some folks went off the deep end with quackery and mysticism. Many others adopted a live-for-today attitude. There were orgies and rapes and robberies and killings by people who figured they had nothing to lose. A quarter of the people in fifteenth-century England didn't marry. That's an amazing statistic in that era.

There was also a move to find someone to blame for the terrible situation people found themselves in. In Europe during the Middle Ages, the people who served as the scapegoats were the Jews. What happened to the Jewish population in the plague era is probably second only in its horror to the Holocaust.† Jews were

---

* If you happen to be Protestant, maybe you consider this development to be a benefit of the Black Death.

† According to the author Henrik Svensen, Jews were almost wiped out of a couple of European nations during this era because of their association with the plague.

accused of poisoning wells to make people sick and thereby take over the Christian world. Victims of the disease itself were also blamed for spreading the disease. People suspected of witchcraft or sorcery were also targets.

At the time the plague struck in the fourteenth century, the population of England was six million souls, what many experts consider to be a maximum carrying capacity for that era. This number was reduced to two million in just a few years. The population would not rebound until the 1700s—more than three hundred years later.

There were subsequent outbreaks of the Black Death, the Great Pestilence, or the Great Mortality, as it was variously called, every couple of years, as though it were returning to claim the lives it had missed the previous go-through. It kept the recovery from really taking hold, because it was only natural for people to assume and plan for the worst.

We can't know how many people in all died. While estimates put the figure at 75 million, countless out-of-the-way farms and towns and even cities may not be included in the final toll. With the total population of western Europe at the time at a bit more than 150 million, this means that about half of the entire population of just that area was wiped out. (A similar percentage today would see more than 300 million people die in Europe alone.)*

The ramifications were extensive. In our modern world—which has seen nothing but exponential population growth to such a degree that it may be threatening the planet's ecosystem—the idea of populations collapsing is hard to imagine.† Once

---

*Based on a European population of 740 million.

†Many places have seen their populations grow steadily since the era of the Black Death. Interestingly enough, though, the collapses can be almost as rapid as the explosions in population. If every couple simply has a single child, a given population will halve in a generation. This isn't conjecture.

again, only in tales of science fiction are themes explored that deal with things like nature reclaiming the cultivated land from humans because the humans have died (as has happened in Chernobyl, for example, post–nuclear meltdown—wildlife and wild vegetation have repopulated the wasted site). Yet that's what was going on in areas hit hard by the plague.

For example, before the pandemic in western Europe, almost no land was available for new farms. That all changed when so many people perished in such a relatively short time. With something like 40 percent of the population gone, peasants who had previously owned nothing of their own moved onto land and into houses that had belonged to the now deceased. Many fields that had once been forests and had been laboriously cultivated now reverted to their natural state. To modern eyes accustomed to the environment succumbing to increasing human encroachment, it seems perhaps somewhat heartening to see a sort of counterattack by nature, taking back the land.

Before the plague struck, peasants were afraid to protest poor working conditions, but after, all bets were off. To paraphrase Barbara Tuchman, modern man may have been born because of the Black Death. Suddenly, the well-ordered class system—one often defended by those who benefited from it as "divinely ordained"—didn't matter so much, and ideas of equality and merit-based advancement seeped in where nobility and lineage had previously held sway. Population disasters always prompt questions about balance, and they are usually the sort of questions that are easier to ask about in the context of animal ecosystems rather than human ones. Recently, for example, an idea was floated that, due to the incredible loss of life during

---

In the 1990s, Russian birth rates took a turn into negative territory, and other developed nations currently have similar demographic trends.

the Mongol conquests in the thirteenth century, Genghis Khan may have shrunk humankind's carbon footprint on the planet. Is that a cause to celebrate? If our ability to massively lower the traditional death rate from disease is part of explaining our highest-of-all-time global population level, perhaps we have somehow thrown a monkey wrench into a self-correcting system that was keeping things in balance?*

Perhaps an optimist (or a pessimist?) would point out that nature is always evolving. This battle of man versus microbe is far from over. As nature regularly reminds us, there's always something new in the microbial pipeline to replace what no longer works.†

In 1918, during a century in which the most modern of societies thought such epidemics were a thing of the past, people got a reminder that even seemingly routine illnesses can be potentially civilization threatening under the right conditions. A malady that would be dubbed the Spanish Flu struck while the devastating First World War was raging, and soon its death toll greatly surpassed that of the war's.‡

Perhaps one of the most astonishing things about this flu was that at the time it hit, humanity had made great strides in medicine. But when American service personnel started showing symptoms, the experts were stumped. The author John Barry

---

*This can take you down the intellectual rabbit hole quickly. Do vaccines short-circuit nature's delicate population-balance mechanisms? Do longer life spans and lower child mortality rates damage the earth? If we decided they did, would we ever voluntarily forsake them to allow "nature to take its course"? Science fiction indeed.

†And as we are all aware from the headlines, even older maladies are increasingly developing tolerances to our current antibiotics.

‡All these death tolls are estimates, but the First World War is usually blamed for between 16 and 19 million deaths. The Spanish Influenza killed tens of millions.

describes in *The Great Influenza* how sailors mysteriously began bleeding from their noses and ears, while others coughed blood. "Some coughed so hard the autopsies would later show they had torn apart abdominal muscles and rib cartilage," Barry writes. Many were delirious or complained of severe headaches "as if someone were hammering a wedge into their skulls just behind the eyes" or "body aches so intense they felt like bones breaking." Some of the men's skin turned strange colors, from "just a tinge of blue around their lips or fingertips" to skin "so dark one could not tell easily if they were Caucasian or Negro."

A couple of months before the appearance of these extraordinary symptoms, autopsies of crewmen from a British ship who had died after experiencing similar trials showed "their lungs had resembled those of men who had died from poison gas or pneumonic plague."

More alarming was the speed and scope of the spreading, Barry writes, despite efforts to isolate and contain those who hadn't even shown symptoms but had merely been exposed: "Four days after that Boston detachment arrived, nineteen sailors in Philadelphia were hospitalized. . . . Despite their immediate isolation and that of everyone with whom they had had contact, eighty-seven sailors were hospitalized the next day . . . two days later, six hundred more were hospitalized with this strange disease. The hospital ran out of empty beds, and hospital staff began falling ill." As the sick overwhelmed the facility, officials began sending new patients to civilian hospitals, while military personnel continued moving among bases around the country, exposing ever more people.

What began in Philadelphia—at least in its most dangerous form—quickly advanced. There was still an international war on, and modern transportation had made great strides, so the virus could get from place to place at a far greater pace than any previous pandemic could. The collision of this outbreak with this first period of true globalization was devastating.* At its height, whole cities in the United States were virtually shut down, as areas where human beings congregated were closed to prevent people from transmitting the illness.† People stayed home from school and work rather than risk exposure, and the gears of society in some places seemed imperiled by the justifiable fear of getting sick.‡ By the time it receded in 1920, modern epidemiologists estimate that the flu had killed somewhere between fifty and one hundred million people; "roughly half of those who died were young men and women in the prime of their life, in their twenties and thirties," Barry writes. "If the upper estimate of the death toll is true, as many as 8 to 10 percent of young adults then living may have been killed by the virus."§

The disease wasn't just remarkable for the number of its victims, but also for the compressed nature of its devastating labors. Although it took two years to come and go, "perhaps

---

*Imagine this epidemic in our modern twenty-first-century international travel environment.

†Theaters, sporting events, festivals, and even elections were subject to disruption to prevent large numbers of people from gathering in ways that might spread disease.

‡It's interesting to examine how people, cities, and societies reacted to this example of a modern plague. It's a rare modern case study.

§It's intriguing to wonder about how losing younger people affects a society differently than losing older ones. One of the oft-mentioned ramifications of the Spanish Flu pandemic was an increase in the popularity of occult practices connected to communicating with the dead. Mediums and séances, for example, were very popular in the postflu period. One senses a desperation that would make more sense for grieving parents or spouses mourning people cut down early rather than those wishing to contact parents or grandparents who had lived full life spans and died old, as nature seemed to intend.

two-thirds of the deaths occurred in a period of twenty-four weeks, and more than half of those deaths occurred in even less time, from mid-September to early December 1918." That amount of damage in that short a period of time is disorienting and potentially destabilizing for a society.

All this happened in an age when we understood a lot about biomedicine. We understood that germs spread disease; we understood how you prevented contact to limit exposure. Indeed, doctors quickly figured out that what was killing sailors in Philadelphia was a strain of influenza, but it was unlike any they had seen before, and nothing they did could contain it. As much as a fifth of the entire population of the planet contracted it, and as much as 5 percent died from it. In sheer numbers, it was the deadliest pandemic to hit humankind, but as a percentage of the human population alive at the time, it wasn't nearly as bad as the Black Death that hit western Europe in the mid-fourteenth century. So, humankind didn't exactly dodge a bullet—the damage was severe and widespread—but it could have been much, much worse.

It still can be. The same sense of hubris affects us today as affected the generation that was blindsided by the Spanish Influenza. A modern epidemic comparable with the great ones of the past is a thing more akin to science fiction to most people living today rather than something seen as a realistic possibility.* But those who regularly work with infectious diseases and see the Black Death–like damage that something like Ebola or Marburg virus can have on a small scale in isolated communities are all

---

* Isn't this what the bad guy Thanos is doing in the Marvel/Disney Avengers movies? Wiping out half of the life in the universe to ease the strains of overpopulation? Perhaps the Thanos character is a metaphor for disease as a maintenance tool.

too aware of how a hemorrhagic fever virus in one global region, or an avian flu mutation somewhere else, could remind us that, just like the *Titanic*, our civilization is not unsinkable. In fact, the culprit need not even be something new.

On September 11, 1978, a British woman named Janet Parker became the last person to officially die of smallpox. It was rather strange that she contracted it at all, since by that time the disease had been almost eradicated worldwide, and on the rare occasions a person was infected it usually was in a last-holdout sort of out-of-the-way location like the rural subtropics. Parker, however, was infected in the modern city of Birmingham in the Midlands of the United Kingdom. She worked in a room over a lab that contained samples of this insanely prolific killer and is thought to have somehow contracted it from there. She had been vaccinated against smallpox during her lifetime, but not recently enough.*

In large part because of Parker's infection, the World Health Organization ordered that all samples of the disease in existence be turned over to one of two extrasecure sites, where two live smallpox samples still reside—one in the United States, and one in Russia.† A debate has been ongoing since then over whether those samples should be destroyed so that the threat will be forever removed. Both the US and Russian governments have opposed the idea, saying the samples are important to study and might be needed someday.‡

---

*This is an understandable rationale one might use today as well. The less you see of a disease, the less you feel an urgency to inoculate yourself.

†When the USSR disintegrated in the early 1990s, fears similar to those of nuclear experts, who worried about lax safeguards for nuclear weapons, concerned biological weapons experts, who worried about Soviet stores of bioweapons and diseases falling into the hands of terrorists or rogue states.

‡For beneficial reasons, creating vaccines, studying genome stuff, etc.

In a *New York Times* op-ed piece in 2011, Kathleen Sebelius, then the secretary of the US Department of Health and Human Services, laid out some chilling reasons the government believes that samples should be retained, including that other nations may have surreptitiously kept their own samples, or that mislabeled or forgotten samples might be lying around somewhere: "Although keeping the samples may carry a minuscule risk, both the United States and Russia believe the dangers of destroying them now are far greater. . . . The global public health community assumes that all nations acted in good faith; however, no one has ever attempted to verify or validate compliance with the WHO request [to destroy live smallpox samples]. It is quite possible that undisclosed or forgotten stocks exist."

In fact, on more than one occasion, we've found some.* Let's hope no terrorists ever do.

The traditional Black Death–type pathogen has already been used in attempts at weaponization. One of the old theories about the Black Death was that the Mongols brought it to Europe and spread it while assaulting urban centers—the claim was that they launched infected corpses over the city walls. While that may or may not be true, there's no doubt that in the 1930s and 1940s the Japanese military deliberately introduced the plague into fleas and then dropped the fleas over Chinese cities.

Bacteriological warfare has come a long way since then. In fact, the concept of airborne pathogens being used against a population is a more frightening and potentially more destructive threat than any other weapon in global arsenals. Nuclear

---

*Multiple times so far, including cases in 2013 and 2014.

and chemical armaments are terrible, but both have limitations to their lethality. With the ability for a killer pathogen to spread from person to person[*] and to continue to kill for generations (or forever), a man-made plague might be worse than anything nature's previously thrown at us.[†]

What about new diseases? New strains of flu are jumping from pigs and poultry and birds to humans just about every year. The Spanish Flu was unknown until it showed up. AIDS was unknown until it showed up.[‡] There are also diseases we've "extinguished" that can reignite their danger due to mutations on their part or the diminishing effectiveness of counterresponses like vaccines, treatments, antibiotics, or antidotes on ours.

While it is natural to focus on the direct effects of a mass death situation resulting from a pandemic, oftentimes the ripple effects are just as potentially influential. Reading today's expert literature makes it clear that modern authorities are as worried about the dangers associated with fear, uncertainty, and irrationality on the part of the public as they are about the actual direct

---

[*] Including, crazily enough, to the population of the attacker.

[†] The US government has already warned of the danger of people replicating killer diseases, pointing out that the genome information for smallpox is posted on the Internet.

[‡] Part of what made AIDS a different sort of plague from something like smallpox or influenza was its long incubation and often longer survival period compared with most traditional epidemic diseases. It gave society more time to adjust than would have been the case if AIDS had killed all the victims it claimed from inception to today in a single year or two. Think of the societal destabilization that would have happened if the estimated thirty-five to forty-two million who have died from AIDS had perished in a matter of months or a year. It was destabilizing enough as it was.

dangers of any future pathogen.* History would suggest they are probably right to be so worried.

Even a slow-moving tragedy like the AIDS outbreak threatened all sorts of panic, backlash, and prejudicial responses when it first took hold in the public consciousness. As bad at it was in the 1980s, imagine how much more acute it would likely have been had AIDS behaved more like cholera or smallpox—infecting people through the air they breathed or the water they drank, and killing them in a matter of days. It's hard to imagine a human society acting rationally or humanely if mortality levels began reaching catastrophic levels. In the past, societies have been reshaped and at times have nearly crumbled under the weight of a pandemic. It's possible that, facing mortality rates of 50, 60, or 70 percent—as people who lived through the Black Death did—we might do as they did: turn to religion, change the social structure, blame unpopular minorities and groups, or abandon previous belief systems. We can learn from how people in other eras responded to a catastrophic situation, and we can

---

*Yet smallpox isn't considered a great disease to use as a weapon to cause casualties. It could easily backfire, and vaccines exist or could probably be easily created. Something like anthrax seems to be much more directly dangerous. But if the intent is to prompt societies to panic and do damage to themselves through fear, smallpox is one of the most scary of pathogens in our collective memory. "The thing with smallpox is that the fear associated with it is not justified," writes the bacteriology expert Hugh Pennington. "Yes it will kill a few people, but it is the panic that comes with it that makes it such an effective tool. It's not a weapon of mass destruction, it's a weapon of mass panic."

In fact, some of the biggest fears about smallpox today seem to be centered on the mass public panic that might occur if a disease with this many deaths to its credit ever broke out again. A smallpox incident in New York in 1947, for example, led to a national effort involving the military to have more than six million New Yorkers—as many people as died in the Holocaust—vaccinated in a supremely short period of time to ward off a pathogen that formerly killed six million people a year rather routinely.

ask ourselves: With all our modern technology and science and medical knowledge, how would we respond? How much would our better understanding of the science behind epidemics help blunt the normal fear and panic that seem to be the normal response to such a threat?

While we have infinitely more tools in the medical toolbox to combat any modern disease, the modern world also confers some advantages to pathogens. After all, we live in a world with a far greater level of interconnectivity than in any past era. Contagion can now spread on a far greater scale and at a far greater speed than ever before. A pandemic-level disease could travel around the world before experts even knew there was a problem.

What's the likelihood that humanity has already experienced the worst plague it will ever encounter? In the famous science fiction classic *The War of the Worlds*, author H. G. Wells has the alien would-be conquerors defeated ultimately by Earth's pathogens. Let's hope those same planetary defense mechanisms don't get us first.

Chapter 7

THE QUICK AND THE DEAD

UNLESS HUMANKIND CAN break patterns of collective behavior that are older than history itself, we can expect to have a full-scale nuclear war at some point in our future. The great regional or global geopolitical rivals at any given time and place have been squaring off with each other since the first cities arose in Mesopotamia, and it seems unrealistic to imagine that this has forever ended. Despite intermittent peaceful eras, there have always been wars. But the next Total War will be the first one in which both sides possess weapons powerful enough to destroy civilization—and efficient enough to do it in an afternoon.

On October 30, 1961, a specially modified Soviet aircraft dropped a nearly 60,000-pound, 50-megaton thermonuclear bomb over a test site in the Arctic. Known then as a "hydrogen bomb," it was by far more powerful than any weapon before or since. Part of the intent of the test was to demonstrate to the United States in no uncertain terms the destructive capabilities possessed by the Soviet Union. It wildly exceeded those goals—it sent a message to future ages.

In fact, the Soviet Union had wanted to use an almost

incomprehensibly powerful 100-megaton weapon instead,* but one of the physicists on the project, the future dissident and peace activist Andrei Sakharov, talked the Soviet leader Nikita Khrushchev out of it. Sakharov was worried enough about what a 50-megaton bomb would do.

The largest nuclear weapon ever used up to that point had been a 15-megaton hydrogen bomb, detonated as part of the 1954 Castle Bravo test conducted by the United States in the Pacific. There were serious questions about possible runaway chain reactions that such a huge blast might trigger, and whether or not the radioactive fallout would affect the entire planet. (What "affect" meant wasn't exactly clear, either.) There was a lot that was still unproved and theoretical about very large bombs, and the Castle Bravo test highlighted the inexact science of bomb power estimation. For a start, it was not supposed to have been that large—the bomb surprised everyone and turned out to be more than twice as powerful as expected. In fact, there was fear among a few scientists that the air itself might catch fire.

The gigantic Soviet bomb—known as "Tsar Bomba" in the West—was described like this by the historian John Lewis Gaddis in *The Cold War*: "[It was] the single largest blast human beings had ever detonated—or have since—on the planet. The flash was visible 600 miles away. The fireball," now quoting someone who saw it, "was powerful and arrogant like Jupiter. It seemed to suck the whole earth into it."

Gaddis continues: "The mushroom cloud rose 40 miles into the stratosphere. The island over which the explosion took

---

*The atomic bomb that exploded at Hiroshima released the energy equivalent of 13 to 18 thousand tons of TNT (kilotons). The largest bomb ever tested by the United States was about 15 megatons (millions of tons of TNT). The USSR's 50-megaton bomb was the equivalent of 50 million tons of TNT.

place was literally leveled, not only of snow but also of rocks, so that it looked to one observer like an immense skating rink. . . . One estimate calculated, on the basis of this test, that if the originally requested 100 megaton bomb had been used instead, the resulting firestorm would have engulfed an area the size of the state of Maryland." It also would likely have killed the crew of any aircraft that dropped the bomb.*

HUMANKIND IS MORE than seventy years into an ongoing experiment. The experiment will answer the question of whether we can handle the power of the weapons we've created. Since the weapons aren't ever going to get any weaker, the only way this experiment will likely ever conclude is if we find out that we can't.

We are an ostensibly adaptable species. Our ability to accommodate changing circumstances has helped *Homo sapiens* overcome countless challenges and achieve our current level of civilizational growth. In the twenty-first century, we are alive and thriving, and there are more of us than ever before. But there are several major problems on the horizon that have the potential to reverse those trends unless we are able to adapt yet again.

We currently live in an era of human history that some have referred to as the Long Peace. There has not been a war for more than seven decades between great powers such as we've seen from Mesopotamia onward—the world wars, the Napoleonic Wars, the Thirty Years' War, the Hundred Years' War, the Punic Wars.

---

*Before missiles became popular, heavy bombers were used to drop such bombs on their target. With very large nuclear bombs, there were always concerns about the planes being able to get far enough away after releasing the bomb to escape damage from the shock waves. Combine a big enough bomb with a slow enough plane, and dropping it becomes a suicide mission.

Large-scale warfare between the most powerful states has been a regular feature of human history right up until about seventy-five years ago—right about the time that humanity's weaponry made a quantum leap forward in power. This is not to say there haven't been bloody conflicts—human violence is, alas, ongoing and constant—but we've managed to avoid major conflicts between the superpowers. Have we seen the last of the big wars?

It's hard to imagine us ridding society of problems relating to any number of baseline human instincts: sex, greed, intoxicating substances, violence . . . war?* Could we give up war? When the adaptation required to avoid the nightmarish outcome involves altering aspects of human behavior that seem almost innate, it's easy to get pessimistic about our chances. Even if we decided it would mean self-destruction and renounced the practice, it would be tough to feel confident that we wouldn't slip back into our old habits. We might be good for a while, but "forever" is a long time to try to maintain vigilance against nuclear conflict.†

Humans have been improving their weapons from the Stone Age forward. Weapons technology sometimes changed little over centuries, and until relatively recent times armies from different eras might still have been competitive if pitted against each other. Spears, archery, and men mounted on horses, for example, had been used for a very long time. (And sometimes the process of military improvement involved things other than weapons.)‡

---

* Is war hardwired into us? I think this is still being studied, assessed, and debated.

† The philosopher Bertrand Russell said about the problem of trying to maintain vigilance, "You may reasonably expect a man to walk a tightrope safely for ten minutes; it would be unreasonable to do so without accident for two hundred years."

‡ Weapons are only one element of creating an effective military. Tactics, training, leadership, logistics, battlefield formations, and other such things

But after about Napoleon's time, the killing power of cutting-edge militaries really began to increase. By the late nineteenth century, industrialization—with its factories and assembly lines and modern science and its continuous technological innovations—was transforming warfare. Armies doubled in size between the Battle of Waterloo in 1815 and the Battle of Sedan in 1870, and then doubled again by the outbreak of the First World War in 1914. The changes to the power of their weaponry was even greater. The largest artillery pieces of the First World War fired *shells* that weighed more than Napoleon's heavy cannons of a century before, and the infantryman's rifle in 1914 outranged those eighteenth-century horse-drawn artillery pieces. All this was backed by the wealth, power, and populations of deep nation-states. The power to kill lots of people had increased almost incomprehensibly in a relatively short time period, and continuously striving to stay cutting edge was more important than it had ever been.* To fall behind on the latest equipment, tactics, and practices was to court military (and perhaps national) disaster.† And this made scientists some of the most important contributors to the war effort.‡

---

have also been part of the evolution process. So while both Assyrians in the eighth century BCE and the Romans in the first century BCE used swords, a lot of other elements in the military system had evolved to make the Roman military far more formidable and dangerous than the biblical-era Assyrians.

* As we've said, for much of human history the pace of change was slower, and older systems could often remain viable and effective for a long time.

† As the French found in the Franco-Prussian War in 1870–71, for example, especially in the much more effective German use of railroads for troop concentration.

‡ "I believe the statement that in this war [World War II] a hundred physicists are worth a million soldiers originated in England," said the physicist Arthur Holly Compton.

The employment of twentieth-century technology in the First World War scared everyone. The damage wrought with purely conventional weapons in that conflict was shocking. Added to that, the new horrors that science had contributed to the world's arsenals included the equivalent of human insecticide—gas and chemicals that treated people like ants.

If this was how bad things had become by that war's end in 1918, what did the future hold? One can understand why there was an effort after that war to see that such a global conflict wouldn't happen again.

Yet less than twenty years later, an astonishingly powerful new weapons class was about to be revealed.

In 1938, with war clouds on the horizon, German scientists made a discovery that foreshadowed the weaponization of the atom. In August 1939, less than a month before the Second World War broke out, Albert Einstein wrote to Franklin D. Roosevelt, the president of the United States, warning about the potential for atomic superweapons. He also made it clear in the note that such potential might be realized soon:

> It may become possible to set up a nuclear chain reaction in a large mass of uranium by which vast amounts of power and large quantities of new radium-like elements would be generated. Now it appears almost certain that this could be achieved in the immediate future.
>
> This phenomenon would also lead to the construction of bombs, and it is conceivable—though much less certain—that extremely powerful bombs of a new type may thus be constructed. A single bomb of this type, carried by boat and exploded in a port, might very well destroy the whole port together with some of the sur-

rounding territory. However, such bombs might very well prove to be too heavy for transportation by air.

It's worth noting that to a highly educated man of that preatomic era like President Roosevelt, this warning would have been difficult to understand.* If you don't understand the information, what do you do with it?† In the case of the president of the United States, he instigated a program to build an atomic bomb.

The Manhattan Project—the multinational cooperative effort to develop a superweapon—was a significant gamble involving precious resources. It cost a huge amount of money, brought together scientists and experts from around the world, and had a small city of people doing secret work to help develop and test a weapon before it was finalized by the other side. Once the war broke out, it almost seemed like a defensive measure—after all, the other side had brilliant physicists, too (Einstein had been one of them before leaving Germany).

Human beings in ancient Egypt or Mesopotamia would have understood the reasoning behind the geopolitical realism of the Manhattan Project. Some of the scientists involved certainly had reservations about creating a monster bomb so that humans could more effectively kill one another, but the idea of the Nazis getting their hands on such a superweapon first was the stuff of nightmares.

---

*Also one that might be *wrong.* Einstein was telling FDR about something that might be possible, not 100 percent certain. Hard enough to make decisions about stuff like this if you *are* a physicist and understand it. FDR wasn't and probably didn't.

†Besides the philosophical question of whether it's smart to forever be increasing the power of weapons, there's the opportunity cost aspect. Might the effort and money that would go toward such an experimental effort be better spent in an area more likely to help win the war?

When, after years of work, the Trinity bomb test was conducted in a desert region of New Mexico on July 16, 1945, not only was the weapon successful (this had not been a given), but it turned out to be more powerful than the physicists who developed it had expected.* When the bomb went off, there was a huge sense of relief and triumph among those involved in creating it, but also mixed emotions. Many of them already sensed that this weapon would only grow in power as time went on.

J. Robert Oppenheimer, sometimes called the father of the atomic bomb, described the moment that the bomb went off in a 1965 interview on a program called *The Decision to Drop the Bomb*:

> We knew the world would not be the same. A few people laughed. A few people cried. Most people were silent. I remembered the line from the end of scripture, the *Bhagavad Gita*. Vishnu is trying to persuade the prince that he should do his duty and, to impress him, takes on his multiarmed form and says, 'Now, I am become death, the destroyer of worlds.' I suppose we all thought that one way or another.

Context is everything, and this bomb test was not occurring in a vacuum. It's important to remember what that last year of the Second World War was like. Many consider it the worst year of the war in terms of the meat grinder–like nature of the conflict. In 1945, cities were being virtually wiped off the map *a couple of times a week*. If there's one thing the Second World War proved,

---

*The device, according to the Atomic Heritage Foundation, was nicknamed "the Gadget." Like the one that would be dropped on Nagasaki, the Gadget was an "implosion-type bomb" fueled by plutonium.

it was that it doesn't matter how many arms treaties nations sign or what limits countries impose during peacetime—when societies are in the midst of a *Total* War, with their survival at stake, there's nothing ethically sacrosanct in the arsenal.* The bombings of cities that had so horrified the world when the war first started were now so commonplace that the moral outrage of 1939 seemed a quaint remnant of a prewar mentality. And to some, this new bomb just seemed like a more efficient and economical way to do with one airplane what was currently being done in raids with hundreds and hundreds of them.

This is a point often not emphasized enough in modern-day discussions of the morality of dropping the atomic bombs on Japan, but it would certainly have loomed large in the minds of those at the time. The plan had been to use the new superbomb on Germany the same way that the Allies had been using conventional bombs to level the Third Reich. Almost every major and midsize German city had been torn up.† In May 1945, two months before the successful Trinity test, Nazi Germany surrendered, but the Allies were still at war with Japan.

By 1945, Japan was getting the same conventional bombing treatment that had been meted out to Germany. Its cities were being systematically burned to the ground, and had atomic bombs not been dropped on Japan, the United States would

---

*People sometimes point out that poison gas wasn't used in a significant way in the Second World War as it had been in the First, but the reason wasn't humanitarian. It wasn't a war-winning tool; if it had been, they'd have used it. There was much talk of using it in certain situations, and several Second World War combatant nations were accused of using chemical weapons at some point or another during the conflict.

†One of the reasons for the popularity of the German city of Heidelberg among tourists today is that the city mostly escaped being badly bombed, and hence it's one of the best-preserved towns showing what the architecture and style of Germany was like before the war.

simply have continued to fight the war the way it had been. In March 1945, five months before Hiroshima, US forces, flying more than three hundred heavy bombers, conducted a fire-bombing raid on Tokyo that killed a hundred thousand people, wounded about a million more, and incinerated seventeen square miles of the capital.* By the time the atomic bombs were dropped in August, Tokyo was already so devastated by previous firebombing raids—fifty to sixty square miles of the city had been burned out—that it had been taken off the priority targeting list. Some sixty-plus other Japanese cities had suffered the same fate.

Today, when we talk about the two atomic bombs† the United States dropped on Japan, we tend to do so in the context of the *morality* of dropping them. The truth is, the decision makers almost certainly didn't have the range of options we often assume (or wish) they had. The idea that President Truman could have done something *other* than use the atomic bomb on Japan is probably a little out of step with the political realities of the time.‡ As the historian Garry Wills wrote in his book *Bomb Power*: "If it became known that the United States had a knock-

---

*These numbers are comparable casualtywise to those of the atomic bombs that would be dropped in August 1945.

†The devices were nicknamed "Little Boy" and "Fat Man." According to the Atomic Heritage Foundation, Little Boy was ten feet long, weighed nearly ten thousand pounds, and was fueled by "highly enriched uranium." It was dropped on Hiroshima on August 6, 1945. Fat Man, a plutonium-fueled implosion-type bomb—the same as the Trinity test bomb—was dropped on the Japanese city of Nagasaki on August 9, 1945. Using just thirteen and a half pounds of plutonium—about the size of a softball—Fat Man's efficiency was deemed "ten times that of Little Boy."

‡Many questions still arise over *how* he employed the bombs. Some physicists and even military figures had wanted a demonstration test in a less populated or unpopulated area (such as over water off the coast of Japan) to show Japan what the bombs could do before using them on human beings.

out weapon it did not use, the families of any Americans killed after the development of the bomb would be furious. The public, the press, and Congress would turn on the President and his advisors. There would have been a cry to impeach President Truman and court-martial General Groves. The administration would be convicted of spending billions of dollars and draining massive amounts of brain power and manpower from other war projects and all for nothing."

Of course, an atomic bombing does have unique horrors associated with it. Those who've lived though twenty-four- or thirty-six-hour conventional bombings have written about how strange it is to emerge from bomb shelters to see a city that had been intact when they descended now transformed into a ruin. Yet there's at least a short span of time, a matter of hours probably, in which a person living through such an event can mentally process what's occurring. In an atomic attack, the initial damage occurs in the blink of an eye. The people who lived through the only two actual bombings carried out on human beings often appeared stupefied. And many would die of their wounds or from the bomb's radiation before they ever had a chance to get their minds around what had happened to them, in any case.

The atomic bombings of Hiroshima and Nagasaki (August 6 and 9, respectively) together probably killed more than two hundred thousand people. Those victims became the only cases in world history of what happens to human beings in a nuclear attack. They were living examples, unwilling guinea pigs.*

---

*Unintentional as well. The bomb's inventors did not drop the weapon to test what it would do to people. They definitely studied the aftereffects, though. The data the attacks provided was a by-product, but it was extremely instructive and was used in all sorts of ways, including as a stark warning about what a global nuclear conflict would do to the individuals on the ground.

It motivated some to publicly share their stories and speak out about how terrible a nuclear war would be.

Others cataloged and immortalized the eyewitness accounts for future generations. The author Susan Southard writes in her book *Nagasaki* that within a second of the bomb being dropped, the resulting fireball was 750 feet in diameter, and the temperature inside it was 540,000 degrees Fahrenheit, higher than at the center of the sun. "Horizontal blast winds tore through the region at two and a half times the speed of a category five hurricane, pulverizing buildings, trees, plants, animals, and thousands of men, women, and children. In every direction, people were blown out of their shelters, houses, factories, schools, and hospital beds; catapulted against walls; or flattened beneath collapsed buildings." And all of it happened in an instant.

One Hiroshima survivor, Hiroshi Shibayama, saw the explosion and ran toward the city center where the bomb had gone off. He wrote, "The people were burned so badly that it was hard to distinguish feature from feature, and all were blackened as if covered with soot. Their clothes were in rags. Many were naked. Their hands hung limply in front of them. The skin of their hands and arms dangled from their fingertips. Their faces were not the faces of the living." The survivors' accounts leave a modern reader slack jawed.

In any third world war, the nuclear survivors would likely have similar experiences.* But as everyone knew after the first two bombs were used, in the next big war nuclear bombs will

---

*Even with bigger, more powerful weapons, the general experience on the ground will probably be similar. The distances from ground zero that will feel the effects will be pushed outward, the kill zone will be extended, but the survivors of the next nuclear bombing will likely look a lot like the ones from the last one.

be bigger, there will be more of them, and both sides will probably have them. What if instead of two small atomic bombs, two hundred large ones are used and we begin to damage things beyond fixing?[*]

Albert Einstein is supposed to have said that he didn't know what sort of weapons the Third World War would be fought with, but the one after it would be fought with sticks and stones. Air Force general Curtis LeMay allegedly coined the phrase "to bomb someone back to the Stone Age."[†] Both quotes, whether said by these men or not, invoke the idea of a future all-out war knocking humanity backward on the civilization scale. For the first time in their history, humans had created weapons so powerful they had the theoretical potential to spawn dark ages.

Humanity hasn't really dealt with a loss of capacity or a backward step for a millennium or more. It's easy to forget that there could be things out there that could do to us what the plagues[‡] or earthquakes or massive volcanic eruptions did to civilizations many centuries ago. And it's unprecedented that a human being could order it done, like an act of God—the civilization-destroying outcomes of any nuclear holocaust would be an act of human beings. If such outcomes were ever to occur, it would be because a person or persons decided that it would. No human being orders a volcano to erupt or a tsunami to strike. The ancient Greeks had

---

[*] The capacity to rebuild to prewar levels is one of the definitions the physicist Nick Bostrom uses for the term "existential risk" in his book *Global Catastrophic Risks*. "An existential risk is one that threatens to cause the extinction of Earth-originating intelligent life or to reduce its quality of life (compared to what would otherwise have been possible) permanently or drastically."

[†] LeMay swore that he never said it.

[‡] If you're skipping around and missed chapter 6, be sure to go back if you'd like to read more about the plagues that wiped out huge portions of humanity.

all sorts of myths connected to humankind getting its hands on godlike abilities.* What human being or collective group of people is capable of responsibly handling power like this?†

The advent of nuclear weapons made it possible for the first time in history for a single human being to destroy tens of millions, maybe hundreds of millions, of lives—and as delivery technology improved to do so in as little as minutes. None of the scariest people in history—Genghis Khan, Alexander the Great, Adolf Hitler—had anything like that kind of capability. If in the thirteenth century the Mongol titan Genghis Khan had decided to smash an empire or state, it was going to take some time. If that state was huge—as, for example, China was—it was probably going to take decades. However, if President Richard Nixon in 1969 decided to launch a nuclear strike on that same place, he could have annihilated one hundred million Chinese people *in an afternoon*.

If humankind treated this new superweapon as it had treated every other effective weapon ever invented, the next world war would be one fought with near godlike destructive capability. Many of the several hundred people who witnessed the birth of the atomic age realized this the minute they saw that Trinity test in the desert. "Now, I am become death, the destroyer of worlds," as Oppenheimer said.

As with the scientists themselves, the reactions of Americans were mixed. If you are mired in a world war, and your

---

*Both the inventor Daedalus and the stealer of fire Prometheus figure in mythological tales of providing godlike power to mortal men.

†And even if such competent people could be found, who eventually replaces them? We're talking about a power or threat that needs to be managed until it isn't a threat anymore. When is that going to be? What are the odds of getting competent people at all times, in all countries, with such weapons?

side acquires the superweapon, it's absolutely going to be seen in a positive light.* In his book *In the Shadow of War*, the historian Michael S. Sherry described Americans' varied reactions after President Truman spoke on television to tell the American people and the world that the bomb had been dropped, and to explain what this new weapon was and why it had been used. "Some stressed pride in American achievement and satisfaction in gaining vengeance against the Japanese." A few wished the war had continued so we could drop more bombs on Japan. "Others—especially soldiers who assumed that an invasion of Japan was the only alternative to the bomb's use—welcomed the peace that the bomb had speeded, and the bomb itself as a tool for enforcing continued peace."

Others saw something else entirely—to them, the bomb was evidence of the scourge of modern war. Still others felt a sense of foreboding about what the future might hold. The CBS newsman Edward R. Murrow put it this way: "Seldom, if ever, has a war ended leaving the victors with such a sense of uncertainty and fear—with such a realization that the future is obscure and that survival is not assured."

THE GENERATIONS THAT grew up in the first few decades after the Second World War had the specter of a nuclear conflict hanging over them—they talked about it, wrote and sang about it, and had nightmares about it. American children often did emergency drills in school that taught them what to do and how to behave during a nuclear attack. The literature and popular entertainment of the period was saturated with themes of atomic (and later thermonuclear) war. "The End of the World"

---

*Much better than the other side getting it, of course. Imagine the American reaction if the Soviet Union had been the first to develop the A-bomb.

became a popular trope, a fantasy. It didn't even matter if you lived in a so-called neutral country, because no region would escape the fallout—literally—if a third world war happened. In the era when the superbombs were new, people from many varied backgrounds—scientific, military, political, artistic, and philosophical—began to think about the odds of this happening as if their very lives depended on it.

This is where the fork-in-the-road question we've been looking at again comes into play. Either things will happen again as they always have, or they won't—meaning either there will be another great war (or wars) in human history, or there never will be again. You're free to choose either scenario.

Realizing that they had delivered the most powerful weapon ever created into the hands of a rather violent species, some of those who helped create the superbomb tried to look at the potential positives. Maybe humanity would finally be frightened enough and motivated enough to renounce war, something that had been with us since the dawn of history. Oppenheimer himself said, "It did not take atomic weapons to make man want peace, but the atomic bomb was the turn of the screw. The atomic bomb made the prospect of future war unendurable." Idealism had become realism (or else).

The physicist Arthur Holly Compton* wrote, "If with such destructive weapons men are to survive, they must grow rapidly in human greatness. A new level of human understanding is needed. The reward for using the atom's power towards man's welfare is great and sure. The punishment for its misuse would seem to be death and the destruction of the civilization that has been growing for a thousand years."

"Must grow rapidly in human greatness" is a wonderful

---

*Who also was involved in helping develop the atomic bomb.

phrase. As is "destruction of the civilization that has been grow-ing for a thousand years." It seems like a nice way of saying that we as a species must become more enlightened or die.

Einstein seemed to be a bit more pessimistic about the adapt-or-die question: "The unleashed power of the atom has changed everything, save our modes of thinking and thus, we drift toward unparalleled catastrophe." He later clarified what he meant:

> Many persons have inquired concerning a recent message of mine that "a new type of thinking is essential if man-kind is to survive and move to higher levels."
>
> Often in evolutionary processes a species must adapt to new conditions in order to survive. Today the atomic bomb has altered profoundly the nature of the world as we know it, and the human race consequently finds itself in a new habitat to which it must adapt its thinking.
>
> In light of new knowledge . . . an eventual world state is not just desirable in the name of brotherhood; it is nec-essary for survival. . . . Today we must abandon competi-tion and secure cooperation. This must be the central fact in all our considerations of international affairs; otherwise we face certain disaster. Past thinking and methods did not prevent world wars. Future thinking must prevent wars.*

This is one fork in the intellectual road. It is the one that says humanity must change profoundly or be destroyed by its own creations. Even the proponents of this viewpoint acknowl-edge how difficult it will be for humankind to stop acting as it

---

*Einstein wrote this in 1946. At that time there were high hopes that the newly established United Nations might turn out to be something akin to a global government at some point. It may have sounded less far-fetched than it does today.

always has,* but they also maintain that we don't have a choice. In essence, this view of the world represents a true test of our vaunted adaptability as a species. We either succeed or face nuclear Armageddon at some point in our collective future.

The other intellectual fork in the road says that humankind will likely act as it always has, and that ancient habits are too ingrained to substantially change. Some people who hold this view argue that the odds are too highly stacked against sufficient adaptation or evolution by our species and believe it's better to try to find strategies to minimize bad outcomes. Still others don't buy into the general premise that these new weapons are inherently bad things; to these adherents of the bomb, it's more about who uses them and how that determines whether they're good or bad.

Once the Second World War was over and emotions had cooled somewhat, questions arose about what to do with this weapons technology. How can it be controlled? What if other countries get the new weapons, too?† Many debates took place within the United States in 1945 and 1946 concerning topics such as who should be in charge of the weapons. The military seemed like the logical choice—it was the one who was going to use them, after all. But President Truman wasn't having it,‡ and

---

*The idea of the nations and peoples of the world acquiescing to something like an actual world government superseding the sovereignty of national governments/nation-states shows the level of the challenge involved. If the question were put more starkly—either humanity consents to the formation of a global single state or humanity gets bombed back to the Stone Age—which side are you putting your money on? Again, your answer depends perhaps on your level of confidence in humanity.

†The United States had a monopoly on these weapons from 1945 to 1949. Its leaders thought the country was going to maintain it for much longer than it did, and this was reflected in their planning assumptions.

‡And he had a good rationale for this. Truman is quoted in James Forrestal's diaries as saying about the bomb that he didn't want to have "some

eventually, it was decided that going forward the US president would have the exclusive power to authorize and order the use of the superweapons.

But this was a level of personal power the constitutional framers of the United States had never foreseen. And that, historian Garry Wills wrote, was one of the side effects of the bomb—it changed the American constitutional system. "Lodging 'the fate of the world' on one man," Wills argues, "with no constitutional check on his actions, caused a violent break in our whole governmental system." But it was a development that "was accepted under the impression that technology imposed it as a harsh necessity." How, for example, would a president have time to consult with other leaders or branches of government if the enemy's missiles were already in the air?

The nature of the presidency, says Wills, was irrevocably altered by this grant of unprecedented power.

While new weapons were changing how the American government did things on a national level, the question of how they might change things on a human level was also being debated. There developed an active attempt to put the nuclear genie back in the bottle, to eliminate atomic weapons from the face of the earth, almost as if they had never been discovered at all.[*]

Indeed, in October 1945, just one month after Japan's surrender, President Truman, in a speech to Congress, said the hope

---

dashing lieutenant colonel decide when would be the proper time to drop one."

[*] And remember, since at this time only one nation had these weapons, had that nation decided in favor of eliminating them, they could simply opt to destroy the ones they had and never make any more. It would be nowhere near as easy to do this today. Of course, that would have done little or nothing to prevent another nation or entity from eventually developing the capability to produce such weapons.

of civilization rested on international agreements to renunciate the use and development of atomic weapons. In November that same year, he began to work with the leaders of Canada and the United Kingdom to formulate a policy to effect limits. It was, according to the nuclear expert Joseph Cirincione, essentially the first nuclear nonproliferation agreement.

The financier Bernard Baruch was tasked with presenting the plan at the first session of the United Nations Atomic Energy Commission on June 14, 1946. He framed the stakes in biblical terms. "We are here to make a choice between the quick and the dead," Baruch said in his speech. "That is our business. If we fail, then we've damned every man to be the slave of fear." His proposal included collecting all the uranium and thorium* in the world, as well as all the explosives and other components that go into the making of bombs, and putting all of it in a central location under the control of what he called an international atomic development authority, "to which should be entrusted all phases of the development and use of atomic energy."

The Soviet Union, quickly morphing into the "other side" in the Cold War† during this era, objected to this plan, in no small

---

*According to the World Nuclear Association, thorium (named after Thor, the Norse god of thunder) is more abundant in nature than uranium. It isn't very radioactive—you can hold it in your hand without injury—but it's "fertile," which means it can absorb neutrons when it's irradiated and transmute into Uranium 233, which is fissile (capable of nuclear fission). "Fissile materials are composed of atoms that can be split by neutrons in a self-sustaining chain-reaction to release enormous amounts of energy," according to the Institute for Energy and Environmental Research. "In nuclear weapons, the fission energy is released all at once to produce a violent explosion."

†Many historians believe that it was a "cold" war and not a hot war because of the existence of atomic (and later, thermonuclear) weapons. A popular counterfactual question is whether a world war three would have happened

part because while the United States was offering to give up its monopoly on atomic weapons, it was asking every other country to renounce them *first*. The deal would allow the United States to keep its nuclear arsenal for several years before dismantling it, thereby allowing it to extend its advantage. Instead, the Soviets suggested the Americans get rid of their nukes immediately, and then the rest of the world could figure out how to keep from developing any more.

The military historian Gwynne Dyer doesn't find the fact that the two superpowers soured toward each other surprising at all. He likens it to earlier geopolitical rivalries and argues that the democracy-versus-communism Cold War dynamic was a lot like the role religion played in the wars of the sixteenth and seventeenth centuries. "Each side has an ideologically watertight explanation for why the adversary behaves with such persistent wickedness and aggression," Dyer writes. "None of the post-1945 developments would seem surprising to a 17th century Spanish or Ottoman diplomat. Neither communism nor liberal democracy would mean anything to him, other than as a useful label for the players, but he would have no trouble understanding why the victorious alliance so quickly fell apart. They almost always do after victory, because the winners are the biggest players left on the board, hence they automatically become the greatest threats to each other's power."

In the immediate postwar period, both sides had ample reason to fear the capabilities of the other. These were, after all, the armies that had recently won the war. But now they might be turned against each other, and they were frankly scary. The Soviets had what was probably the strongest land force that

---

between the victorious Second World War powers had atomic weapons not been discovered.

had yet existed in global history—the Red Army, even after partially demobilizing in 1945, remained large, powerful, and threatening.* Where the Western Allies had used a wide array of tools to achieve battlefield superiority (airpower was a crucial component, for example), the Soviets put most of their emphasis on lots of very heavy armor, masses of artillery, and lots of men. This was not a finesse force; it was an army built to steamroll opponents, as it had the German Wehrmacht, which had been considered the best army in the world up to its defeat.† And they were perched along the farthest limit of the territory they had taken over in wartime, occupying unwilling populations in places like Poland, Romania, Hungary, and the Baltic states.

The West, however, had fantastic air forces and complete naval supremacy. On the ground their land armies had many electronic, signals, logistics, and communication advantages over the somewhat technologically simpler Red Army. And they had the atomic bomb.

Over the ensuing decades, it became an article of faith among many that war with the Soviet Union wasn't just a possibility, but an inevitability. For the United States, such

---

*At its numerical height during the Second World War, the Red Army had more than eleven million men. After its demobilization in 1945, it shrunk to closer to three million. The US Army had had nearly six million in uniform during wartime; this had shrunk to just under a million by 1947, and only about a hundred thousand men were stationed in Germany after its postwar demobilization.

†A sometimes overlooked but key point is that the armies on both sides had lots of institutional combat experience. Even when inexperienced, or "green," troops were used (such as the US soldiers when the Korean War broke out), the officers and leadership all had recent wartime experience. The Red Army in the early Cold War was in part so dangerous because it was led by experienced veterans and had a ton of combat-hardened officers in its ranks. The same was true for its counterpart in the West.

pessimism colored its decision making. If the premise that war was inevitably going to happen was accepted, more than five thousand years of political and military history said it would be best if such a war happened at a time and place of one's choosing, and when one's strengths were maximized. Since the end of the Second World War, no greater disparity in weapons technology has ever existed than when the United States had a monopoly on nuclear weapons right after it. How many leaders in world history would have taken advantage of such circumstances?

Some of the more aggressive voices at the time argued for doing just that, acting before the advantage narrowed. General George Patton famously suggested before demobilization began that, since the Western Allies already had mobilized forces over in Europe, ready to fight, they ought to confront the Soviets right away. No one knew how long that window of opportunity was going to last.* Only a fool, some thought, would squander such a chance.

There were differing opinions about what to do with the United States' atomic monopoly. President Truman's secretary of war, Henry Stimson, described the advantage of the monopoly in poker terms: The bomb was the equivalent, he said, of a royal straight flush. How do you resist playing with a hand like that? What would Julius Caesar or Alexander the Great—or Hitler, for that matter—have done with a monopoly on nuclear weapons? *Not* use them? If you gave the great Carthaginian general Hannibal nuclear weapons in his life-or-death struggle with the Roman Republic, handed him the button, and said, "If you push this, all of Rome will be

---

*General Leslie Groves, the military head of the Manhattan Project, thought it would be two decades before the Soviets got the bomb.

devastated," does he push it, or does he say, "Maybe I should think about this"?*

Conversely, what might a very enlightened people do with such force? Could they turn it into a tool for righteousness? The fact that the West saw itself in a Manichaean good-versus-evil face-off with the USSR also colored how the weapons were seen. They were often viewed as the counterbalancing force offsetting the conventional power of the Red Army, and thus as the most powerful weapon protecting the free world from Soviet tyranny.

Even concerned scientists and pacifists were worried enough about the Soviet threat to consider the potential value of a preventative nuclear war. The British philosopher and mathematician Bertrand Russell, who was such a proponent of peaceful approaches to conflict that he was jailed for opposing the First World War, wrote just after the Second, "There is one thing and only one thing which could save the world, and that is a thing which I should not dream of advocating. It is that America should make war on Russia during the next two years and establish a world empire by means of the atomic bomb."† Russell went on, in a speech to the House of Lords, to theorize that after the next war—which he deemed imminent—civilization would have to be rebuilt anew. (He believed this effort would take five hundred years.)‡

---

*What if Hannibal had lived through two world wars, witnessed the fighting at Verdun, the siege of Stalingrad, the firebombing of Dresden, or the aftermath of Hiroshima and Nagasaki, and then you hand him the button and say, "Do you still want to nuke Rome?" Maybe in order to "grow into greatness," humanity has to experience the growing pains.

†Is this Einstein's concept of a global government, but one formed the old-fashioned way, by conquest and force rather than cooperation, a modern version of the Pax Romana to keep atomic war from breaking out?

‡Russell gave another speech soon afterward, recounted in William Poundstone's *Prisoner's Dilemma*, in which he told the House of Lords of

It is relevant that Russell and others spoke such thoughts at a time when everyone was still traumatized by the war. Today, humanity still faces its share of potential calamities,* but the tension level is different now than in those immediate postwar years.

People understood that war could break out with little or no warning, too—the leading nations on both sides of the Cold War had entered the Second World War as a result of being on the receiving end of devastating surprise attacks: Operation Barbarossa, the massive German surprise invasion of the Soviet Union in June 1941 (in violation of the German-Soviet Nonaggression Pact of 1939); and Pearl Harbor, the Japanese surprise bombing raid on the US territory of Hawaii in December of the same year.†

Between 1946 and 1952, the bomb would fundamentally transform the US government into an entity that would in many ways be unrecognizable from the one that was attacked at Pearl Harbor in 1941. Not only did the fate of the world rest in the hands of a single individual, as the author Garry Wills has described, but in just a few years a series of new policies and laws such as the Truman Doctrine,‡ the National Security Act

---

his nightmare scenario, one so terrible that it would turn a committed pacifist into a person advocating a preventive nuclear strike: "As I go about the street and see St. Paul's, the British Museum, the houses of Parliament and the other monuments of our civilization, in my mind's eye I see a nightmare vision of those buildings as heaps of rubble with corpses all round them."

*Climate change, for example, could cause immense problems for humanity. This will happen, though, over time and in the future. A nuclear war could do its damage all at once, and tomorrow.

†Can nation-states get the equivalent of a collective case of post-traumatic stress disorder? If so, the United States after Pearl Harbor might have had a slight case of it. The Soviets after Barbarossa had a much more severe case, though. The trauma from that June 1941 surprise attack and its aftermath was enormous and played into future distrust in international relations.

‡The Truman Doctrine committed the United States to aid other nations "who are resisting attempted subjugation by armed minorities or by outside

of 1947, and the Marshall Plan* created a new national security state at home and reoriented US foreign policy abroad, making the containment of communism its top concern. This was also the era when the CIA, the NSA, and the National Security Council were born, all part of a massive redesign of the US government, one intended to protect secrets, spy on our enemies, and run an increasingly globally focused military command.

While these may have been understandable changes, given the state of the world at the time, they do seem to run counter to what many scientists had been arguing about preventing a third world war through bringing about a new level of human understanding. It certainly was a very different approach from what some physicists had suggested should be done in late 1945 and 1946—sharing atomic secrets with the Soviet Union and thereby easing tensions. This idea was seen by its adherents as a trust-building move, a demonstration of good faith that could usher in a new postatomic spirit of cooperation in order to ward off catastrophe. To our modern mind-set, it seems more like the equivalent of giving military secrets to terrorists. It sounded just as crazy to the military class after the war.

For President Truman in the immediate postwar years, practical questions went along with the philosophical questions. For one thing, although the United States didn't let on, it actually had very few of these bombs in its arsenal. In addition, it had no particularly good way to deliver them to their targets.

So, over the next couple of years, the United States focused

---

pressures." Essentially, it was a pledge to attempt to contain Communist expansion into non-Communist states.

*Formally called the European Recovery Program, the Marshall Plan (named after the man who came up with it, US secretary of state George Marshall) was a $12 billion American program to help rebuild war-ravaged Western Europe.

on developing a system to deliver Armageddon on command, if that was deemed necessary. The official name of this intricate weapons-delivery system was the Strategic Air Command (SAC). SAC was part of a brand-new branch of the US military known as the air force.* SAC's job, if called on to do it, was to destroy the Soviet Union's major population centers, infrastructure, and industries with atomic weapons, making it the most destructive weapons system that had ever existed so far—if used, it would have killed *at least* tens of millions of people. Here we can see that in the space of less than two years we had gone from discussions about crafting legislation to rid the world of the scourge of atomic weaponry to the president being asked to approve air force plans for a strategy commonly referred to as the "atomic blitzkrieg."

One might think that in a situation as important to humanity's future as potential global nuclear war, the modern equivalent of philosopher-kings would meet, together with the most intelligent physicists and ethicists and others, in some sort of unprecedented global forum, where they could quietly and wisely (one hopes) discuss how to meet this potentially existential challenge. Instead, the reality of normal life and pedestrian concerns intervened. Politics was an obvious element that affected decision making, but matters like budgetary concerns and interservice rivalries within the military also influenced the outcomes. Indeed, there is a pretty good argument to be made—and many have made it—that one of the primary reasons for adopting the atomic blitz strategy in the first place was budgetary—it was a cost-saving move. If you have an air force with lots of atomic

---

*During the Second World War, US air assets had been part of the army and navy, respectively. The American bombers wreaking havoc over Germany and Japan were officially part of the US Army Air Forces, or USAAF.

bombs, maybe you don't need to keep buying all the other expensive military equipment like tanks or cannons.

This was a theoretical question at the time, since there were no data or metrics on the subject of cost savings. One thing President Truman *did* know was that after the war ended, the United States couldn't long keep funding the military as it had at its astronomical wartime levels; he was faced with cutting funding by 70 percent, while still maintaining the capability to fight a third world war should it come (and, again, many people thought it surely would).

Adopting and embracing a military strategy that put tens (if not hundreds) of millions of civilians in the crosshairs of the US armed forces understandably didn't sit well with a lot of people. Some of them happened to be those who would be called on to do the killing—that is, members of the military itself.

In October 1949, at congressional hearings about the air force's atomic blitz plan, the "Revolt of the Admirals" revealed the strong feelings held by those faced with doing the dirty work. As Eric Schlosser writes in *Command and Control,* "One high-ranking admiral after another condemned the atomic blitz, arguing that the bombing of Soviet cities would be not only futile but immoral." Admiral William F. "Bull" Halsey—a commander of the South Pacific during the war, and a man whose battle group got Lieutenant Colonel James Doolittle's planes close enough to Japan for them to bomb Tokyo in 1942—testified thus: "I don't believe in mass killings of noncombatants." Admiral Arthur W. Radford—commander of the northern carrier group and eventual vice chief of naval operations during the war—said, "A war of annihilation might bring a pyrrhic military victory, but it would be politically and economically senseless." And Rear Admiral Ralph A. Ofstie, who had toured the burned-out cities of Japan after the war, described the atomic blitz as the "random mass slaughter of men, women, and children." The whole idea, he said, was "ruthless and barbaric and contrary to American values."

It's hard to really know how much of the navy's opposition was truly based on morality, or how much might have been an effort to defend the necessity and relevance of its branch of the military services in the face of those looming budget cuts. (Indeed, the moral complaints would be notably muted later when navy submarines began to carry nuclear weapons.)

The admirals' testimony elucidated a key moral question that the world still wrestles with decades later: Is there an ethical way to fight a nuclear war? Is there a way to bomb cities and civilians with atomic weapons and have it square with American values and the values the Cold War West was trumpeting as a hallmark of its moral superiority over the "godless Communists"? In the view of the time, Stalin was as bad as Hitler had been. He was ruthless, and "the Reds" were on the move globally. But if you kill tens of millions of civilians to thwart the perceived evils of a totalitarian superpower, how much evil do you get splashed onto you in the process?* And to complicate the ethical dilemma ever more, what if the side that purports to occupy the moral high ground strikes *first*?†

It is crucial to recall that we today have the luxury of knowing how things in that era turned out; that is, that there was no third world war or nuclear conflict with the Soviet Union. Assessing what happened, and the decisions taken in safety, as we do, is one thing, but the folks making those decisions at the time

---

*One is reminded of Friedrich Nietzsche's line: "He who fights with monsters should be careful lest he thereby become a monster."

†As even the pacifist Bertrand Russell suggested was the only way to avoid a third world war. In all fairness to Russell, he would later change his opinion on this.

felt anything but safe. We also now know many things today that were hidden then.

The United States and others argued that Soviet ruthlessness[*] had to be met with a similar level of resolve. By 1948, Truman had already had minor standoffs with the Soviets in several locations around the globe[†]—and each time the Soviets gave in. But Stalin would further test that resolve in the summer of 1948 when he shut down the rail lines, roads, and canals into West Berlin, denying the United States, France, and Great Britain access to their respective sectors of the divided city.

This is the first crisis that raised truly practical questions about whether or not to use an atomic bomb. Truman had already allegedly played the nuclear bluff game[‡]—a strategy known as "escalation dominance"[§]—with Stalin. What if he threatened Stalin with atomic bombs over Berlin and Stalin didn't back down? Would the United States and its allies attack the Soviet Union and precipitate World War III? Was it even possible to launch a nuclear attack? Were there planes in place?

[*] In February 1948, for instance, the Czechoslovakian government was overthrown in a coup and that country became part of the Communist bloc, the last independent government in Eastern Europe to do so. Moreover, the foreign minister of the overthrown government was found dead outside his apartment in the foreign ministry building. The official story at the time was suicide. It wasn't until 2003 that a forensic expert named Jiri Straus said the evidence was conclusive that he was pushed out the window, as had long been suspected.

[†] In Iran in 1946, for example.

[‡] Michio Kaku and Daniel Axelrod make this claim in *To Win a Nuclear War*.

[§] This strategy essentially goes back to caveman times. In its crudest form it simply means the willingness of one side to take things to the next, most extreme level in order to get what it wants. It works best when the side doing the threatening has more powerful weapons. It theoretically works really well with nuclear weapons—until it doesn't.

How many bombs were available? What would the targets be, and if those targets were bombed and destroyed, would the attack achieve the overarching goal?

How well would such an attack play in the increasingly important court of global public opinion? If the US nuclear arsenal did only half the damage of its own estimates, it would kill untold numbers of men, women, and children.* Western "resolve" might be proved, but at a very high cost. The Soviets hadn't physically attacked anybody—they had simply closed off supply routes and thereby indicated that the next geopolitical chess move was the West's.

At this point, Truman brought together various people to have fundamental discussions, the kind they hadn't had before. And there were broad differences of opinion. The military men (by and large) were under the impression that if the nation went to war, the United States would use the new weapons just as they had used the conventional ones previously. But others, including David Lilienthal, the head of the Atomic Energy Commission, counseled the president not to use nuclear weapons. As Michio Kaku and Daniel Axelrod write in *To Win a Nuclear War*, the secretary of the army, Kenneth Claiborne Royall, "spoke for the hard-liners when he said, 'We have been spending 98 percent of all the money for atomic energy for weapons. Now if we aren't going to use them, that doesn't make any sense.'"

Some wanted to rely on a strategy that would eventually be-

---

*And they wouldn't necessarily even be the civilians of the other side in the war. The likely battlefield would be the territory of the people the United States (for example) was trying to defend. A French premier had said, "The next time you come you will probably be liberating a corpse." That ups the resolve tab even more.

come known as deterrence.* For deterrence to work, however, the side being deterred must truly believe that these weapons will be used against it. This meant that any nation seeking to lean on deterrence couldn't ever publicly say anything like, "These weapons are awful, and we'll never use them." Yet this is exactly what the United States had said right after the war in 1945. Was the United States ready to blow up Russian cities and slaughter so many of its people if Stalin called its bluff? If he did call the bluff, and the United States backed down, its future ability to use atomic bombs as a threat would be greatly diminished—and thereby the value of its nuclear arsenal, too. This is a conundrum that would outlive most of the officials debating it in 1948.

The fight over Berlin never exploded into a nuclear conflict because both sides managed to walk a delicate tightrope for almost a year. The West began tentatively attempting to fly into the city the supplies it needed to keep citizens from starving or freezing; when Stalin didn't attack the nonmilitary aircraft, the effort was expanded. The blockade would last until May 1949; the airlift itself would go on for months after that. By the time it ended, the United States and the Western Allies had flown 1.5 million tons of coal, fuel, and other necessary products into the city on nearly 200,000 flights. In geopolitical chess terms, Stalin had made a move fraught with land mines for the other side to trigger, and, by using the airlift, the West had managed to avoid them. In the early history of humankind trying to live with nuclear weapons technology—let's call it the "toddler years"—each time a crisis was averted without events tipping into disaster, much was learned. That said, if the Third World War had broken out as

---

* Deterrence is a strategic concept that predates nuclear weapons. In fact, in one form or another it's probably almost as old as humans are. It basically means using threats of some sort to prevent or deter others from taking unwanted actions.

a result of the Berlin Blockade, only one side was going to have atomic weapons used on it. If you're a member of the American public sweating out the increasing tensions between the superpowers, you could at least take comfort in knowing you were still safe from atomic weapons because your own government was the only one that had them.

Until it wasn't.

The Berlin situation calmed down in the spring of 1949, but everything else seemed to ratchet up in intensity that year. In fact, 1949 may have been the most dangerous year of the Cold War.* That was the year that Chinese Communists (the "Red Chinese") finally gained victory in their long-running civil war over the Nationalists and took over all of mainland China. The Soviet Union—already the largest land power in the world geographically—had now added to its ideological ranks a country roughly the size of the United States, and which contained a full quarter of the world's population. That year, in order to begin to cobble together a united defense strategy among countries still trying to recover from the damage of the Second World War, the North Atlantic Treaty Organization (NATO) was formed. Tensions only deepened.

Nineteen forty-nine was also the year the Soviets got the bomb.

On August 29, the Soviets conducted their first atomic bomb test in a central Asian desert—about sixteen years sooner than Western scientists had predicted. Suddenly, the whole dynamic changed. The United States now had to worry about having atomic bombs dropped *on it*. The oceans that had long shielded the North American continent no longer provided safety; in

---

*One shudders to think of what the events and tension level of 1949 would have been like if both sides possessed the technology and arsenals of 1969. We might still be trying to rebuild our societies today.

turn, the American nation and its populace had never faced a threat even remotely like it.

Thus ended that brief period at the beginning of the nuclear age when atomic power rested in the hands of a single country. It's notable, given the evidence of past human history, that with its monopoly, the United States didn't use that advantage to dominate the world.* Perhaps this means that in an ethical sense there had indeed been human progress—a "growth in human greatness." But perhaps, too, as Bertrand Russell would point out,† this was a single victory in an endless struggle. The first round went to humankind's ethical and evolutionary growth because the United States avoided bombing the Soviet Union when it was the only country to have the bomb,‡ but now two countries had it.

And one of the things that happened right away was that there was a new good argument for starting a preemptive nuclear war as soon as possible.

We've been living ever since with the fact that both sides— and others, now—have the nuclear option. Russia's announcement that it had the bomb signaled the end of the era of the United States having what the secretary of war had called the royal straight flush. Predictably, the question of how to respond ran the gamut; even sober, humanitarian-minded scientists tried to figure out if the balance of rational thought had swung

---

*A case can certainly be made that the United States did in fact dominate the world and did use these weapons as leverage to do so. But it's a far cry from how the Roman Empire probably would have used nuclear weapons.

†He said, as quoted earlier, "You may reasonably expect a man to walk a tightrope safely for ten minutes; it would be unreasonable to do so without accident for two hundred years."

‡And this monopoly lasted less than five years. Had it lasted fifty, would this restraint have held?

toward the idea of striking the Soviets preemptively. In his book
Prisoner's Dilemma, William Poundstone quotes a letter from
William Golden, one of President Truman's science advisers,
who, in trying to come up with rational approaches to this unprecedented civilizational challenge, did his best to imagine
how a man from Mars (in other words, somebody who didn't
have any skin in the game) might view the geopolitical situation:

> This brings up the matter of immediate use, or threat
> of use, of our weapons. Let us not delude ourselves, to
> bring about a true international control agreement with
> Russia we would have to use them. The consequences
> would be dreadful indeed, even though I assume that
> the Russians have so few A-bombs now that they could
> do little or no damage to the U.S.A. even if they could
> put them on the target.* In theory we should issue an
> ultimatum and use the bombs against Russia now: For,
> from here on, we inevitably lose ground. And this is true
> no matter at how much greater a rate we produce no
> matter how much more potent weapons. For once Russia
> is in a position to put A-bombs on our cities, no matter how
> inefficient those bombs may be and how few in number,
> she is in a position to do us unspeakable injury. That we
> can retaliate a hundredfold, or wipe out every Russian,
> will not repair the damage. So, a good, though amoral,
> case can be made by the disinterested man from Mars for
> our shooting at once.

*This was the rationale for striking immediately. There was a time lag
between the testing of an initial nuclear device and the point when there
would be a stockpile of such weapons available and delivery systems in
place. The idea was to attack before the Soviets were in a position to do
much damage with their new nuclear capability.

Golden then goes on to say, however, that the United States and the West wouldn't carry out a plan like this, regardless of the alternative, because the public would never support it. Whether or not Golden is correct about public support for preventative nuclear war, it's still interesting to consider what it might mean if he were right. One is tempted to see it as some sort of ethical evolutionary change. After all, would public opinion in an ancient Bronze Age civilization have hesitated for even a minute?*

That said, if it's possible to argue that we're adapting the ancient playbook to account for the power of atomic weapons, we nevertheless continue to follow other patterns that have always made logical military sense, but which now greatly increase the chances we will kill ourselves. What's the proper move if you're the United States, and you just had your atomic monopoly destroyed? Traditional realpolitik would probably mandate regaining technological superiority or dominance. You keep inventing and improving, and you develop the next system. The last thing you want to do is risk falling behind the other side, which could spell your eventual doom.

But if you haven't yet figured out how to deal with the power of the weapons you have recently developed, does it make sense to pursue even more powerful ones?

After the Soviets successfully tested their first A-bomb, in October 1949 Truman asked for some help from physicists—including J. Robert Oppenheimer†—on the question of whether

---

* Public opinion would have mattered a lot less in most Bronze Age societies than it does in the modern world.

† Oppenheimer's opinions are often hard to conclusively nail down. Usually he seems pretty pacifistic when it comes to nuclear weapons, but he can swing over to the other viewpoint for various reasons and at various times. Nonetheless, the general opinion among Truman and several

to build the next generation of superbombs (what today we call thermonuclear weapons and what then were often referred to as "the Super"). Some of the questions asked were: Should we develop the next level of weaponry above atomic weapons? What are the chances of success if we try?[*] And if we do succeed, would it actually help solve our problems? The physicists came back with a report telling the administration *not* to build the new weapon. If built, this "hydrogen bomb" would be thousands of times more powerful than the bombs dropped on Hiroshima and Nagasaki.[†] Humans did not need, and might not be able to handle, such a force, they said.

"We believe a super bomb should never be produced," the report found. "Mankind would be far better off not to have a demonstration of the feasibility of such a weapon, until the present climate of world opinion changes." (Is that code for "until we evolve more"?)

This idea that we should not develop stronger weapons rubs against the grain of traditional human behavior, and as such, it signaled an entirely new dilemma confronting our species. Could humanity, if faced with potential extinction, decide to cap weapons research and development?[‡] This would mean avowing to never try to discover anything more powerful and deadly than the weapons of our current capabilities. How does

---

associates was that Oppenheimer was "too much of a poet" to have good judgments on most hardheaded geopolitical questions.

[*] Scientists like Edward Teller had already been working to prove that it could be done.

[†] The nuclear expert Joseph Cirincione described the hydrogen bomb as the equivalent of bringing a literal piece of the sun onto the earth. There is no upper limit to such bombs' power.

[‡] Very imperfect analogies exist. Japan's decision to minimize the impact of firearms on its warfare and social system is often raised, for example.

a civilization shut off information like that? And who is qualified to make such a decision?

Oppenheimer and his like-minded associates had essentially assessed how the "growing into greatness" civilizational experiment had been going in the five years since Hiroshima and Nagasaki, and the results did not seem to be encouraging enough to recommend adding exponentially more power into the mix. The world was already akin to a clueless toddler playing with a pistol, and now it was being asked if it favored replacing the pistol with a machine gun.

Elsewhere in the report, the scientists also seemed to suggest that this moment provided a chance to break the patterns of the past to survive. "In determining not to proceed to develop the super bomb," the report read, "we see a unique opportunity of providing by example some limitations on the totality of war and thus limiting the fear and arousing the hopes of mankind."

Enrico Fermi and another physicist penned an even more apocalyptic response, arguing that these weapons would be able to create the equivalent of giant natural catastrophes.

> A decision on the proposal that an all-out effort be undertaken for the development of the "Super" cannot in our opinion be separated from considerations of broad national policy. A weapon like the "Super" is only an advantage when its energy release is from 100–1000 times greater than that of ordinary atomic bombs. The area of destruction therefore would run from 150 to approximately 1000 square miles or more.
>
> Necessarily such a weapon goes far beyond any military objective and enters the range of very great natural catastrophes. By its very nature it cannot be confined to

a military objective but becomes a weapon which in practical effect is almost one of genocide. It is clear that the use of such a weapon cannot be justified on any ethical ground which gives a human being a certain individuality and dignity even if he happens to be a resident of an enemy country. It is evident to us that this would be the view of peoples in other countries. Its use would put the United States in a bad moral position relative to the peoples of the world. Any postwar situation resulting from such a weapon would leave unresolvable enmities for generations. A desirable peace cannot come from such an inhuman application of force. The postwar problems would dwarf the problems which confront us at present.

Those who saw such weapons in a more positive light often thought that these scientists lived in a fantasy world. But David Lilienthal from the Atomic Energy Commission—who pushed back against using atomic bombs during the Berlin Airlift— wrote in his diary about the way the government was leaning, and it was not in the direction the physicists wanted. "More and better bombs, where will this lead is difficult to see. We keep saying we have no other course. What we should say is we're not bright enough to see any other course."

But Truman, as usual, had many more pressures weighing on him than just the opinion of his scientific advisers. David Lilienthal, again in his diary, records a comment by Senator Brien McMahon, who describes how the American people would likely react if they found out that the Communist superpowers had an H-bomb, but the United States didn't: "Why, a President who didn't approve going ahead on the H-bomb all out would be hanged from a lamppost if the Russians should get it and we hadn't."

It's hard not to be struck here by the width of the intellectual chasm between the people who were to create these superweapons and the people who would make the decision whether to use them. But even if elected figures were more competent to make such a choice than the electorate was, the court of public opinion was still strong—and are we comfortable with such decisions being made by the average Joe and Jane?*

In January 1950, after reading the report from Oppenheimer and his fellow scientists telling him not to build the super-superbomb, Truman decided to build it anyway.

The reasons given all revolved around this: the Russians were going to get it, so we had to have it. Even if one bought into Oppenheimer's argument that more powerful weapons weren't needed (i.e., that a nation can just employ A-bombs against the other side's H-bombs),† the psychological effect on the American people was unacceptable to a chief executive who depended on keeping power through the ballot box.

To gauge how unusual any other choice would have been, you have to imagine humankind declining to research and develop more powerful weapons systems. No doubt there are überpacifistic groups on the planet that would do so, but when you think of the most powerful nation-states, it's hard to imagine any of them saying, "Yes, we know our global adversaries and competitors have much bigger and more powerful weapons

---

*One can't help but wonder how a society that voted on everything, as ancient Athens did at one point in its democratic era, would handle the power of nuclear weapons. Would it be more or less likely to employ them if the people got to vote on it? It could go either way.

†In making his case that no one needed the H-bomb, Oppenheimer pointed out that the destruction level was already at the point where each side would be taking out the other's cities. If it took four A-bombs to take out a city that one H-bomb could destroy, did this meaningfully change anything? Even if it did, did that outweigh the possible negative effects?

than we have, but we're okay with what we currently possess. We don't need that bigger weapon."

Growing into greatness isn't easy.

Humanity had the bad luck to begin this civilizational experiment in extremely tense times. If nuclear weapons had been invented in a more peaceful era, instead of during the worst year of the worst war in human history (followed by a decades-long potentially existential standoff—the Cold War), the evolution of this great high-stakes experiment may have turned out differently. Instead, half a year after Truman decided to proceed with development of the Super, the United States found itself in a ground war in Asia against a Communist country supported by the Soviets. For the first time in history, a nuclear-armed state found itself going to war, and against a country whose friend and benefactor had just successfully conducted its own nuclear test the year before.

In the 1930s, the "isolationist" US republic boasted only a small volunteer army that avoided "foreign entanglements."[*] At the dawn of the 1950s, it stood astride the world like a colossus. Several major laws, acts, doctrines, and policy changes had reoriented American foreign and military policy in those years into the very opposite of isolationist.[†]

NSC-68, presented to Truman in April 1950, was one of the most important documents of this period.[‡] It laid out the stakes for the United States in apocalyptic terms: "The issues that face us are momentous," the document stated, "involving

---

[*] A phrase used by some early American leaders to represent the traditional diplomatic attitude of the United States regarding things like permanent alliances.

[†] We already mentioned such things as the National Security Act of 1947.

[‡] NSC-68 was known more officially as the United States Objectives and Programs for National Security.

the fulfillment or destruction not only of this Republic but of civilization itself." The policy recommendations of NSC-68 were breathtaking and included, among other things, going ahead with the H-bomb development. It also advocated *tripling* conventional defense spending.*

What NSC-68 did in paragraph after paragraph was spot the holes in the entire US defense strategy, which basically relied on making atomic threats. If the threats failed to gain the desired result, the United States would either have to nuke the other side and kill millions of people or back down. The document's authors pointed out that this line in the sand could be tested. Would the United States, for example, be willing to use nuclear weapons against a nation that just sort of gobbled up its neighbor a little at a time? Allies were worried about this, too, because they were starting to think that maybe the United States would be willing to use nuclear weapons and kill millions of non-American civilians if its own safety was directly on the line, but that it wouldn't be willing to do so to defend allied nations.

"The risk was having no better choice than to capitulate or precipitate a global war," NSC-68 said. In other words, leaders and strategists had no flexibility at all—it was nukes or nothing. With that in mind, the document advocated a huge increase in spending on conventional weapons, tanks, planes, ships—but it didn't back off the nuclear weapons expenditures, either. The cost and scope of the recommendations made it unlikely to be accepted; it was surely too sweeping and too expensive. Had

---

*This upset the budgetary hawk Truman, but one of the arguments made was that the lack of conventional weapons made nuclear war more likely. If you had enough conventional weapons to defend yourself, you might not resort to WMDs if you ended up not needing them. If you did not have enough conventional capability, you almost certainly would use nuclear weapons.

this not been such a tense time, maybe NSC-68 would have gone nowhere—instead, the Korean War broke out, World War III appeared closer than ever, and a tripling of spending on conventional weapons didn't seem like such a luxury anymore.

In June 1950, when the North Koreans invaded South Korea, the question of how to fight a war in the nuclear age was no longer merely theoretical. It's hard enough to figure out how to live with this new überpowerful weapons technology in peacetime; it's a completely different sort of challenge to try to deal with the temptation, fear, and uncertainty involving it in wartime. When a nation's soldiers are dying, the pressure to employ whatever means are at the nation's disposal is extreme. And there were also reputations on the line—for both proponents and opponents of the bomb.

And if there was ever a conflict that would tempt a leader to use atomic weapons, the Korean War seemed tailor made for it. Whether early in the conflict when US troops and allies found themselves in dire straits on the battlefield, or later in the war when the idea of using nuclear bombs to break the frustrating World War I–style entrenched stalemate had taken hold, the temptation to use what to some seemed like game-changing weapons was great. After all, people were dying in Korea every day. The war itself started out like a bar brawl, as North Korean Communist forces swarmed down from the northern border and drove the South Korean forces south toward the water. Everything was happening very quickly, and soon the entire South Korean army was in danger of defeat. Within days, the United States was sending forces to aid the South Koreans.*

---

*Normal UN Security Council practice would have been for one of the permanent members on the council to veto any resolution pushing for the use of force. But the Soviets were boycotting the council at the time, and so they couldn't veto anything. This led to a singularly muscular use of force by the "UN."

Eventually the US/UN forces commanded by the legendary Second World War general Douglas MacArthur conducted an amphibious landing behind enemy lines at Inchon, only to trigger a Chinese response soon afterward that sent a ton of Chinese "volunteers" unofficially into the fighting.

It was at this point that it became apparent that, to keep the Korean War from becoming World War III, all the major powers had to create some plausible deniability so that nobody had to admit this *was* World War III.

There is a theory that says that even without nuclear weapons there was a decent chance Korea *would* have turned into World War III. But it appeared to some that Joseph Stalin in the Soviet Union, Mao in Red China, and Harry Truman in the United States all bent over backward to claim that all the air strikes and amphibious naval operations and the millions of soldiers shooting at one another wasn't "war."

When the fighting broke out—the worst since the Second World War—a news reporter asked the American president, "President Truman, is this war? Are we at war?" Truman answered, "No, we are not at war." "So what is this? Is this like a police action?" the reporter asked, and Truman said, "Yes. That is exactly what it amounts to." And forever after, it was called a "police action"—as though wars might call for nuclear weapons, but police actions would not.

(Also, if the situation in Korea wasn't a "war," Truman could argue that he didn't have to go to Congress and ask it to declare it so.)*

---

*The US Constitution puts the power to declare war in the hands of the Congress and the power to wage it as commander in chief to the president. This keeps the power to take the country to war out of a single person's hands. Theoretically, the United States should not be in a war that the Congress has not declared. Police actions, though, aren't spelled out in the

The reason the Korean War is such an important test case for how war between major powers can be conducted without triggering the use of nuclear weapons is explained by the historian John Lewis Gaddis: "The rule quickly became that neither the United States nor the Soviet Union would confront the other directly or use all available force; each would seek instead to confine such confrontations within the theaters in which they had originated. This pattern of tacit cooperation among bitter antagonists could hardly have emerged had it not been for the existence, on both sides, of nuclear weapons."

Part of the adaptation the war forced was in clarifying lines of authority and power between civilian and military leaders. At one point in the conflict, Truman precipitated a near-constitutional crisis by firing Douglas MacArthur, his military commander. General MacArthur had been accused of insubordination for disagreeing with the way the president was micromanaging the war,* but Truman was worried about more than the war in Korea—he was clearly trying to restrain the use of force to keep things from spiraling out of control and into World War III.

Someone who disagreed with this caution was Air Force general Curtis LeMay. LeMay's attitude was shared among a lot of generals, especially the First and Second World War veterans—men who considered the most damaging aspect of modern war its duration. Because casualties reliably mounted every day, anything that could be done to limit the length of the war was humanitarian by its very nature—even if what it took to do that

---

Constitution. It's a bit of a gray area. The United States has not declared war since the Second World War was being fought. It may never again.

*It might be quite a bit more complicated than this, as recent works depict MacArthur perhaps working at odds with Truman, and his actions coming to Truman's attention via secret intercepts. Insubordination, regardless.

was a shocking amount of violence in a very short time. LeMay had wanted to unleash his heavy bombers, as he had over Japan in the Second World War, and he testified after the war was over that to do so would have been a more humanitarian approach. This is the philosophy/logic of strategic bombing, as contradictory as it may sound, highlighted by the nomenclature: the new bomber that was slated to carry out any possible nuclear destruction of places like the Soviet Union in 1950 and 1951 was the brand-new B-36, nicknamed the "Peacemaker."

Neither side—not the Truman backers who wanted to shy away from nuclear war, nor the Total War enthusiasts like the air force's Curtis LeMay—was able to conclusively win its arguments. By the middle of 1951, both sides were at the armistice table talking and working out a deal, which Truman's supporters could claim as a victory of sorts. Military hawks could counter that the talks would go on for two long years, and soldiers and civilians died on both sides the entire time.

Perhaps the final word, though, goes to the Truman supporters, who could point out that by walking a diplomatic and military tightrope World War III was averted. That's a pretty strong mic drop.

In October 1952, a third player in the nuclear game joined when the United Kingdom exploded its first atomic bomb. It was understood by all that the Brits would hardly be the last power to join the nuclear club. In the coming years, it seemed clear that human beings might have to manage a world with ten, fifteen, maybe as many as twenty nuclear powers.

And just as minds started to contemplate a world with multiple nuclear powers, the power of the weaponry itself got supercharged once again.

Less than a month after the United Kingdom joined the club, the United States demonstrated that it had the technology and the working capability to build a thermonuclear weapon, the "Super": the H-bomb. This megabomb was detonated just a couple of days before the US presidential election of 1952. The power of the bomb—even to a world getting accustomed to the mushroom cloud of atomic weapons—was truly paradigm shifting.

When the bomb exploded on an island in the Pacific, it created a fireball more than three miles wide. Lightning crackled inside it. The subsequent crater measured more than 6,000 feet across, and the hole was more than 150 feet deep. This "Super" was somewhere between four hundred and five hundred times more powerful than either of the bombs that were dropped on Japan in the Second World War.

But with the extraordinary power of this new bomb came new problems. Thermonuclear weapons are so powerful that they effectively work against the idea that you can use them as a deterrent, because the bigger they get, the less likely your adversary is to think you'll use them. Joseph Stalin was quoted* as saying that he thought that public opinion and the peace movement around the world would rein governments in—no one was going to use a multi-megaton-strength weapon, because world opinion wouldn't stand for it.† But if you're the military and you *want* to be able to use these weapons, or you're the intellectuals and the political associates of the president and you want your deterrence to still be effective, you must figure out a way around the dilemma of nuclear weapons too big to use.

The way around the dilemma was to make smaller nuclear

---

*In the Soviet newspaper *Pravda*.

† And not just for moral reasons. These weapons were huge radioactive pollution creators. Their use affected the health and safety of noncombatant states.

weapons.* "Tactical" nuclear weapons are those which are small enough to be used in situations that have a potential battlefield utility. Nuclear artillery shells fired from cannons or nuclear mines are two examples. One such weapon was even designed to be fired by a soldier from a bazooka-like recoilless cannon.† J. Robert Oppenheimer even helped develop them, saying later that he mistakenly thought he was improving the situation because the weapons were at least smaller.

Despite Oppenheimer's hope that smaller weapons were better than those that were included in what he called "the most God-damnedest thing I ever saw" (he was referring to the air force's war plan for 1951, a plan that called for five hundred atomic bombs to be dropped on the Soviet Union in a very short time), tactical nuclear weapons actually opened up the door to a very quick escalation to the very big bombs that Oppenheimer hoped would never be used. Rather than one instead of the other, experts worried that you would likely just get both.

The speed at which all this happened makes it seem at times like an out-of-control technological train, with humankind along for the ride until the inevitable crash. It's fair to ask which of several developments from the year 1952 was potentially the most destabilizing. Was it the fact that nuclear proliferation had now begun, and more countries were getting the bomb? Was it the invention of the hydrogen bomb and the incredible growth, virtually overnight, of humanity's destructive capacity? Or was it the beginning of the revolution in what we today refer to as tactical nuclear weapons?‡

The rest of the 1950s would see plenty of changes. Truman

---

* And not "instead of" but "in addition to" the larger nukes.

† Known as the "Davy Crockett." They made a couple thousand of them.

‡ Also called battlefield nuclear weapons.

would be replaced by the Republican president (and former general) Dwight David Eisenhower, and Stalin would die in office and be replaced by Nikita Khrushchev. This was also the height of what is known as the "Red Scare" in US history, when anti-communism reached levels of fear and paranoia that it had never reached before or would again.* It certainly didn't make cooperation between the nuclear adversaries any easier. The tech, as always, was progressing, and missiles were a key development, adding yet another dimension to the concept of a nuclear war. With them came the idea of "pushing the button" and unleashing a nuclear war automatically.†

Once again, the movement arguing that nuclear weapons must be eliminated, and humankind must alter its long-standing patterns of behavior and "grow into greatness," gained momentum.‡

The intellectual counterpoint to those calling for unprecedented changes in human behavior also gained momentum in the 1950s. Those who didn't believe humanity was likely to change to the degree required instead took the position that it would be smarter to look for approaches to manage the danger; strategies to effectively ride the nuclear tiger, as it were. The

---

* Officially, it was the "Second Red Scare," the first being a short one in 1919.

† There was always more to it than this, such as launch codes and other procedures. But certainly, unlike bombers, missiles once launched cannot be recalled or ordered to stand down, and they make it to their targets much more rapidly than aircraft would, thus shrinking any potential reaction window.

‡ Aided in part by a radiological disaster in the wake of the unexpectedly large Castle Bravo thermonuclear bomb test. Emerging nations began to assert a growing collective clout on the world stage to have a voice in the nuclear standoff between the superpowers. In his introductory statement as part of the 1955 Russell-Einstein Manifesto, Bertrand Russell began with the powerful line, "I am bringing the warning pronounced by the signatories" (their manifesto) "to the notice of all powerful Governments of the world in the earnest hope that they may agree to allow their citizens to survive."

holders of such beliefs became an alternative intellectual school of thought to what some considered the unrealistic "poets" like Oppenheimer. Eventually many of them would make careers working for defense-related think tanks theorizing about every aspect of nuclear war imaginable. Getting superintelligent people into a building together and tasking them with finding solutions, or at least long-term coping mechanisms, to some of the great problems of the age seems like a worthwhile idea.[*]

At their best, some of the figures who would eventually be called "defense intellectuals" were supergeniuses. John von Neumann was one of the most prominent of these early figures. Von Neumann has been called one of the most intelligent people of the twentieth century.[†] His list of accomplishments is mind boggling. He's a foundational figure in computing and physics. He worked on the Manhattan Project "as an extracurricular activity."[‡] It was clear from the time he was a young child that he was not a normal person.

The author William Poundstone wrote of him in *Prisoner's Dilemma*: "From childhood, von Neumann was gifted with a photographic memory. At the age of six, he was able to exchange jokes with his father in classical Greek.[§] The Neumann family sometimes entertained guests with demonstrations of Johnny's ability to memorize phone books. A guest would select a page and column of the phone book at random. Young Johnny read the

---

[*] From a logic perspective, this idea makes sense whether or not it actually produces good or usable ideas. This could be considered an attempt by society to use its collective best intelligence to adapt to the power of its weaponry.

[†] A statement like this is always debatable.

[‡] "Both the computer and the [atomic] bomb were extracurricular activities for von Neumann," Poundstone writes.

[§] That's ancient Greek, not what they speak in Athens today.

column over a few times, then handed the book back to the guest. He could answer any question put to him (who has number such and such?) or recite names, addresses and numbers in order."

The knock on people like this from detractors, however, is that while brilliant, they were somehow machinelike when it came to the human, emotional side of things like nuclear war and millions of dead. They were what you might call Spock-like, people who could logically and mathematically work on plans that might make Armageddon likely. The author Fred Kaplan wrote a book about them and called it *The Wizards of Armageddon*.

Von Neumann is credited with inventing something we today call game theory.* He was a game player himself (poker especially) and was fascinated with how games worked. He was particularly interested in the human element. As Poundstone explains it, "As von Neumann used the term, a 'game' is a conflict situation where one must make a choice knowing that others are making choices too, and the outcome of the conflict will be determined in some prescribed way by the choices made. Some games are simple. Others invite vicious circles of second-guessing that are difficult to analyze. Von Neumann wondered if there is always a rational way to play a game, particularly one with much bluffing and second-guessing. This is one of the fundamental questions of game theory."

By the 1950s, von Neumann was working with some of the other most brilliant thinkers in the world at a think tank called the RAND Corporation. There they put serious effort into studying the "game" that the fate of civilization hinged on. They were trying to develop theories for how this game of geopolitical chess or atomic poker worked, and what moves

---

*The standard definition of game theory is "a mathematically precise method of determining rational strategies in the face of critical uncertainties."

made sense in which situations, analyzing every move and possible countermove, every variable that might crop up.

Military leaders like Curtis LeMay argued that once political leaders had blundered somehow into war, the nuclear plan should be carried out by the military leadership ASAP, and the hundreds of bombs should start falling. Game over. Some of the civilian defense intellectuals analyzing the "game" countered that not only was the game *not* over after war broke out, but how it was played from that point onward could mean the difference between tens of millions of deaths or potentially hundreds of millions.

For example, Bernard Brodie, another of the wizards of Armageddon and one of the founding fathers of nuclear military strategy, clashed with the military's plan to bomb everything right away, saying that the enemy's people were more valuable as hostages than as corpses. LeMay's plan created millions of corpses almost right away. Brodie wanted to preserve flexibility even after the atomic bombs dropped. Fred Kaplan writes, "Brodie reasoned that the final surrender of the Japanese in the Pacific War resulted not from the atom bombs dropped on Hiroshima and Nagasaki, but from the implicit threat of more atom bombs on their way if the Japanese did not give up then.

"Likewise," Kaplan writes, paraphrasing Brodie's argument, "the Soviets would more likely stop fighting after receiving some destructive blows, knowing that if they did not stop, their cities would be the next targets to get hit. If, however, we blew up their cities at the very outset of the war, the bargaining lever would be blown up along with them. Hostages have no value once they are killed. Consequently, the Soviets would feel no inhibitions about blowing up American cities in return, hardly an outcome that would serve the interest of American security."

It's a combination of the dispassionately logical and, at the same time, in its own way (especially when compared with the atomic blitz plan the air force had in place), the humanitarian.*

But the wizards of Armageddon trying to find ways to use humans' intelligence to avoid killing ourselves with our own weapons were running into the same problem that those who wanted to see humankind evolve completely away from war were running into—the speed of the pace of change. Everything kept evolving so quickly that the minute you thought you had this atomic poker game figured out playing with a single deck, somebody decided to add a second. Then a third. It upset the paradigm on a regular basis and increased the complexity and number of variables enormously.

Within the efforts between the superpowers to normalize relations and reduce the hair-trigger element of their relationship, every decrease in tensions was countered with a new challenge to make up for it. The nuclear expert Joseph Cirincione ran down the growth in weapons technology in the ten years between 1950 and 1960:

> While Atoms for Peace† was promoting nuclear technology for peaceful purposes, the U.S. military was equipping their troops with thousands of nuclear weapons, adapting them for use in nuclear depth charges, nuclear torpedoes, nuclear mines, nuclear artillery, and even a nuclear bazooka. This infantry weapon, called the Davy Crockett, would fire a nuclear warhead about half a mile.

---

*The United States commissioned a war plan in 1955 to check out how many people would die if America carried out its proposed strikes against the Soviet Union when World War III broke out. The number came back to be sixty million. That's roughly on par with the total World War II death tolls and ten times the number of Jews killed in the Holocaust.

†A program/policy purporting to push for the peaceful application of nuclear technology.

Both the United States and the Soviet Union developed strategies to fight and win a nuclear war, created vast nuclear weapon complexes, and began deploying intercontinental ballistic missiles and fleets of ballistic missile submarines. The effective abandonment of international control efforts and the race to build a numerical and then a qualitative nuclear advantage resulted in the American nuclear arsenal mushrooming from just under 400 weapons in 1950 to over 20,000 by 1960. The Soviet arsenal, likewise, jumped from 5 warheads in 1950 to roughly 1,600 in 1960. The United States was ahead but afraid.

It didn't take a genius to realize that if controlling nuclear weapons was hard when there were a mere relative handful, and they were all of one sort, it would be exponentially more difficult now.

By the time the 1960 presidential election rolled around, fifteen years into the atomic age, one might have thought that the only thing American voters should have cared about was getting this sword of Damocles question right. After all, the entire world's prosperity and perhaps survival depended on it. But that's not how human beings function in any system in which they're allowed to have an opinion.*

The nuclear issue would certainly be one of the factors in the electorate's decision about whom to elect as someone one could potentially describe as "the most dangerous person in all of human history," but it wouldn't be their only consideration. There were still plenty of quotidian issues such as domestic policy and taxes and political party affiliation to contend with.

---

* Again, this is why some were/are pessimistic about humanity's chances with ever-increasingly destructive weapons technology. Did Einstein or Oppenheimer favor "the people" making decisions about who was qualified to wield such godlike destructive capability?

And as superficial as it might sound when deciding who should be vested with the most awesome power in global history, personal charisma and likability would also factor into this decision. From an outsider's point of view—here comes our Martian again—this could appear to be a very strange reality. In a game of geopolitical multideck atomic poker, with the stakes as high as they were, humans would potentially pick the guy with the best hair?*

It turns out that in 1960, the more glamorous candidate won,† even though he was less experienced than his adversary, Richard Nixon, and by presidential standards, very young. In fact, at forty-three years of age, John F. Kennedy was the youngest man ever elected to the office.‡ The outgoing two-term president, seventy-year-old Dwight D. Eisenhower—a five-star general who had commanded the Allied invasion at Normandy and who had been the supreme Allied commander in Europe in the Second World War—turned over the nuclear launch codes to a successor whose detractors considered him merely a millionaire playboy—a guy who hung out with cats like Frank Sinatra, and who was a political and intellectual lightweight—a kid.

The Soviet premier, Nikita Khrushchev, had, in fact, wanted

---

*Underappreciated factoid: Americans have not elected a bald man president since Eisenhower. Even this might have been an anomaly, because Eisenhower's Democratic opponent in both presidential elections was Adlai Stevenson, a man with even less hair than Eisenhower.

†This doesn't mean he wasn't also the better choice. But in as historically close an election as the 1960 contest was, John Kennedy's charisma, which was off the charts, must have been enough of a factor to put him over the top. It wouldn't have taken much.

‡To be fair, his opponent, Richard Nixon, was himself just forty-six. He would go on to win the presidency eight years later, and resign in 1974 during the Watergate scandal. At one point he would show off the sheer power of the office, telling members of the press corps, "I can go back into my office and pick up the telephone and in twenty-five minutes seventy million people will be dead."

JFK to win over his Republican opponent, Richard Nixon, a man who had been Eisenhower's vice president and was known to be a virulent anti-Communist. But no president takes office with a completely clean slate, and Kennedy inherited projects and plans that had been started by the previous administration.

One of them was the CIA-backed invasion of Communist Cuba by Cuban exiles. The plan was designed to topple Fidel Castro, but he routed the invasion and killed or captured the US-backed fighters. Kennedy would be deeply affected by what happened in the event known as the Bay of Pigs. Advisers during meetings would catch him staring off into space, saying, "How could I have been so stupid?"

JFK's biographer Robert Dallek writes:

"How could I have been so stupid?" was his way of asking why he had been so gullible. He puzzled over the fact that he had not asked harder questions and had allowed the so-called collective wisdom of all these experienced national security officials to persuade him to go ahead. He had assumed, he later told [adviser Arthur] Schlesinger, that "the military and intelligence people have some secret skill not available to ordinary mortals." The experience taught him "never to rely on the experts." He told [journalist] Ben Bradlee: "The first advice I'm going to give my successor is to watch the generals and to avoid feeling that just because they were military men their opinions on military matters were worth a damn."

If this can be called a learning experience, what it taught Kennedy may have prevented a nuclear holocaust, though it greatly enraged the Soviets, who were friendly with Castro and his government. It also further strained relations between the young president and his cabal of august, older (and in some cases legendary) military chiefs and advisers.

Payback for the attempted coup would be meted out at a 1961 summit in Vienna. There, the savvy sixty-seven-year-old Soviet leader—a man born a peasant who had no formal education, but who had risen to be the longtime underling to Joseph Stalin before assuming Soviet leadership—met the wealthy forty-four-year-old Harvard graduate and Massachusetts socialite. And almost ate him alive. Describing the experience afterward to James Reston of the *New York Times*, Kennedy said that the summit meeting had been "the roughest thing in my life. He just beat the hell out of me. I've got a terrible problem if he thinks I'm inexperienced and have no guts. Until we remove those ideas, we won't get anywhere with him."

But according to Vladislav Zubok and Constantine Pleshakov in their book *Inside the Kremlin's Cold War*, this face-to-face meeting had changed Khrushchev's view of the man and what he could get away with and what he might decide to try. The Soviet leader had initially hoped to push for better relations but instead ended up telling advisers after JFK's weak performance that the favorable situation of a less formidable US leader must be exploited. It was too good of an opportunity to pass up, even in a nuclear world.

But as Kennedy theorized, when neither side wants war, you're likely to have one break out only if there's a significant miscalculation on someone's part. Khrushchev's was to believe that Kennedy was weak.

Tensions rose after the Vienna summit, and both sides resumed testing nuclear weapons.* This is the period when the

---

*There had been an unofficial testing moratorium going on. These tests in this period did provide useful data, but they were also in part about sending messages to the other side.

Soviets set off the largest man-made explosion in world history (the "Tsar Bomba"). The United States made up for its lack of size with numbers, carrying out ninety-eight nuclear tests in a single month in 1962.*

Sometime that same year, in a breathtaking example of high-stakes[†] gambling, Khrushchev solved a bunch of his problems in one move by secretly beginning to put nuclear weapons on the island of Cuba. In many ways, it was a brilliant idea, but it all hinged on a single and very slender reed: The Soviets needed to get the missiles and nuclear warheads into Cuba and activate them before the United States knew they were there. If the Americans found out, they would bomb the unfinished missile sites or invade the island, and the entire plan would fall apart. If, however, the missiles became functional before that could happen, any action the United States took would likely prompt the launching of those missiles against the US mainland.[‡] With global thermonuclear war as the stakes, how is it that Khrushchev was comfortable hinging a plan on such a gamble?

On the morning of October 16, 1962, Kennedy's advisers brought him photographs showing the construction of missile sites under way in Cuba. The United States had been watching suspicious activity among Russian handlers off-loading ships

---

*This number is according to the author Donovan Webster. To date more than two thousand nuclear test explosions have taken place in global history.

[†]Some might go so far as to say "reckless," and one of the knocks on Khrushchev later was that he was too much of a gambler.

[‡]Part of the reason for the significance is that unlike in the 1970s and 1980s, when both sides could reach virtually anywhere on the planet with their nukes, the Soviets' capabilities in the early 1960s were such that being able to station missiles in Cuba made much more of the United States vulnerable to a nuclear attack.

already, and Kennedy had asked the Soviets if they were doing anything. The Soviets, in turn, had assured Kennedy nothing was up, but U-2 spy plane photos confirmed everyone's worst fears. Kennedy's CIA advisers thought there would be operational nuclear missiles ninety miles or so off the US coast sometime the following week.

Everything revolved around the operability of the Soviet missiles on Cuba. But there were so many unknowns, and the alarming questions mounted. Were any of the missiles any-where ready to be fired? Were there other sites on the island that hadn't been discovered? Were there nuclear warheads on the island? If so, how many? Were more weapons en route?

Within hours of seeing the photos of the construction sites in Cuba, President Kennedy called a meeting on October 16 of what would become known as the EXCOMM, a group of hand-picked national security advisers, along with some other influ-ential voices whom Kennedy wanted to hear from, including the attorney general, his younger brother Robert.

Unbeknownst to any of the participants at that morning meeting (except his brother), the president taped the meetings.* And at one point, Kennedy reminded everyone there that they were talking about the potential for strikes on American urban

---

*These so-called EXCOMM tapes are some of the most amazing historical primary sources that have ever existed. They recorded the deliberations and decision making of the leadership of one side in what might have been global nuclear Armageddon. They are publicly available to listen to today online. And what's crazy when you listen to them is that they are a com-bination of boring, monotonous office meeting–type conversations with a subject matter that makes the hair on the back of your neck stand up. Even during the most stressful periods, nobody's screaming and yelling. It sounds like a traditional board of directors business meeting. But when you listen to what they're saying, you realize they're talking about death totals that reach Second World War levels in an afternoon.

centers that could cause eighty to one hundred million deaths.[*] Has there ever been a more important series of conversations in the history of the world?

As events unfolded, and with hindsight available to us, it's hard not to be impressed with President Kennedy's ability to push back against the most hawkish of his civilian and military advisers.[†] Since the invention of nuclear weapons, the US military had had its aggressive advocates for their use.[‡] Had Truman heeded them, he'd have used them during the Berlin Blockade and in the Korean War. Eisenhower had multiple occasions when nuclear hawks counseled using the H-bomb. At the EXCOMM meetings, Kennedy's decision against launching air strikes targeting installations on Cuba was opposed *unanimously* by his military advisers.[§]

Yet the young American president played things with extreme care, initiating a blockade on Cuba rather than attacking it. It was an imperfect solution, because it did nothing to disrupt the assembly of the missiles on the island, but like Stalin's play in Berlin in 1948, it threw down a geopolitical card and forced Khrushchev to make a move. Would *he* push things toward war?

---

[*] And that's just for the United States. The Soviet capital of Moscow alone was to be hit with more than a hundred nuclear warheads in the US war plan. President Eisenhower had once said that you could never have a nuclear war because there wouldn't be enough bulldozers to clear the corpses off the streets.

[†] This is where some point to the lessons of the Bay of Pigs and JFK learning to take the hawkish military counsel he'd been getting with a bigger grain of salt.

[‡] The same goes for their counterparts in the Soviet Union.

[§] Many of the civilian advisers agreed with the military. JFK was going against a ton of advice in this situation. Said JFK to his aide David Powers (as quoted by the historian Sheldon M. Stern), "These brass hats have one great advantage in their favor. If we listen to them and do what they want us to do, none of us will be alive later to tell them that they were wrong."

Up to this point, the world had been unaware of the exact details of what was going on, but it's pretty much impossible to make a secret of a blockade, so Kennedy went on television to explain the situation.

Kennedy's speech to the world did two things almost instantaneously: The first was to confirm what the Soviets were already suspecting, that the United States had found their missiles, so the jig was up. The second thing was to inform the world that there might be a global nuclear war in the very near future.

There's never been a public announcement like this in the history of the world. One analogy for the effect this statement had might be that of aliens arriving in a spacecraft over Earth—there's every chance that the world would witness a not unreasonable mass freak-out. If you thought you might not wake up tomorrow and most other people around you were having the same sort of thought, how does that change things in your life? The first lady, Jackie Kennedy, famously said that she didn't want to be evacuated from Washington, DC—if nuclear annihilation was going to happen, she wanted to die with her children and her husband. There are many accounts of people thinking similar things.*

The rest of what history calls the Cuban Missile Crisis played out in real time in front of a global audience. The entire affair lasted about two weeks, and at several points things looked to be tipping toward the abyss. Both Kennedy and Khrushchev had moments of high moral action, and by the later stages of the crisis, both seemed desperate for a way out.

At one point in a communication to the US president, Khrushchev wrote, "Mr. President, we and you ought not now to pull on the ends of the rope in which you have tied the knot of

---

*Bob Dylan supposedly kept working on a song because he wanted to make sure to finish it before he died if nuclear war broke out.

war, because the more the two of us pull, the tighter that knot will be tied. And a moment may come when that knot will be tied so tight that even he who tied it will not have the strength to untie it, and then it will be necessary to cut that knot, and what that would mean is not for me to explain to you, because you yourself understand perfectly of what terrible forces our countries dispose."

Perhaps against the odds, the situation was resolved without war breaking out. At seemingly the last moment, the Soviets accepted a secret quid pro quo missile deal and agreed to remove the nuclear arms from Cuba.

But the affair had mortally terrified everyone. It was likely the closest the world has ever come to nuclear war, and the near miss led to many changes—now based on experience, rather than theory—that would lessen the chances of such a thing happening again.*

By the mid-1960s, while the threat of Armageddon continued, enough lessons had been learned, enough changes made, enough practical experience accrued, and any number of complex systems created that the world didn't seem quite so much like a toddler playing with a machine gun anymore.

THE END OF our world was almost televised.†

At the moment of highest tension and drama during the Cuban Missile Crisis—with Soviet ships approaching the US naval quarantine line—enormous crowds stood in Times Square, reading the electronic news crawl flashing on the

---

*For example, as crazy as it seems now, while the world was teetering on the edge of nuclear disaster, the two superpowers had no good way to directly communicate with each other. They often did so indirectly through media broadcasts, for example. The famed "hotline" telephone system would be set up after the Cuban Missile Crisis, so that when things got frightening, the two sides could speak directly.

† Imagine how this would be with today's media. The graphics alone!

side of the buildings. All three US broadcast networks gave the crisis the equivalent of wall-to-wall-coverage. Primitive hand-drawn little maps behind the news broadcaster Walter Cronkite, with little paper ship counters occasionally being moved closer and closer to that line of quarantine, provided a countdown to catastrophe. The president and his people were watching this coverage, too, and the nation was holding its collective breath.

This was quite a bit different from Edward R. Murrow's groundbreaking live radio broadcast from London as the bombs were dropping on the city during the 1940 Blitz, because unless you lived in London, this didn't have a direct effect on your life. The audience for this live event in 1962—regardless of where they lived—was watching to find out whether or not they would wake up the next morning, and whether or not their children would get to grow up.

The historian H. W. Brands pointed out how this changed the entire equation from anything we human beings had experienced in our previous history:

> When people had labored toward distant goals in the pre-nuclear era, they could console themselves with the knowledge that though they might not live to see their objectives realized, their children or grandchildren might. If the goals were beyond human grasp, each succeeding generation could at least approach a bit closer than the one before. The invention of nuclear weapons changed the situation entirely.
>
> Now, there existed a real possibility that the whole human experiment would be cancelled midway. In that event, not even future generations—because there wouldn't be any—would know how things turned out.

Under the nuclear cloud, the meaning of human existence grew murkier than ever.

Samuel Johnson is supposed to have said, "When a man knows he is to be hanged in a fortnight, it concentrates his mind wonderfully." For that two-week period, when all seemed near lost, humankind treated the threat with the level of gravity it had always deserved. In a perfect world, we would be able to do this continuously, but history has shown that the lesser aspects and banalities of life have a way of intruding.

It's very human, isn't it? Perhaps even a form of survival skill acquired over the ages. How ironic if it turned out to be the reason we took our focus off Bertrand Russell's tightrope long enough to lose our collective balance.

Chapter 8

THE ROAD TO HELL

HOW DID IT come to this? That's the question that would be on everyone's mind had a nuclear war occurred and hundreds or thousands of nuclear weapons been used. Had a full-scale nuclear war broken out, especially after about the late 1960s,[*] we would still be trying to recover today. Hundreds of the world's most important cities would have been hit and transformed instantly into vast, corpse-strewn ruins. The radiation would still be in everything.

A descendant of ours reading a history in the future would be justified in thinking us to be the functional equivalent of the stereotypical reckless and childish "barbarians" that the Romans wrote of, although in possession of absurdly strong weapons they couldn't hope to control. It would be unfair, though, if they thought us evil. The road to hell, it is said, is paved with good intentions, and if a nuclear holocaust had happened, or ever eventually occurs, evil was never why people poured their lives and reputations into such endeavors. So many who helped pave the way to this reality, rather than being murderous Adolf

---

[*] Because of the numbers of weapons on both sides and the modern missile delivery systems.

Eichmann–type monsters, were instead hoping their efforts would lead to better outcomes.*

Start with the famous arms merchant and inventor of dynamite Alfred Nobel,† who did as much as anyone to create the modern growth in weapons power since Napoleon's day. Yet he famously told countess Bertha von Suttner, "Perhaps my factories will put an end to war sooner than your (peace) congresses: on the day that two army corps can mutually annihilate each other in a second, all civilised nations will surely recoil with horror and disband their troops." His sentiment that modern war would be so terrible it might make war impossible is also how many viewed what the new technologies and weapons might do. Such a rationale helps explain why good, ethical people could find themselves part of such a potentially catastrophic outcome. It can also make all sorts of horrible things sound like good ideas.

HOW MUCH WOULD it affect your feelings about a murderous event from history if you found out that you were alive today only because of it? How many strangers' lives from the past is your life today worth? There is no answer to this question, but feeling uneasy about it might not be a bad thing.‡

Many veterans and others who lived through the Second World War believed that the dropping of the atomic bombs on Japan saved their lives. The feeling at the time was that those two detonations over the cities of Hiroshima and Nagasaki in August

---

*One of the weird aspects of history is that it's likely even a person like Eichmann was hoping that his actions would lead to "better outcomes." Of course, his conception of better outcomes was a monstrous one.

†The man the modern peace prize is named after.

‡And take note of the fact that someday, future people could ask whether a ton of *our* current lives are worth a single life of *theirs*.

1945—which cost more than two hundred thousand Japanese lives, including women and children—potentially saved the lives of a million Allied soldiers who might have perished had a land invasion of Japan been necessary. Those veterans might also point out that using the atomic bombs was not wrong under the rules of engagement at the time. But might we also ask how it ever got to the point where those *were* the rules of the game? How did we seemingly modern, ethical people decide that dropping atomic bombs on civilians in cities was okay?

The rules of the game when it comes to modern* warfare are complicated, often contradictory, and, during wartime, usually in flux.† If you had been an American or British general in the Second World War, for example, and had continually ordered your ground forces to destroy the structures and rip up the infrastructure of enemy cities while deliberately yet indiscriminately killing large numbers of the civilian noncombatants, you would have been removed from command. The Allied armies did not engage in this sort of deliberate conduct,‡ but aerial bombing, which accomplished the same thing, was considered acceptable, even routine. In fact, if an air commander could get such results reliably, he very well might have been promoted.

On the surface this looks like a level of hypocrisy Genghis Khan could drive a genocide through.§ It's a difference in

---

*"Modern" requires defining, so let's say after about 1890, when some of the first international conferences were held to discuss such matters.

†Look at the difference in the horrified global reaction to the bombing of cities at the start of the Second World War versus the almost blasé attitude at the end of it.

‡Isolated incidents did happen on smaller scales, but this is a generally true statement.

§The equivalent perhaps of atrocity laundering.

methods, not outcomes. But the architects of such catastrophes were not sadists—most thought (or told themselves) that they were *saving* lives, both friendly and enemy. Many of the Allied ground troops and their loved ones at home agreed with this position. There was scant pushback over ethical concerns while the conflict was raging and people were killing and dying on every front, in every military theater, every day.

The late stages of the Second World War were the last time this planet has seen a case of Total War. Total War is to states what a no-holds-barred death match is to individuals. Ethical lines that might be respected in a limited war* get crossed with impunity in Total War. The stakes are so high that the lens through which everyone begins to view things is a simple one: life or death.

When you think of the old gods of war—Ares in Greek mythology, Mars in Roman—you'll note that they display elements of borderline madness. Combat creates a different reality and different rules, rules that might appear less rational in peacetime. Combat also exerts pressures on the human psyche, tapping into fight-or-flight response and various biochemical releases† that help humans survive dangerous situations. Such conditions and such pressures are not the most conducive to reflective thought. It is for this reason that distinctions are made between actions carried out in "hot blood" versus ones carried out in "cold blood."

But this aspect of individual warriorhood in a battlefield situation is a different beast from the insanity that sometimes operates at the decision-making level. The commanders—the Napoleons, Rommels, Caesars, or Grants—are not battle

---

* "Limited war" is the opposite of Total War.

† How about a little adrenaline, for example?

crazed. They make hard decisions, but they try hard not to make crazy ones. In fact, they often make choices that under the same circumstances we ourselves might make. In war, rational decisions are made for less than rational situations.

By our current peacetime standards, the ethics of Total War might seem hard to justify and easy to condemn. But it's extremely difficult to imagine what it was like to be alive during the last years of the Second World War. Decision makers were faced with often terrible choices. That war was the worst conflict in human history, and it caused suffering on an unimaginable scale all over the world.

What extreme actions would you be willing to contemplate if you could potentially end that war at the very start? Had the British or the French been in possession of a single atomic bomb at that time, would you have been in favor of their dropping it on Berlin once Germany invaded Poland? Such a decision would have doomed about a million Germans to a fiery death, including a ton of women, children, and the elderly and infirm. It would also destroy a cultural center of historic and generational importance. But it might have ended the war on the first day. If it had, many more lives would have been saved than had been sacrificed to that one bomb. The numbers are staggering: thirty million souls lost on the eastern front alone; six million lost in the Holocaust. What is the right move?

Nobody had the chance to make such a decision, because the bomb wasn't successfully tested by anyone until 1945. When it was, though, the Second World War was in its worst year, and such a weapon might well have hastened its end. The man who made the decision to use it (and the only man who ever has) was President Truman, and he was new on the job when he made it. He had been Franklin D. Roosevelt's vice president for only three months when FDR died suddenly, and it was only then that Truman even learned of the atomic bomb's existence.* That's one hell of a thing to lay at the feet of a new president.

This is what he wrote in his diary about a meeting with Stalin and Churchill at Potsdam on July 25, 1945, just two months after taking office:

> We have discovered the most terrible bomb in the history of the world. It may be the fire destruction prophesied in the Euphrates Valley era, after Noah and his fabulous ark. Anyway, we "think" we have found the way to cause a disintegration of the atom. An experiment in the New Mexico desert was startling, to put it mildly. Thirteen pounds of the explosive caused a complete disintegration of a steel tower sixty feet high, created a crater six feet deep and twelve hundred feet in diameter, knocked over a steel tower a half mile away, and knocked men down ten thousand yards away.
>
> The explosion was visible for more than two hundred miles and audible for forty miles and more. This weapon is to be used against Japan between now and August 10. I have told the secretary of war, Mr. Stimson, to use it so that military objectives and soldiers and sailors are the target and not women and children. Even if the Japs are savages, ruthless, merciless, and fanatic, we, as the leader of the world for the common welfare, cannot drop this terrible bomb on the old capital or the new.
>
> He and I are in accord. The target will be a purely military one, and we will issue a warning statement asking the Japs to surrender and save lives. I'm sure they will not

---

*Truman was FDR's third vice president, and he was, shall we say, not invited to every meeting.

do that, but we've given them the chance. It is certainly a good thing for the world that Hitler's crowd or Stalin's did not discover this atomic bomb. It seems to be the most terrible thing ever discovered, but it can be made the most useful.

The official line was indeed that both of the atomic bombs dropped on Japan were dropped on military targets and that the civilians who died were unavoidable collateral damage. How do you drop a bomb knowing it's going to kill fifty thousand or a hundred thousand civilians and say that's an *acceptable* level of collateral damage? From our modern vantage point, after generations of relative peace (and don't forget it's all relative), that would seem a very dubious moral call. But context is everything, and by 1945 the world had been enduring the bloody cost of Total War for six years. To a multitude of very intelligent, even empathetic people all over the world, this seemed like the right decision at the time. And a large part of the reason why is that it was little different from what was already being done.

On the night of March 9–10, 1945, months before the atomic bombs were dropped, Tokyo was bombed with incendiary bombs by more than three hundred US aircraft. Anyone who has ever read accounts of this event (dubbed a "firebombing") understands why an atomic bomb seemed little different from conventional bombing. It doesn't seem possible that conditions could ever be any worse than on the ground after the Tokyo strike, so an atomic bomb was simply a more economical way to accomplish the same outcome. Tokyo was one of the most densely populated places in the world, so even though plenty of military assets in the city were targeted, more than a hundred thousand mostly noncombatants were burned to death. The heat was so intense that liquid glass rolled down the street.

In his book *Bombs, Cities, and Civilians*, Conrad Crane writes:

> Thousands suffocated in shelters or parks. Panicked crowds crushed victims who had fallen in the streets as they surged towards waterways to escape the flames. Perhaps the most terrible incident came when one B-29 dropped seven tons of incendiaries on or around the crowded Kokotoi Bridge. Hundreds of people were turned into fiery torches and splashed into the river below in sizzling hisses. One writer described the falling bodies as resembling tent caterpillars that had been burned out of a tree.
>
> Tail gunners were sickened by the sight of hundreds of people burning to death in flaming napalm on the surface of the Sumida River. A doctor, who observed the carnage there, later said you couldn't even tell if the objects floating by were arms and legs or pieces of burnt wood. B-29 crews fought super-heated updrafts that destroyed at least ten aircraft and wore oxygen masks to avoid vomiting from the stench of burning flesh.

These sorts of bombings had been happening all over Japan. More than sixty Japanese cities were burned off the map by war's end. These firebombing raids were so terrible that several people in high command positions of the US Army Air Forces said that the best thing the atomic bomb did was put an end to them.

TO ANSWER THE question of how people thought it was okay to use nuclear weapons on cities, we need to delve into why they thought bombing noncombatants with any sort of deadly munitions was also ethically supportable. To understand how the rules of warfare change—moving, basically, from shielding noncombatants in their homes to specifically targeting those homes for destruction—we need to see the historical progression of war from the air.

When the First World War ended, the beginnings of the weapons systems that would factor heavily into the fighting of the next world war could be seen. Submarines, for example, were just starting to reveal their potential. Submarines were controversial weapons at the time, though, because of the practice of sinking merchant and commercial vessels with noncombatants on board. Deliberately targeting civilians was, if not unheard of, then heavily frowned upon by the ethical standards of the time. But nothing changed conventional military morality as much as the growing importance of airpower, which was just starting to come into its own in 1918.

Humans have accrued thousands of years' experience and knowledge in the use of land forces and equipment. From the Greeks and Romans to the Chinese and Ottomans, there are endless examples of new technology being introduced into the conduct of land warfare. We have a similarly long history in the fundamentals, physics, and tactics of naval warfare. But by the time the Second World War broke out, airpower was not even fifty years old.[*]

The development of airpower was a tremendously destabilizing force to the more genteel laws of the "limited war" era in the 1800s, at least among European powers fighting other European powers. There were still massacres and other atrocities, but relatively speaking, the states had been fairly civilized with one another

---

[*] It's older if you count zeppelins, but if you're talking about airplanes, the Wright Brothers' first flight at Kitty Hawk, North Carolina, was in 1903.

in war, with professional armies doing the fighting and the civilian populations generally treated well. When air elements, such as hot air balloons, first appeared, they were used for reconnaissance and the like, rather than conflict.

But people feared airpower for its potential role as a weapon system in the future. That fear was a popular subject in science fiction at the time. Jules Verne's novel *Robur the Conqueror* (also known as *The Clipper of the Clouds*), describes a giant gasbag of a ship armed with a gun that could fire down on the world. And H. G. Wells's *The War in the Air* depicts a German zeppelin fleet flying across the Atlantic to bomb New York.

In 1899, Tsar Nicholas II of Russia* called a meeting that would come to be known as the Hague Convention, the first of many to be held on the establishment of international law regarding armaments. There, representatives of more than two dozen countries took up the issue of airships, with the Russians proposing a ban on all bombing from the air. The American delegate counterproposed that the ban last only five years, since the science might improve to allow for precision bombing, which might prove humane insofar as it could shorten wars. This philosophy of airpower's war-shortening potential would become one of the key arguments made by its proponents, but it's also the loophole by which a sort of logical insanity is made possible: If airpower could, through the damage it inflicts, end a war the day or week it began, how much nastiness would it spare the combatants compared with a long war?

The idea of deliberately killing lots of noncombatants to achieve this laudable goal was not what anyone had envisioned before

---

*He would be the last Russian tsar; he stepped down in 1917 at the beginning of the Russian Revolution, and he and his family would be executed in 1918.

the First World War; the genteel, and by modern standards even quaint, people would have recoiled at the concept. Instead, airpower's proponents envisioned air elements attacking the enemy's military installations and targets only. But determining where the line between military and civilian targets existed proved very difficult. Given the technology at the time, accurately hitting the target would also be close to impossible, making any distinction moot. This issue remained mostly theoretical until the First World War broke out in 1914.

When that war did erupt, the populations of the major belligerents were terrified, because they'd been reading about these new air capabilities for years. In one publication, a French aviator explained that the coming war would be over in five minutes—which was good, in his mind—but he predicted that Paris and Berlin and other places would be wiped off the map in the process.

Indeed, early in the war, there were some very small German attempts to bomb Paris via a little rickety plane with an open cockpit and a single person inside who dropped a bomb or two by hand, followed by leaflets that read, "Surrender." A few people were killed on the ground in what can only be described as a terror bombing. (At least, that's what you call it when the other side is doing it to you; it's morale-targeted bombing if you're doing it *to* someone.) The US president, Woodrow Wilson, issued a public rebuke of Germany for what amounted to a crime against humanity (by nineteenth-century standards).*

The French would attempt to target military locations by air,

---

*In 1914 a US president harshly condemned a tiny bomb or two dropped by a lone prop plane. That's a mere twenty-six years before the Luftwaffe was bombing London day and night during the Blitz, and three decades or so before German and Japanese cities were being erased. That's a long moral chasm crossed in a short span of time. Two world wars can do that.

sending in a couple of bombers to take out a bullet factory, for example. The Americans also ultimately embraced this precision-bombing idea even though there was nothing precise about any of it and hitting the right target proved to be a crapshoot.

By 1915, the war had bogged down on the western front, and all sides were looking for ways to get past the stalemate.

For a long time, the Germans had kept their zeppelin fleet under wraps rather than trying to use it, letting it serve as a deterrent. By 1915, however, they were attempting to find more aggressive ways to employ the technology. That year, the Germans sent the lighter-than-air fleet to Britain to bomb from the skies, H. G. Wells style, and they killed civilians. Given President Wilson's reaction to the earlier minibombing in Paris, this was a monumental moment, and Germany's opponents used it in their propaganda. Back in Germany, the commanders thought their bombing effort might actually end the war.[*]

The reality of these giant gasbags filled with flammable hydrogen was that they were vulnerable, so once the British developed a way to attack the zeppelins, the German losses mounted, and the attacks trailed off. Nonetheless, the zeppelin attacks had been an unnerving harbinger of things to come.

Later in the war, the Germans would build giant prop-driven bombers, some of them with wingspans almost as large as those of the World War II B-17 "Flying Fortress." These Gotha bombers would fly in large numbers over Britain, releasing their bombs. They did surprisingly little damage, but people on the ground were extremely shaken. These attacks would provide some of the earliest evidence that, in contrast to the pro-bombing theories that suggested that civilians would petition their government to end a war because they couldn't

[*] Of course, they turned out to be wrong.

stand the aerial assault, such attacks actually strengthened the resolve of their victims.

But bombing's proponents had a legitimate excuse for why airpower wasn't more decisive in the First World War—the technology* simply wasn't there yet. Had early twentieth-century air forces been capable of inflicting late–Second World War levels of destruction, perhaps the story would have been different. If the early Gotha raids, for example, had sparked a firestorm that killed forty thousand Londoners in 1918, while torching a huge part of the historic city, it might have shocked people enough to have perhaps broken the stalemate. Instead, a case can be made that being early victims of strategic bombing in the First World War had a toughening effect on Britons and helped them weather the Second World War's aerial storm when it came.

Nonetheless, by the end of the First World War, the future importance—not to mention the potential frightfulness—of airpower was clear. Fascinating proposals were advanced after the war to put airpower solely in the hands of the international community for safekeeping via the League of Nations (the forefather of the United Nations). If one nation started causing trouble, the league would use the only air force in existence and bomb the troublemaker into swift submission, to enforce the will of the world community.

The stalemate on the western front and the relentless daily mounting of the death toll seemed to reinforce an old military maxim that the worst of all evils is a prolonged war. Anything that might shorten a conflict will save lives. Proponents of airpower were convinced it would do just this.

Given that most of global public opinion before the Second

---

*The doctrine wasn't, either. But before you figure out how to employ the effective planes, you need to have them.

World War considered the deliberate bombing of civilians in cities to be a war crime, influential aerial thinkers like the Italian Giulio Douhet were advocating that strategies that amounted to war crimes[*] be employed when the next war broke out. His motives were to prevent what he and many others considered to be the greater war crime—another long modern war like the First World War. Douhet was one of many aerial thinkers who considered it their job to prevent another long, meat grinder–like war like the one that had just ended. He said that airpower would decide a future war before the armies and navies of the combatants even had a chance to mobilize. He suggested that, when war broke out again, three kinds of bombs be dropped on the enemy's cities: the first were to be high explosives, which would blow things up; the second, incendiary bombs, which would light on fire everything that had been shattered and scattered by the first bombs; and the third, gas weapons, which would make the area uninhabitable—even firemen wouldn't be able to go in and put the fires out, so the city would burn down.

Doing all this, Douhet wrote, would mean the home front, the factories, and the war-making capabilities of any enemy city would all be destroyed, but "the effect of such aerial offensives upon morale may well have more influence upon the conduct of the war than their material effects."

Consider the possible effect of Douhet's ideas on the civilians of cities not yet struck but possibly subject to such bombing attacks. What civil or military authority could keep public order, maintain essential services, and continue industrial production under such a threat? And even if a semblance of order was maintained and some work done, would not the sight of a single enemy plane be enough to stampede the population into panic?

[*] By the standards of that era.

In short, normal life would be impossible in this constant night-mare of imminent death and destruction.

Douhet predicted that a country "subjected to this kind of merciless pounding from the air" could not help but experience a "complete breakdown of the social structure." If only to stop "the horror and suffering, the people themselves, driven by the instinct of self-preservation, would rise up and demand an end to the war," and they would do it quickly, "before their army and navy had time to mobilize at all."

In making the logical case for what his more genteel con-temporaries might consider an insanity, Douhet wasn't worried about morality or feasibility—he was concerned only about effectiveness, an effectiveness that would greatly shorten any war, which would be the most moral outcome possible.

IT WAS DURING the interwar period that air weapons were developed with the expectation that a future war would be fought with them. In countries that had been traumatized by the First World War, military thinking assumed the public would support the use of these weapons to avoid their being used against them first.

American air theorists, on the other hand, were under the impression that American public opinion would not allow the development of an air arm designed to blow up women and children and cities. These theorists believed that American sensibilities would support only the idea of *precision* air-power, the kind that would target things and not people. As the American airpower expert Conrad Crane wrote, "Preci-sion bombing doctrine, attacking factories instead of women and children, offered a way for the Air Corps to be decisive in war without appearing immoral."

The giant B-17 heavy bombers—destined to be one of the

most well-known planes of the Second World War—first rolled off the production line in 1936. B-17s were designed to deliver strategic, high-level bombing, and a lot of them had been already built by the time the United States joined the conflict in 1941. And the highly touted Norden bombsight,* installed in the B-17, would supposedly allow precision bombing from thousands of feet up in the air. The Americans and the French led the way on this idea of targeting rail yards and docksides and factories while trying to avoid civilian casualties.

In Britain, the air theorist James Spaight similarly felt that airpower was a necessary evil, because at the time it was believed that there was no defense against the bomber. The British therefore concluded that an "if you hit me, I'll hit you" deterrent was the best guarantor of their cities' safety, even though it would lead to what we now call mutually assured destruction.

There is some logic to this idea. In the later stages of the First World War, the Germans stopped their heavy bombing campaign against Britain because British capabilities had advanced to the point where they would soon be able to do to German cities what the Germans were doing to the British. In the years after the war, the British continued to build a strategic air capability—not to incinerate enemy cities per se, but as a way to stop the enemy from doing it to them first.

After the war, Spaight came up with an idea that's since been used as a science fiction premise: he suggested that one could warn the enemy to evacuate a targeted city ahead of time.

The historian Lee Kennett writes that Spaight considered the effect in "the City," London's historic financial district. "The day population of [the City's] 675 acres was over four hundred thousand people; at night that figure dropped to

---

*Many feel it was overrated.

fourteen thousand. If arrangements could be made to lodge those fourteen thousand elsewhere, the City would become an area in which enemy bombers could do enormous material damage, but at the same time spare human life."

While such theoretical discussions were going on, tensions around the world began to greatly increase. Fascism came to power in Italy, and then in Germany. This added to the global tension already in place because of the radical revolutionary Bolshevik state called the Soviet Union centered in the former Russia and the growing violence between the Japanese and Chinese. The Great Depression was also hitting across the globe. And the entity that was meant to ensure such pressures didn't lead to another world war was failing dramatically.

The earlier suggestion of relegating the control of military aircraft solely to the League of Nations had never been realistically considered, and the problems airpower posed plagued the league during the interwar years. Some of the great powers, for example, used airpower to keep down tribal natives in European colonies. It turns out that airpower was far more effective than troops on the ground for controlling people. The league chastised Fascist Italy for its air tactics in its war with Ethiopia, slapping the country with economic sanctions, but nothing ultimately changed. The Japanese virtually sneered at the League of Nations when it tried to address Japanese aggression in China. Even Britain and France weren't keen on the league telling them what to do in their colonial territories. The United States—which had been a prime mover in creating the postwar organization—essentially abandoned it when the Senate neglected to ratify the treaty or join the league.

Then, in 1936, there came an opportunity to test, employ, and perfect what might be called the beta version of Second World War airpower. In the Spanish Civil War, several future

World War II belligerents began aiding one side or the other, with Hitler's Germany and Mussolini's Italy, for example, offering training, equipment, supplies, and even pilots to the Nationalists in their rebellion against the Republican government; while the Soviets, Mexicans, and French (in a clandestine way at least) gave aid to the Republicans.

Germany would learn a lot about air warfare in Spain, especially from the bombing of the Basque city of Guernica, an incident immortalized in the Picasso painting of the same name. The Italians and the Germans claimed to have been after military targets, especially a bridge, but it was allegedly a market day, which meant the city would have been more crowded than usual. Here is how the historian David Clay Large describes the afternoon attack by the German Condor Legion commanded by Wolfram Freiherr von Richthofen:[*]

At about 4:40 p.m., two nuns on the roof of La Merced Convent in Guernica rang a bell and shouted "Avion! Avion!" According to witnesses, within a few moments of that warning, a single plane appeared over the eastern end of town. The aircraft, a Heinkel 111, passed once over the city, then returned and dived in the direction of Renteria bridge.

Though there was no flak—Guernica had no antiaircraft guns—the plane's bombs landed not on the bridge but about 300 meters to the southwest in a plaza fronting the railroad station. One bomb tore up the Julian Hotel across the plaza. A volunteer fireman saw women and children blown high into the air and then raining

---

[*] Cousin of Manfred von Richthofen, a.k.a. "the Red Baron," the renowned First World War flying ace.

down in "legs, arms, heads, and bits of pieces every-where."

About twenty-five minutes later, three more Heinkel 111s appeared low in the sky. Their bombs, released at about 2,000 feet, hit a candy factory near the Renteria bridge, igniting cauldrons of sugar syrup and turning the factory into an inferno. Young female workers, some of them on fire, began stampeding from the building. The central marketplace, not far away, was also hit. Two bulls, sprayed with burning thermite, charged through the canvas-walled stalls, setting the entire market ablaze.

Next, five pairs of Heinkel 51 fighters zoomed in very low over parts of the town not yet obscured by smoke. According to one witness, two of the planes "just flew back and forth at about one hundred feet, like flying sheep dogs rounding up people for the slaughter." One plane zeroed in on a woman and her three small children, killing them all in a single burst. Another wiped out the town band.

At about 6:00 p.m., the first bombers—Junkers 52s and Italian Savoys—neared the target. They came in groups of three, wave after wave, carrying among them almost 100,000 pounds of high explosives. These they dropped helter-skelter through the smoke and dust hanging over the town. One bomb hit a *pelota frontón*—a jai alai court; another blew up the Bank of Vizcaya; and still another demolished an orphanage. By the time the last of the bombers had headed back to their bases, roughly two-thirds of the buildings in Guernica were leveled or on fire.

Pictures of dead babies appeared in the media around the world; the German and Italian governments were embarrassed. While the number of casualties was not that heavy—fewer than the number of people killed on 9/11, for example—the indiscriminate nature of the attacks prompted outrage.

The governments might have been shamed, but the architects of the attack were elated. The German commander, von Richthofen, wrote in his diary, "Absolutely fabulous. City was completely closed off for at least 24 hours that would have guaranteed immediate conquest if troops would have attacked right away, but at least we had a complete technical success with our 250s and firebombs."

As nasty as the attack on Guernica was, it probably wouldn't have been prohibited by any of the major militaries of the day. The historian Tami Davis Biddle has considered what some of the military manuals from just before the Second World War say on the matter. The British Royal Air Force (RAF) manual rules that it's not only okay to go after public and private buildings, but it's part of what you do to induce the enemy to surrender — which is a nice way of saying that you can pound them into submission. A German military manual specifically rules that it's permissible to go after the morale of the enemy at its root . . . oh, and also strike military installations.

The British aviator James Spaight pointed out that when it came to bombing, the rules of war had loopholes you could pilot a B-17 through. The number-one loophole was the question of military installations. Everyone agreed that it was permissible to use airpower to hit military targets. The problem was that the accuracy of the technology at the time didn't allow aircraft to reliably hit military targets. British tests right before the Second World War showed that fewer than two-thirds of bombers placed their bombs within five miles of an intended target. With accuracy like that, allowing bombing in civilian areas in order to go after military targets was the same as saying it was legal to kill civilians.

———

THE AIR WAR didn't break out the way many had imagined it would. When the British prime minister Neville Chamberlain announced on the radio that Britain was at war, air raid sirens went off in London, but the Luftwaffe didn't come. Nonetheless, after the fall of France in June 1940, things looked grave; Britain's very national survival was at stake.

Once the Battle of Britain* began, the stakes were as high as could be imagined: a German invasion. But this could happen only if the Luftwaffe won control of the air. The British fleet could halt any channel crossing as long as its ships weren't bombed to the bottom of the sea. And if the Germans crossed the channel and started splashing up on British beaches, Churchill planned on using poison gas. Is anybody going to cry "war crime" if the Nazis are landing fifty miles from your house?

The early targets identified by the Germans for air attacks were radar installations and airfields; and, for a time, the Luftwaffe seemed to be gaining the upper hand. Then the "we don't deliberately bomb cities" moral line was breached supposedly due to a tit-for-tat mix-up that had the Luftwaffe accidentally bombing London, followed by a British retaliatory raid on Berlin, followed by a full-bore deliberate assault on British cities by the Germans in response.†

On September 4, 1940, Hitler, playing the victim, said in a speech, "I have tried to spare the British. They have mistaken my humanity for weakness and have replied by murdering German women and children. If they attack our cities, we will simply erase theirs."

---

*The air war that began between the Luftwaffe and the Royal Air Force after the fall of France in 1940.

†Some claim that German ordnance had been released accidentally and struck London. The British then bombed Berlin in a token retaliation.

The Luftwaffe's foray into bombing British cities, especially the Blitz in London, marked the beginnings of strategic bombing in a way that would become horribly familiar—first in England, then in Germany, then in Japan. Places like Warsaw and Rotterdam had been bombed earlier in the war in single incidents, but the Blitz was not a strike, it was an ongoing ordeal that lasted for months.

Generally, the bombers of the Second World War were of medium size, but some were huge. The US B-29 Superfortress, built in the final years of the war, was the size of a modern commercial airliner. Picture hundreds of them in the sky over your city, dropping bombs that would create an unholy inferno when they hit the ground. It's a horrifying image.

The author Hermann Knell, himself a survivor of World War II strategic bombing attacks, wrote about the German raids on the British capital during the Blitz in his book, *To Destroy a City*:

From September 7 until November 13, London was bombarded every night. A total of 13,000 tons of high explosives and 12,000 incendiary canisters were dropped. Other cities were raided, too, and the most famous raid is the one on Coventry on 14 November 1940, when 450 bombers discharged 500 tons of high explosives and 880 incendiary canisters. Civilian losses were appalling, mainly because there were few adequate air raid shelters.

The attacks failed both to stop the British raids over Germany and to squash morale. Indeed, the whole idea of using bombers to destroy civilian morale was flawed for several reasons. One may have been the bravery of the citizenry. Studies showed that, at first, victims just got angry at the enemy and hoped their own air force would strike back. When it got really nasty, and the people had been bombed to near oblivion, a resigned, just-trying-to-survive kind of depression crept in. What was avowedly not happening, though, were marches demanding an immediate end to the war.

Morale bombing turned out not to work, but too many people had too much invested in it to change course. As writes Len Deighton, a former RAF member, when the RAF was confronted with evidence that the British population didn't crack under the Blitz, what made its leadership think the Germans would do so? The RAF's response was that British civilians were stronger than Germans.

Air Marshal Arthur "Bomber" Harris—the man who would become known for leading Britain's bombing campaign in Germany—said, "There are a lot of people who say that bombing can never win a war. Well, my answer to that is that it's never been tried yet, and we shall see." (Harris would go on to pay the Germans back exponentially for what they did to Britain.)

Forty thousand British civilians were killed in strategic attacks during the war, a horrific number of people, but there are few accounts in the history books of the true nastiness of what those people went through—it's difficult to find photos of British casualties, or even graphic descriptions of the carnage. The British focused their reports on how much damage to historic buildings was done but rarely talked about the people who were killed. Doing so, it was felt, wouldn't be good for morale, and Churchill wouldn't allow anything in newspapers or magazines that didn't show Britain pluckily holding up under the German barrage.

The Germans, on the other hand, would send a plane over to take pictures of the damage, then rush the pictures to headquarters, where air scientists and theorists and pilots would determine how well the raid had done.*

The diabolical nature of strategic bombing—whether via atomic bombs or conventional bombs—reveals itself in the nitty-gritty details involved in the craft. Delayed-fuse bombs, for instance, which were dropped with timers so they didn't go off until hours after they hit the ground, had two roles: first, to kill any rescuers; second, to tell people not to bother sending rescuers next time. And remember: this was all done, and justified, in the name of shortening the war by making it worse.

The physicist Freeman Dyson, who worked for the RAF's Bomber Command, said years after the war, "I felt sickened by what I knew. Many times, I decided I had a moral obligation to run out into the streets and tell the British people what stupidities were being done in their name. But I never had the courage to do it. I sat in my office until the end, carefully calculating how to murder most economically another hundred thousand people."

It takes time to get to a point of logical insanity. It doesn't happen the moment war breaks out; it ratchets up over the course of time and events. No one wanted to be the first to drop bombs on cities from the air, but then the other side did it, so they responded. They said they'd go after only military targets, until they figured out they couldn't fly bombers in daylight because they'd get massacred by air defenses and fighters, so they decided to bomb at night. The problem was that they already couldn't hit their targets in daylight, so when they decided to fly bombers at night, it was with the implicit acknowledgment that they were just randomly dropping bombs on cities.

---

*The British would start to do this later, as would the Americans.

"In theory, they were still trying to bomb a list of targets much like the ones they failed to hit in daylight," Len Deighton writes about the Germans' change of strategy. "In practice, they did as the Royal Air Force Bomber Command was doing. They tried to find a big city center and set light to it."

In June 1941, the British officially said they were going to start targeting the morale and living arrangements of the enemy's workers, and they were going to drop their bombs at night. ("Terror bombing" when the Germans did it, remember; "morale bombing" when the British did it.) For the British, this was one of precious few remaining methods they possessed at that time in the war to strike at Germany.

The German author Jörg Friedrich called the fleet of the Combined Bombing Offensive "the most ominous weapon ever to have been aimed at humans." (After the war, Air Marshal Harris, who oversaw the effort, firmly believed it had saved an entire generation of British soldiers.)

The majority of the air leaders during the Second World War had fought in the First World War as pilots or soldiers, from the Luftwaffe's Hermann Göring to Air Marshal Harris to US Army Air Force general Curtis LeMay, and to them anything was better than what they had experienced on the front lines twenty years earlier. Harris makes a point that the Royal Navy in the First World War allegedly starved eight hundred thousand mostly noncombatant Germans—all under the laws of war during the British naval blockade—and that this was considered morally acceptable because it was done to save the lives of soldiers fighting on the western front.[*]

Tami Davis Biddle asks in her essay "Air Power and the Law

---

[*]Not by everyone, of course. German attitudes differed markedly and understandably from British ones.

of War," "How does one weigh the lives of one's own soldiers against the lives of enemy civilians?" And when Britain began bombing Germany, some pacifist clerics brought up the question of when it was better to lose a war than to cross a certain moral threshold to win it.

US Army Air Force leader Henry "Hap" Arnold said after hundreds of thousands of civilians had died, "When used with the proper degree of understanding, the bomber becomes, in effect, the most humane of all weapons." The worst carnage occurred when the conditions were just right.* Under certain circumstances the bombing could create a phenomenon known as a firestorm, which can happen when there are many blazes in a given area—in this case, a city—and they merge into one huge inferno. When that happens, a giant updraft of heat pulls the air upward, and all the cooler air on the ground gets sucked into the vortex, creating hurricane-force, superheated winds.

In a situation like this, people can meet their end in any number of ways. A person could be killed by the blast itself—the lungs burst, the veins and nerves absorb the shock, and death follows. Victims could be burned to death from flames or crushed under giant pieces of concrete or buildings (unlike a bullet, which creates a personal wound that may prove fatal, bombs destroy the world around the victim, too). Many were asphyxiated by the carbon monoxide that blew into bomb shelters or were deprived of oxygen after the firestorm sucked the air from a room. (Photos of such scenes exist; beware, they are gruesome.)

The worst night of the London Blitz was so bad that a firestorm developed, creating perhaps the worst conflagration the city had seen since the Great Fire of 1666. Yet this paled in

---

* Or wrong, if you are the nation being bombed.

comparison with the payback delivered against German cities.* The first really terrible attack happened in Hamburg in 1943; an estimated forty to fifty thousand people were incinerated.

Kate Hoffmeister was nineteen years old in 1943, writes Gwynne Dyer in his book *War*, when she survived a bombing raid. Hers is among the most extreme human experiences imaginable. On leaving the shelter, Hoffmeister entered a world that had become a burning inferno. People's gas masks had melted onto their faces. Dyer quotes Hoffmeister's experience: "We couldn't go on across the Eiffestrasse because the asphalt had melted. There were people on the roadway, some already dead, some still lying alive but stuck in the asphalt. They must have rushed on to the roadway without thinking. Their feet had got stuck, and then they put out their hands to try to get out again. They were on their hands and knees screaming."

Once these firestorms started happening, a precedent had been established that could not be broken. Forty thousand people died in the London Blitz over a period of eight months (that's more than most militaries in premodern times lost in a whole war); the Germans in Hamburg lost that many in one evening. If there was ever a time to look into the abyss and turn away, that would have been it.

Few were in a position to do so, but the prime minister of Great Britain might have been one of them. Winston Churchill is supposed to have reacted in horror when viewing film from the nose camera of a plane of the damage being done to these German cities. According to an Australian military attaché who

---

*The Luftwaffe, which early on in its development had flirted with a doctrine emphasizing strategic bombing, had switched by the war's outbreak to more of an emphasis on tactical air attacks. Tactical attacks focus more on the battlefield level than a citywide level. When German Stuka dive-bombers attack tanks, that's an example of tactical bombing.

was with him at the time, Churchill sat bolt upright in his chair and said loudly, "Are we beasts? Are we taking this too far?" This is the same Churchill who is quoted as saying in 1940, "A fire in his own backyard will force Hitler to retreat, and we will make Germany a desert, yes, a desert."

Churchill was also concerned with the loss of European heritage that the bombing was causing. Even after the people being directly affected by the war were dead and gone, their great-great-great-grandchildren would still suffer the loss of their heritage going back to Roman times. Their cultural inheritance was being destroyed by this logical insanity. And it wasn't just Europe. It was happening in Japan and China and lots of other countries.*

FDR held two different positions on bombing enemy cities: in public, he was against it; in private, he was for it. On August 4, 1941, he made a statement recorded by US treasury secretary Henry Morgenthau (as quoted by Conrad Crane): "Well, the way to lick Hitler is the way I've been telling the English but they won't listen to me. I've suggested again and again that if they sent a hundred planes over Germany for military objectives that ten of them should bomb some of these smaller towns that haven't been bombed before. There must be some kind of factory in every town. That's the only way to break German morale."

By 1943, the casualties were mounting at a horrifying pace, and the number continued to grow. The United States would lose more people in the final year of the hostilities than it lost in the entire rest of the war.

General Douglas MacArthur hated the firebombing. One of

---

*It continues into very recent history, as bombings in, say, Iraq damaged ancient Babylonian and Assyrian sites.

his aides, essentially writing on his behalf, called it "one of the most ruthless and barbaric killings of noncombatants in all history." MacArthur actually put his troops in harm's way and lost men in order to protect civilians and not bomb civilian targets, a decision even today some would argue was wrong.

Some of the most powerful people in the world seemed powerless to halt the momentum of these atrocities. George Marshall, the top US general conducting the war, and Henry Stimson, the US secretary of war, both didn't like what was happening and yet couldn't stop it. Stimson said that the Manhattan Project physicist J. Robert Oppenheimer thought it was appalling that there wasn't more public outrage in the United States over the firebombings and attacks on civilians—he didn't want the attacks to stop, necessarily, he was just disturbed that more people weren't upset about it.

It is a sign of the insanity of the times that the very people who had designed a precision-oriented air force because public opinion before the war wouldn't condone the targeting of women and children had by 1944 largely shed those concerns. But cities had lots of military targets, so if you wiped an entire city off the map, you were taking out lots of military targets.

Japan, in a move that unwittingly came at unfathomable cost, decided to spread its industry among civilian areas. The Japanese made every block have a small factory on it, so that production wasn't concentrated where bombers could destroy it. This, naturally enough, turned out to provide a convenient justification for leveling everything.

Technology now provided physical distance from the damage being inflicted, too. Army lieutenant colonel Dave Grossman, an expert in military psychology, writes about how distance makes killing possible and how the farther away one is from the target, the easier it is to kill. None of what was done to Japan and to

Germany, nor what the Germans did to Britain, would likely have happened had the soldiers been required to inflict it face-to-face by hand.

Grossman writes about one of the raids that killed seventy thousand people from the air in an evening: "If bomber crew members had to turn a flamethrower on each one of these seventy thousand women and children, or worse yet slit each of their throats, the awfulness and trauma inherent in the act would have been of such a magnitude that it simply would not have happened. But when it is done from thousands of feet in the air, where the screams cannot be heard and the burning bodies cannot be seen, it is easy." American aircrews returned from one of the Tokyo fire raids smelling like burning people. The bottoms of their planes were scorched, and they supposedly handed in their after-action reports with shaking hands.

Conrad Crane quotes a US official on the use of the air force to target civilians: "Isn't that the same as ordering ground forces to kill all the civilians and destroy all the buildings as they fight?"

Well, sort of, except that, as we've said, ground forces, like naval forces, have the benefit of thousands of years of codified behavior in war and an understanding of what's permissible and what's not.

By February 1945, there were complaints that there was nothing left to bomb in Germany, that all the Allies were doing was making the rubble bounce—and yet it didn't stop them from continuing. After the war, at the Nuremberg war crimes trials, the defendants—most of whom would be hanged for crimes against humanity—complained about the Allied bombings of German cities. One of the Allies' chief counsels said the aerial bombardments had "become a recognized part of modern warfare as carried on by all nations." So the horse was out of the barn on that ethical question.

If the Allies didn't stop bombing the Germans when they were effectively defeated, how could anyone have stopped attacks in the Pacific theater, where the Japanese were, relatively speaking, stronger?* Indeed, the idea of a "death blow from the air," once floated as a tool against Germany, would resurface in August 1945. The day-to-day casualties were horrific at that point, and every day the war was shortened, thousands and thousands of lives could be saved.

Days after the two atomic bombs were dropped on Japan, and before the surrender was finalized, a thousand planes dropped firebombs on Tokyo. Again.

To focus on the Allied bombing attacks in a vacuum, however, is to forget the stakes, and the nature of the opponents. The air force historian Bruce Hopper, after visiting the Buchenwald death camp in April 1945, wrote: "Stench everywhere: piles of human bone remnants at the furnace. Here is the antidote to qualms about strategic bombing." At the 1899 Hague Convention, it had been the American delegation who had said that bombers could someday be made precise enough that they wouldn't hurt civilians, meaning that they would be a humanitarian weapon. It was the United States, too, that felt that its citizens wouldn't stand for a military policy that indiscriminately killed so many noncombatants. How ironic that this was the same nation—the only nation—that used an atomic bomb, perhaps the most indiscriminate killer of civilians in world history.

The logic of Total War is brutal.

Fast forward fifteen years and, by codifying the rules after the war that using bombs and high-altitude explosives on

---

*The Germany First policy of the Allies had prioritized attacks on the Third Reich. By early 1945, Germany was in a much more precarious position than the still uninvaded Japan, with multiple enemy armies fighting on German soil and every major German city in ruins.

inhabited areas was legal—after all, everyone was doing it—the United States had opened itself up to being targeted by nuclear weapons during the Cold War. The magnitude of the logical insanity would grow exponentially when world leaders started talking about whether it was morally acceptable or justifiable to exterminate 100 million human beings to save the lives of 300 million.

It is certainly logical to try to minimize death totals, especially if you save 300 million people in the process. But it would be difficult to put a spin on the violent deaths of 100 million human beings at the hands of your weaponry in any way that looks sane and beneficent.

If humankind ever spawns another dark age because we engage in a global thermonuclear war, perhaps we will all feel as Charlton Heston did when he screamed, "You maniacs! You blew it up!" But if that is the outcome we get, it won't be because that's what anybody wanted at the time.

AFTERWORD

THE FERMI PARADOX is named after the famous physicist Enrico Fermi, who did the math and figured out that, statistically speaking, the universe should contain a ton of intelligent life. So, he asked, where were they? He and others then started speculating about all the reasons that might explain why extraterrestrial life might not be here, and one of them was that they didn't survive long enough to migrate beyond their home world.* This idea is part of an aspect of the Fermi Paradox known as the Great Filter. It's possible most life on other planets never made it through the great filter.

I was born in 1965. At that time the world lived in justifiable fear that a nuclear war might end modern civilization. It wasn't long afterward that a mass understanding of the many threats facing the global environment began to take hold. This double sword of Damocles still hangs above us today. Perhaps they are both part of our great filter test.

Whether you are optimistic or pessimistic about our civilization's long-term chances may depend on your view of how much we human beings can change. We laud ourselves for the adaptability of our species, but these are difficult challenges that may

---

*Economist Robin Hanson, for example, who is also involved with the fascinating Oxford University Future of Humanity Institute.

have sunk many other intelligent life forms before us. If we do what we have always done, we can depend on outcomes that are disastrous. If we engage in another total war between the great powers, we will do damage on a scale that has no comparable historical analogy. If we cannot change enough to deal with the modern global version of the environmental damage that human beings traditionally do to their immediate surroundings, we will cause ramifications that affect almost every aspect of life. Either one of these scenarios could cause the sort of downstream problems like starvation, disease, mass migration, geopolitical upheaval, piracy, and systems collapse that we dealt with in some of the earlier chapters of this book.

If we wish to look on the bright side, we can hope for innovations and discoveries to create conditions in which we can continue to live as we do and not kill ourselves—the invent-our-way-out-of-it scenario. Then there's also the possibility that Fermi's paradox could get blown out of the water and beings from other solar systems could arrive and begin to use their advanced technology to solve our problems. Of course, that's quite a bit to depend on.

But, should the worst happen, perhaps humans will adjust to the new conditions. Be it the post–World War III world or an apocalyptic overpopulation/environmental wasteland, maybe the idea that tough times make tough people will remind us that we as a species are survivors. Children will be raised differently, expectation levels will change, and we could easily see people adapt as much to fit into their less rosy world as we have seen humans adjust and evolve into the world created once the era of computers and cell phones began.

The possibility also exists that our ecological system will be the one to adjust, giving the people who rely on it no say in the matter. It's certainly conceivable that nature has its own ways to rebalance itself. If there are far too many people for the ecosystem to support at modern consumption levels, maybe something like a modern plague "fixes" things by halving global population levels in a decade. Would that be a good thing?

Or maybe the next Dark(er) Age is one we trigger intentionally. It's certainly possible that someday environmental problems could necessitate society forcibly cutting things like energy use (as one example) or any of the other elements of modern society that require the high voltage of the twenty-first-century lifestyle. What if there were far less power and energy available in the world a hundred years from now? Fewer electronics or devices or conveniences like refrigeration, sure, but what if it's to combat a potentially existential threat? If our children do not have our level of capabilities because the power doesn't exist, does that mean they live in a worse time? Or is it a better time because they are possibly making headway against extremely significant, potentially extinction-related problems we are currently far from solving? If their situation allows them to progress through the Great Filter successfully, but ours doesn't, who is really ahead?

Yet even this characterization is simplistic. If the true threat to humanity turns out to be something more like a virus or an asteroid, it might be the very societies that most endanger us environmentally or militarily that have the advantage in dealing with the danger. It would be incredibly ironic if a civilization-killing asteroid that has been on target to hit Earth for perhaps millions of years was only thrown off course at the last minute by the timely use of a nuclear weapon. A bomb developed to kill millions, shot into space on a missile similar to the ones that would have devastated our cities in any Third World War, saves everyone and (historically speaking) was developed just in time to play that role.

That scenario sounds about as plausible to my ears as the likelihood of my alternative book title coming true. It was going be called *And They All Lived Happily Ever After.* How do I define "happily"? Humanity living in an age when, for once in our existence, it is not the case that the end is always near.

ACKNOWLEDGMENTS

IT WOULD PROBABLY take up less page space to list those to whom I do not owe a debt of thanks for this book rather than the reverse. I hate to single people out, though, so I am ditching that idea. Also, since I've decided that I have too many friends, I will keep this brief. Instead, I will take the conventional route because in my case it happens to be true. Without my family there is no book or anything else. My endlessly patient wife, Brittany; my daughters, Avery and Liv; my über-talented mom, my mother-in-law, my sister, my brothers, my sisters-in-law, and my brothers-in-law. It is no cliché to say they make my life worth living.

Being a history geek, how can I leave out those who are not here now but who are also in large part responsible for me.* I had both a father and a stepfather that any person would have been lucky to get in an either-or deal. They helped me so much and I miss them terribly. I never knew my dad's dad, but my maternal grandfather was Batman.† Proof indeed that the apple *can* fall far from the tree. I miss him greatly, too. At his funeral the man who knew him giving the eulogy said of his wife, my

---

*Note, these are also the people to *blame*, depending on the point-of-view.

†For all intents and purposes. A chain-smoking, drinking, Irish, curly-haired ginger Batman.

grandmother, that had it not been for my grandfather she would have been president of the United States. So she was really something herself (and more proof about the apple tree thing). I miss her fiercely as well.

I've never officially confirmed the existence of my longtime podcasting partner Ben, nor am I doing so now, but even if he's the equivalent of Elwood Dowd's white rabbit, Harvey, there's no book without all that he's (seemingly) done. Thanks, buddy.

My co-writer, Elizabeth Stein, turned working with an impossible person and impossible material into something possible. I have always enjoyed watching gifted people plying their trade and she was so good at what she does. I appreciate the many things she did to make this book a reality. I owe my sanity to her on at least a few occasions.

My literary agent Andrew Stuart was the actual genesis of this work. Somebody has to eventually say, "Ever thought of writing a book?" for a project to get started, and that's how this one began. Unfortunately for Andrew the work for him didn't stop there, but he's infinitely patient and like Liz Stein excellent at his craft.

My extreme thanks to both of my editors: Luke Dempsey, who I so wanted to work with that he enticed me to HarperCollins and set the tone for the work, and Eric Nelson, who took over the project before publication and had to finish all that difficult heavy lifting that traditionally happens as a book nears publication. Lifting that I gladly would have helped more with were I my grandfather's grandson. I am thankful for the both of them.

Finally, and I say this all the time but that's because I think about it all the time, my thanks to the avid listeners of the podcasts we do. You have supported us, promoted us, encouraged us, and helped us mold the work into its current form. You have been doing this since 2005. Every day I realize how fortunate I am. Where on earth would we be without you?

FURTHER READING

Want to know more? Here are a few places you can start.

Chapter 1: Do Tough Times Make for Tougher People?

Delbrück, Hans. *Warfare in Antiquity.* Vol. 1 of *History of the Art of War.* Translated by Walter J. Renfroe Jr. Omaha: University of Nebraska Press, 1990.

Diamond, Jared. *Collapse: How Societies Choose to Fall or Succeed.* New York: Viking, 2005.

Durant, Will. *The Story of Civilization.* 11 vols. New York: Simon & Schuster, 1935–1975.

Gavin, James M. *War and Peace in the Space Age.* New York: Harper, 1958.

Gibbon, Edward. *The History of the Decline and Fall of the Roman Empire.* 6 vols. 1766–1788. Reprint ed. New York: Everyman's Library, 2010.

Herodotus. *The Histories.* Translated by Aubrey De Selincourt. New York: Penguin Classics, 2003.

Hoover, Herbert. *The Great Depression, 1929–1941.* Vol. 3 of *The Memoirs of Herbert Hoover.* New York: Macmillan, 1952.

Starr, Chester G. *A History of the Ancient World.* New York: Oxford University Press, 1965.

Steinbeck, John. "The Dubious Battle in California." *The Nation*, September 12, 1936.

——. *The Grapes of Wrath*. New York: Viking, 1939.

——. "The Harvest Gypsies." 7 pts. *San Francisco News*, October 5–12, 1936.

Xenophon. *Anabasis: The March Up Country*. Translated by H. G. Dakyns. Independently published, 2017.

——. *Cryopaedia: The Education of Cyrus*. Translated by H. G. Dakyns. CreateSpace, 2012.

Also: *Young Frankenstein*, directed by Mel Brooks, story and screenplay by Mel Brooks and Gene Wilder, Twentieth Century Fox, 1974.

Chapter 2: Suffer the Children

Delbrück, Hans. *History of the Art of War*. 4 vols. Translated by Walter J. Renfroe Jr. Lincoln: University of Nebraska Press, 1975–1990.

deMause, Lloyd. *The Emotional Life of Nations*. New York: Other Press, 2002.

——, ed. *The History of Childhood*. New York: Psychohistory Press, 1974.

Shahar, Shulamith. *Childhood in the Middle Ages*. London: Routledge, 1990.

Chapter 3: The End of the World as They Knew It

Arnold, John H. *History: A Very Short Introduction*. New York: Oxford University Press, 2000.

Drews, Robert. *The Coming of the Greeks: Indo-European Conquests in the Aegean and the Near East*. Reissue ed. Princeton, NJ: Princeton University Press, 1994.

——. *The End of the Bronze Age: Changes in Warfare and the Catastrophe ca. 1200 BC*. 3rd ed. Princeton, NJ: Princeton University Press, 1993.

Fischer, Peter M., and Teresa Bürge, eds. *"Sea Peoples" Up-to-Date: New Research on Transformations in the Eastern Mediterranean in the 13th–11th Centuries BCE*. Vienna: Austrian Academy of Sciences Press, 2014.

Givas, Nick, "Rubio Leads Bipartisan Backlash After De Blasio Quotes Castro Ally Che Guevara," Fox News, June 27, 2019. https://www.foxnews.com/politics/de-blasio-apologizes-for-che-guevara-quote-seiu.

Homer. *The Iliad*. Translated by Caroline Alexander. New York: Ecco, 2015.

Homer. *The Odyssey*. Translated by Emily Wilson. New York: W. W. Norton, 2018.

Knapp, Bernard A., and Sturt W. Manning. "Crisis in Context: The End of the Late Bronze Age in the Eastern Mediterranean." *American Journal of Archaeology* 120, no. 1 (January 2016): 99–149.

Liverani, Mario. *The Ancient Near East: History, Society and Economy*. New York: Routledge, 2014.

Pickworth, Diana. "Excavations at Nineveh: The Halzi Gate" in *Iraq* 67, no. 1, Nineveh. Papers of the 49th Rencontre Assyriologique Internationale, Part Two (Spring 2005), pp. 295–316. British Institute for the Study of Iraq, https://www.jstor.org/stable/4200584.

Plato. *Timaeus and Critias*. Translated by Robin Waterfield. Oxford, UK: Oxford World's Classics, 2009.

Robbins, Manuel. *Collapse of the Bronze Age: The Story of Greece, Troy, Israel, Egypt, and the Peoples of the Sea*. Bloomington, IN: iUniverse, 2001.

Shaw, Garry J. *War & Trade with the Pharaohs: An Archaeological Study of Ancient Egypt's Foreign Relations*. Barnsley, UK: Pen and Sword Archaeology, 2017.

Starr, Chester G. *A History of the Ancient World*. New York: Oxford University Press, 1965.

Tainter, Joseph. *Collapse of Complex Societies*. Cambridge University Press, 2007.

Van De Mieroop, Marc. *A History of the Ancient Near East ca. 3000–323 BC.* 2nd ed. Oxford, UK: Blackwell Publishing, 2006.

Wiener, Malcolm H. "Causes of Complex Systems Collapse at the End of the Bronze Age," in *"Sea Peoples" Up-to-Date: New Research on Transformations in the Eastern Mediterranean in the 13th–11th Centuries BCE*, edited by Peter M. Fischer and Teresa Bürge. Vienna: Austrian Academy of Sciences Press, 2014.

Also: *Planet of the Apes*, directed by Franklin J. Schaffner, story by Pierre Boulle, screenplay by Rod Serling and Michael Wilson, Twentieth Century Fox, 1968.

Chapter 4: Judgment at Nineveh

Durant, Will. *Our Oriental Heritage.* Vol. 1 of *The Story of Civilization.* New York: Simon & Schuster, 1935.

Farrokh, Kaveh. *Shadows in the Desert: Ancient Persia at War.* Oxford, UK: Osprey Publishing, 2007.

Ferrill, Arther. *The Origins of War: From the Stone Age to Alexander the Great.* Rev. ed. New York: Routledge, 2018.

Frahm, Eckart. *A Companion to Assyria* (Blackwell Companions to the Ancient World). Hoboken, NJ: Wiley-Blackwell, 2017.

Gavaghan, Paul F. *The Cutting Edge: Military History of Antiquity and Early Feudal Times.* New York: Peter Lang, 1990.

Healy, Mark. *The Ancient Assyrian.* Oxford, UK: Osprey Publishing, 1992.

Olmstead, A. T. *History of Assyria.* New York: Charles Scribner's Sons, 1923.

Roux, Georges. *Ancient Iraq.* 3rd ed. London: Penguin, 1993.

Saggs, H. W. F. *Everyday Life in Babylonia and Assyria.* New York: Putnam, 1967.

Xenophon. *The Persian Expedition.* Translated by Rex Warner. New York: Penguin Classics, 1950.

Chapter 5: The Barbarian Life Cycle

Barbero, Alessandro. *Charlemagne: Father of a Continent.* Translated by Allan Cameron. Berkeley: University of California Press, 2004.

Collins, Roger. *Early Medieval Europe, 300–1000.* 3rd ed. New York: Palgrave Macmillan, 2010.

Delbrück, Hans. *The Barbarian Invasions.* Vol. 2 of *History of the Art of War.* Translated by Walter J. Renfroe Jr. Rev. ed. Omaha: University of Nebraska Press, 1990.

Dennis, George T., trans. *Maurice's Strategikon: Handbook of Byzantine Military Strategy.* Philadelphia: University of Pennsylvania Press, 2001.

Durant, Will. *The Age of Faith: A History of Medieval Civilization—Christian, Islamic, and Judaic—from Constantine to Dante, AD 325–1300.* Vol. 4 of *The Story of Civilization.* New York: Simon & Schuster, 1950.

———. *Caesar and Christ.* Vol. 3 of *The Story of Civilization.* New York: Simon & Schuster, 1944.

Einhard. *The Life of Charlemagne.* Ann Arbor: University of Michigan Press, 1960.

Fell, Christine E., and David M. Wilson, eds. *Northern World: The History and Heritage of Northern Europe.* New York: Harry N. Abrams, 1987.

Ferrill, Arther. *Fall of the Roman Empire: The Military Explanation.* London: Thames & Hudson, 1986.

Gibbon, Edward. *The History of the Decline and Fall of the Roman Empire.* 6 vols. 1766–1788. Reprint ed. New York: Everyman's Library, 2010.

Gregory of Tours. *The History of the Franks.* Translated by Lewis Thorpe. London: Penguin, 1974.

Heather, Peter. *The Fall of the Roman Empire: A New History of Rome and the Barbarians.* New York: Oxford University Press, 2006.

James, Edward. *The Franks.* Oxford, UK: Basil Blackwell, 1988.

Lendon, J. E. *Empire of Honour: The Art of Government in the Roman World*. Oxford, UK: Oxford University Press, 1997.

Riche, Pierre. *Daily Life in the World of Charlemagne*. Translated by Jo Ann McNamara. Philadelphia: University of Pennsylvania Press, 1978.

Suetonius. *The Twelve Caesars*. New York: Penguin Classics, 2007.

Tacitus. *Agricola and Germania*. New York: Penguin Classics, 2010.

Ward-Perkins, Bryan. *The Fall of Rome and the End of Civilization*. Oxford, UK: Oxford University Press, 2005.

Wells, Peter S. *Barbarians to Angels: The Dark Ages Reconsidered*. New York: W. W. Norton, 2009.

Wickham, Chris. *The Inheritance of Rome: Illuminating the Dark Ages, 400–1000*. New York: Viking, 2009.

Williams, Hywel. *Emperor of the West: Charlemagne and the Carolingian Empire*. Reprint ed. London: Quercus, 2011.

Chapter 6: A Pandemic Prologue?

Barry, John M. *The Great Influenza: The Story of the Deadliest Pandemic in History*. New York: Viking Penguin, 2004.

Bostrom, Nick, and Milan M. Ćirković, eds. *Global Catastrophic Risks*. New York: Oxford University Press, 2008.

Docherty, Campbell, and Caroline Foulkes. "Toxic Shock." *Birmingham Post* (UK), October 4, 2003.

Durant, Will. *The Age of Faith: A History of Medieval Civilization— Christian, Islamic, and Judaic—from Constantine to Dante, AD 325–1300*. Vol. 4 of *The Story of Civilization*. New York: Simon & Schuster, 1950.

Kolata, Gina. *Flu: The Story of the Great Influenza Pandemic of 1918 and the Search for the Virus That Caused It*. New York: Farrar, Straus and Giroux, 1999.

Littman, Robert J. "The Plague of Athens: Epidemiology and Paleopathology." *Mount Sinai Journal of Medicine* 76, no. 5 (October 2009): 456–67.

McCullough, David. "There Isn't Any Such Thing as the Past." Interview with Roger Mudd in *American Heritage Presents Great Minds of History* 50, no. 1 (February/March 1999).

McNeill, William H. *Plagues and Peoples.* New York: Doubleday, 1977.

Orent, Wendy. *Plague: The Mysterious Past and Terrifying Future of the World's Most Dangerous Disease.* New York: Free Press, 2004.

Rosen, William. *Justinian's Flea: The First Great Plague and the End of the Roman Empire.* New York: Viking Penguin, 2007.

Sebelius, Kathleen. "Why We Still Need Smallpox." *New York Times,* April 25, 2011.

Svensen, Henrik. *The End Is Nigh: A History of Natural Disasters.* London: Reaktion Books, 2011.

Thucydides. *The Landmark Thucydides: A Comprehensive Guide to the Peloponnesian War.* Touchstone ed. New York: Free Press, 1998.

Tuchman, Barbara. *A Distant Mirror: The Calamitous 14th Century.* New York: Alfred A. Knopf, 1978.

Chapter 7: The Quick and the Dead

For more information about the atomic bombs dropped on Japan at the end of the Second World War, see the Atomic Heritage Foundation website: https://www.atomicheritage.org/history/little-boy-and-fat-man.

Baruch, Bernard. Speech before the first session of the United Nations Atomic Energy Commission, Hunter College, New York, June 14, 1946.

Blight, James G., and Janet M. Lang. *The Armageddon Letters.* Lanham, MD: Rowman & Littlefield, 2012.

Bobbitt, Philip. *The Shield of Achilles: War, Peace, and the Course of History.* New York: Alfred A. Knopf, 2002.

Bostrom, Nick, and Milan M. Ćirković, eds. *Global Catastrophic Risks.* New York: Oxford University Press, 2008.

Bradley, John. *World War III: Strategies, Tactics and Weapons.* New York: Crescent, 1982.

Brands, H. W. *What America Owes the World: The Struggle for the Soul of Foreign Policy.* Cambridge, UK: Cambridge University Press, 1998.

Cameron, Rob. "Police Close Case on 1948 Death of Jan Masaryk—Murder, Not Suicide." Radio Praha Broadcast Archive, June 1, 2004. https://www.radio.cz/en/section/curraffrs/police-close-case-on -1948-death-of-jan-masaryk-murder-not-suicide.

Cirincione, Joseph. *Bomb Scare: The History & Future of Nuclear Weapons.* New York: Columbia University Press, 2007.

Codevilla, Angelo, and Paul Seasbury. *War: Ends and Means.* 2nd ed. Washington, DC: Potomac Books, 2006.

Compton, Arthur Holly. *Atomic Quest: A Personal Narrative.* 1956.

Crane, Conrad C. *American Airpower Strategy in World War II: Bombs, Cities, Civilians, and Oil.* Lawrence: University of Kansas Press, 2016.

Dallek, Robert. *An Unfinished Life: John F. Kennedy, 1917–1963.* New York: Little, Brown, 2003.

Dobbs, Michael. *One Minute to Midnight: Kennedy, Khrushchev, and Castro on the Brink of Nuclear War.* New York: Alfred A. Knopf, 2008.

Donovan, Hedley. *Roosevelt to Reagan: A Reporter's Encounters with Nine Presidents.* New York: HarperCollins, 1985.

Dunnigan, James F. *How to Make War: A Comprehensive Guide to Modern Warfare in the 21st Century.* 4th ed. New York: Harper Perennial, 2003.

Durant, Will, and Ariel Durant. *The Lessons of History.* New York: Simon & Schuster, 1968.

Dyer, Gwynne. *War: The Lethal Custom.* Reading, UK: Periscope, 2017.

Eden, Lynn. *Whole World on Fire: Organizations, Knowledge and Nuclear Weapons Devastation.* Ithaca, NY: Cornell University Press, 2003.

Einstein, Albert. Letter to President Franklin Delano Roosevelt, August 2, 1939. Available via the Atomic Heritage Foundation, https://www.atomicheritage.org/key-documents/einstein-szilard-letter.

"Fissile Material Basics." Institute for Energy and Environmental Research, 2019. https://ieer.org/resource/factsheets/fissile-material-basics/.

Forrestal, James. *The Forrestal Diaries.* Edited by Walter Millis. New York: Viking, 1951.

Fursenko, Aleksandr, and Timothy Naftali. *One Hell of a Gamble: Khrushchev, Castro, and Kennedy, 1958–1964: The Secret History of the Cuban Missile Crisis.* New York: W. W. Norton, 1997.

Gaddis, John Lewis. *The Cold War: A New History.* New York: Penguin Press, 2005.

———. *We Now Know: Rethinking Cold War History.* Oxford, UK: Oxford University Press, 1997.

Gavin, Francis J. *Nuclear Statecraft: History and Strategy in America's Atomic Age.* Reprint ed. Ithaca, NY: Cornell University Press, 2012.

Gray, Colin S. *War, Peace and Victory: Strategy and Statecraft for the Next Century.* New York: Simon & Schuster, 1990.

Greene, Jack C., and Daniel J. Strom, compilers. *Would the Insects Inherit the Earth? and Other Subjects of Concern to Those Who Worry About Nuclear War.* Oxford UK: Pergamon Profession, 1988.

Hachiya, Michihiko. *Hiroshima Diary: The Journal of a Japanese Physician, August 6–September 30, 1945 (Fifty Years Later).* Translated by Warner Wells. 2nd ed. Chapel Hill: University of North Carolina Press, 2011.

Holloway, David. *Stalin and the Bomb: The Soviet Union and Atomic Energy, 1939–1956.* New Haven, CT: Yale University Press, 1994.

Howard, Michael. *The Invention of Peace: Reflections on War and International Order.* New Haven, CT: Yale University Press, 2000.

Kahn, Herman. *On Thermonuclear War.* Princeton, NJ: Princeton University Press, 1960.

Kaku, Michio, and Daniel Axelrod. *To Win a Nuclear War: The Pentagon's Secret War Plans.* Boston: South End Press, 1999.

Kaplan, Fred. *The Wizards of Armageddon.* Stanford, CA: Stanford University Press, 1983.

Kennedy, Paul, ed. *Grad Strategies in War and Peace.* New Haven, CT: Yale University Press, 1991.

Kennett, Lee B. *A History of Strategic Bombing: From the First Hot-Air Balloons to Hiroshima and Nagasaki.* New York: Scribner, 1982.

Khrushchev, Nikita Sergeevich. *Khrushchev Remembers.* Translated by Strobe Talbott. Boston: Little, Brown, 1970.

Kozak, Warren. *LeMay: The Life and Wars of General Curtis LeMay.* New York: Regnery, 2009.

Lilienthal, David E. *The Atomic Energy Years, 1945–1950.* Vol. 2 of *The Journals of David E. Lilienthal.* New York: Harper & Row, 1964.

Martel, William, and Paul L. Savage. *Strategic Nuclear War: What the Superpowers Target and Why.* Santa Barbara, CA: Praeger, 1986.

McNamara, Robert S., with Brian VanDeMark. *In Retrospect: The Tragedy and Lessons of Vietnam.* New York: Times Books, 1995.

Poundstone, William. *Prisoner's Dilemma: John von Neumann, Game Theory, and the Puzzle of the Bomb.* New York: Doubleday, 1992.

Schlosser, Eric. *Command and Control: Nuclear Weapons, the Damascus Accident, and the Illusion of Safety.* New York: Penguin Press, 2013.

Sekimori, Gaynor, trans. *Hibakusha: Survivors of Hiroshima and Nagasaki.* Tokyo: Kosei, 1989.

Sherry, Michael S. *In the Shadow of War: The United States Since the 1930s.* 2nd ed. New Haven, CT: Yale University Press, 1997.

Shiotsuki, Masao. *Doctor at Nagasaki: My First Assignment Was Mercy Killing.* Tokyo: Kosei, 1989.

Southard, Susan. *Nagasaki: Life After Nuclear War.* New York: Viking Penguin, 2015.

Stern, Sheldon. *Averting 'The Final Failure': John F. Kennedy and the Secret Cuban Missile Crisis Meetings.* Stanford, CA: Stanford University Press, 2003.

———. *The Cuban Missile Crisis in American Memory: Myths Versus Reality.* Stanford, CA: Stanford University Press, 2012.

———. *The Week the World Stood Still: Inside the Secret Cuban Missile Crisis.* Stanford, CA: Stanford University Press, 2005.

Thomas, Evan. *Ike's Bluff: President Eisenhower's Secret Battle to Save the World.* New York: Little, Brown, 2012.

US Congress. *The Effects of Nuclear Weapons.* Washington, DC: US Congress Office of Technology Assessment, 1959.

Van Creveld, Martin. *Technology and War: From 2000 BC to the Present.* New York: Free Press, 1991.

Webster, Donovan. *Aftermath: The Remnants of War: From Landmines to Chemical Warfare—the Devastating Effects of Modern Combat.* New York: Pantheon, 1996.

Whitfield, Stephen J. *The Culture of the Cold War.* 2nd ed. Baltimore: Johns Hopkins University Press, 1996.

Wills, Garry. *Bomb Power: The Modern Presidency and the National Security State.* New York: Penguin Press, 2010.

Zaloga, Steven J. *The Kremlin's Nuclear Sword: The Rise and Fall of Russia's Strategic Nuclear Forces, 1945–2000.* Washington, DC: Smithsonian Books, 2002.

Zubok, Vladislav, and Constantine Pleshakov. *Inside the Kremlin's Cold War: From Stalin to Krushchev.* Cambridge, MA: Harvard University Press, 1996.

Chapter 8: The Road to Hell

Biddle, Tami Davis. "Air Power and the Law of War," in *Laws of War*, edited by Michael Howard, George Andreopoulos, and Mark Shulman. New Haven, CT: Yale University Press, 1994.

Carey, John, ed. *Eyewitness to History.* Reprint ed. New York: William Morrow Paperbacks, 1997.

Cowley, Robert, ed. *Experience of War: An Anthology of Articles from MHQ: The Quarterly Journal of Military History.* New York: W. W. Norton, 1992.

Crane, Conrad C. *American Airpower Strategy in World War II: Bombs, Cities, Civilians, and Oil.* Lawrence: University Press of Kansas, 2016.

Deighton, Len. *Blood, Tears, and Folly: An Objective Look at World War II.* New York: HarperCollins, 1993.

Douhet, Giulio. *The Command of the Air.* Translated by Dino Ferrari. Center for Air Force History. Originally published in 1921 under the auspices of the Ministry of War. Reprint ed. CreateSpace, 2015.

Dyer, Gwynne. *War: The New Edition*. Toronto: Vintage Canada, 2005.

Dyson, Freeman. *The Fire: The Bombing of Germany, 1940–1945*. New York: Columbia University Press, 2008.

Edoin, Hoito. *The Night Tokyo Burned: The Incendiary Campaign against Japan, March–August, 1945*. New York: St. Martin's, 1989.

Ferguson, Niall. *The War of the World: Twentieth-Century Conflict and the Descent of the West*. New York: Penguin Press, 2006.

Friedrich, Jörg. *The Fire: The Bombing of Germany, 1940–1945*. Translated by Allison Brown. New York: Columbia University Press, 2006.

Giangreco, D. M. *Hell to Pay: Operation DOWNFALL and the Invasion of Japan, 1945–1947*. Annapolis, MD: Naval Institute Press, 2017.

Grossman, Dave. *On Killing: The Psychological Cost of Learning to Kill in War and Society*. Reprint ed. New York: Back Bay Books, 2009.

Hopper, Bruce. TK

Howard, Michael, George Andreopoulos, and Mark R. Shulman, eds. *The Laws of War: Constraints on Warfare in the Western World*. New ed. New Haven, CT: Yale University Press, 1997.

Kennett, Lee B. *A History of Strategic Bombing: From the First Hot-Air Balloons to Hiroshima and Nagasaki*. New York: Scribner, 1982.

Knell, Hermann. *To Destroy a City: Strategic Bombing and Its Human Consequences in World War II*. New York: Da Capo, 2003.

Martin, Douglas. "Thomas Ferebee Dies at 81; Dropped First Atomic Bomb." *New York Times*, March 18, 2000.

MHQ: The Quarterly Journal of Military History 2, no. 4 (Summer 1990).

Obit. Directed by Vanessa Gould. 2016. (Documentary about the *New York Times* obituary section.)

Salmaggi, Cesare, and Alfredo Pallavisini. *2,194 Days of War: An Illustrated Chronology of the Second World War*. New York: Barnes and Noble, 1993.

Truman, Harry S., diary.

Wells, H. G. *The War in the Air*. Originally serialized in *The Pall Mall Magazine*, 1908. Reprint ed. CreateSpace, 2013.

Ziegler, Philip. *London at War, 1939–1945*. New York: Knopf, 1995.

INDEX

ABOUT THE AUTHOR

DAN CARLIN is a pioneering podcaster and the king of long-form audio content. In his *Hardcore History* shows, which sometimes last over six hours, Carlin humanizes the past and forces the audience to "walk a mile in that other guy's historical moccasins." *Hardcore History* has been downloaded over one hundred million times.